# A European Politics of Education

*A European Politics of Education* proposes a sociology of education establishing connections between empirical data coming from European-scale comparative surveys, normative assumptions structuring actors' representations and interpretative judgements, and a specific focus on lifelong learning policy areas. It invites readers to think about the place of standards, expertise and calculations in the European space from a common perspective, supported by a tradition of critical sociology and European political studies.

The book:

- addresses an important agenda: how the policies and politics of supranational Europe are making a European educational space;
- contains a response to the emergence of new epistemic governance and instruments at European level;
- contains contributions from the EU and the UK, which give a comprehensive selection of perspectives and analysis of the field as it concerns Europe.

The complexity of the contemporary European education policy space is addressed here with new lines of inquiry as well as a reflexive outlook, on standardisation, policy-making and actor engagement. Students and researchers of European policy studies, education policy analysts and theorists will all be particularly interested readers.

**Romuald Normand** is Professor of Sociology at the University of Strasbourg, Research Unit SAGE (Societies, Actors and Government in Europe), France.

**Jean-Louis Derouet** is Professor Emeritus of Sociology at the Ecole Normale Supérieure, Lyon, France.

## Studies in European Education Series
Series Editors
Martin Lawn, *University of Oxford, UK*
Romuald Normand, *University of Strasbourg, France*

The European dimensions of education constitute a field of growing distinctiveness and importance, with a speed, scale and complexity reflecting the rise of international and transnational policies and flows of data and public and private experts around Europe.

The European policy space for education describes the emergence of a dense web of relations, data and people. Its speed and scale has been transformed by the push for a competitive Europe through the Lisbon Process, and by using a common set of benchmarks and networks, to governing European education through comparison.

This series intends to create a space for scholars of European education policies and politics in education studies, political science, sociology and European integration studies, and to develop interpretive studies about new European institutions, and the interplay between policy-makers, stakeholders and experts. The series encourages research on education and its links with mobility, migration, finance, standardisation and norms, knowledge and governing, and new technologies and software.

**Shaping of European Education**
Interdisciplinary approaches
*Edited by Martin Lawn and Romuald Normand*

**Governing by Inspection**
*Edited by Sotiria Grek and Joakim Lindgren*

**A European Politics of Education**
Perspectives from sociology, policy studies and politics
*Edited by Romuald Normand and Jean-Louis Derouet*

# A European Politics of Education

Perspectives from sociology, policy studies and politics

Edited by Romuald Normand and Jean-Louis Derouet

Routledge
Taylor & Francis Group

LONDON AND NEW YORK

First published 2017
by Routledge
2 Park Square, Milton Park, Abingdon, Oxon OX14 4RN

and by Routledge
711 Third Avenue, New York, NY 10017

*Routledge is an imprint of the Taylor & Francis Group, an informa business*

*British Library Cataloguing in Publication Data*
*A catalogue record for this book is available from the British Library*

*Library of Congress Cataloguing in Publication Data*
Names: Normand, Romuald, editor. | Derouet, Jean-Louis, editor.
Title: A European politics of education : perspectives from sociology, policy studies and politics / edited by Romuald Normand and Jean-Louis Derouet.
Description: New York, NY : Routledge, 2016. | Series: Studies in European education | Includes bibliographical references and index.
Identifiers: LCCN 2016000855 (print) | LCCN 2016011335 (ebook) |
ISBN 9781138669079 (hardback) | ISBN 9781315618326 (ebk) |
Subjects: LCSH: Education and state–European Union countries. |
Educational sociology–European Union countries. |
Education, Higher–European Union countries.
Classification: LCC LC93.A2 E95 2016 (print) | LCC LC93.A2 (ebook) |
DDC 379.4–dc23 LC record available at http://lccn.loc.gov/2016000855

ISBN: 978-1-138-66907-9 (hbk)
ISBN: 978-1-315-61832-6 (ebk)

Typeset in Galliard
by Out of House Publishing

Printed and bound by CPI Group (UK) Ltd, Croydon, CR0 4YY

# Contents

*Notes on contributors*                                                          vii

1   Introduction                                                                    1
    ROMUALD NORMAND AND JEAN-LOUIS DEROUET

2   Standards and standardisation in European politics of education              13
    PAOLO LANDRI

3   Policy transfers in Europe: the European Union and beyond                    31
    MAGDALÉNA HADJIISKY

4   The praise of mutual surveillance in Europe                                   53
    LUÍS MIGUEL CARVALHO AND ESTELA COSTA

5   Policy learning and expertise in European education                          73
    ROMUALD NORMAND

6   Ranking and structuration of a transnational field of
    higher education                                                              92
    NIILO KAUPPI

7   Higher education: from 'unclear technologies' to human
    resources management techniques                                             104
    JEAN-ÉMILE CHARLIER AND SARAH CROCHÉ

8   Universities, the risk industry and capitalism: a political
    economy critique                                                            122
    SUSAN L. ROBERTSON AND CHRIS MUELLERLEILE

9   'Silencing the disbelievers': games of truth and power
    struggles around fact-based management                          140
    ISABELLE BRUNO

10  Compliance and contestation in the neoliberal university:
    reflecting on the identities of UK social scientists            155
    ALAN CRIBB, SHARON GEWIRTZ AND ANIKO HORVATH

11  Losing the plot, plotting the lost: politics, Europe, and the
    rediscovery of lifelong learning                                176
    JOHN HOLFORD

12  How are European lifelong learning systems changing?:
    An approach in terms of public policy regimes                   194
    ERIC VERDIER

    *Index*                                                         216

# Contributors

**Isabelle Bruno** is Associate Professor in political science at the University of Lille (France) and member of the Lille Centre for European Research on Administration, Politics and Society (CERAPS, CNRS/Lille 2). Her research interests are twofold: she worked on benchmarking as a technology of government and on EU processes of quantification; since 2013, she has focused on sociology of elites and socio-spatial segregation. She recently co-edited with E. Didier and T. Vitale 'Statactivism: State Restructuring, Financial Capitalism and Statistical Mobilizations', *Partecipazione e Conflitto. The Open Journal of Sociopolitical Studies* (vol. 7, no. 2, 2014; <http://siba-ese.unisalento.it/index.php/paco>) and with F. Jany-Catrice and B. Touchelay, *The Social Sciences of Quantification: from politics of large numbers to target-driven policies* (London: Springer, 2016).

**Luís Miguel Carvalho** is Professor of Education Policy and Administration at the Institute of Education, University of Lisbon (IE-UL). His recent research focuses on the circulation of educational knowledge and policies, and on the role of knowledge in the fabrication and regulation of education policies. He is currently coordinator of the 'Research and Training Area of Education and Training Policies' at the IE-UL. His recent books are: *O Espelho do Perito: Inquéritos Internacionais, Conhecimento e Politica em Educação* (Fundação Manuel Leão, 2011), as editor and co-author; *Knowledge and Regulatory Processes in Health and Education Policies* (Educa, 2012) as co-editor.

**Jean-Émile Charlier** has a PhD in sociology. He is a professor at the Catholic University of Louvain (UCL Mons) in French-speaking Belgium and co-tenured the UNESCO chair in educational sciences at the University Cheikh Anta Diop of Dakar in Senegal. He has worked on a wide range of issues, including the sociology of religion, the religious education in Africa, the orientation in secondary education. For 10 years, his research has concerned the effects of the Bologna Process on European and African higher education systems and the resistance to international injunctions in education. Relevant publications: Charlier J.-É., Croché S. and Leclercq

B. (eds) (2012) *Contrôler la qualité dans l'enseignement supérieur.* Louvain-la-Neuve: Academia.

**Estela Costa** is Assistant Professor of Education Policy and Administration at the Institute of Education, University of Lisbon (IE-UL). Presently, she is Deputy Director of the IE-UL, and belongs to the 'Research and Training Area of Education and Training Policies'. She develops her research activities in the field of educational administration and policy. Her research and publications focus on school evaluation, school management and the trans-nationalisation of education policies. She has papers published in Portugal and abroad on these issues.

**Alan Cribb** is Professor of Bioethics and Education and Co-Director of the Centre for Public Policy Research at King's College London. His research relates to applied philosophy, health and education policy. Alan has a particular interest in developing interdisciplinary scholarship that links philosophical, social science and professional concerns.

**Sarah Croché** has a PhD in political and social sciences and a PhD in educational sciences. She is an associate professor at the University Picardie Jules Verne (UPJV) in France. In her thesis, she studied the role of the European Commission in the Bologna Process. More recently, her research has taken two directions: she studies the truth discourses in competition in African education and she studies the effects of quality assurance mechanisms on academics. Her last publication is: Croché S. (Coord.) (2014) Concurrence des discours de vérité à l'école, Éducation et Sociétés, *Revue internationale de sociologie de l'éducation*, LLN: De Boeck, n°33.

**Jean-Louis Derouet** is a former student from the Saint-Cloud Ecole Normale Supérieure. He has a history 'agrégation' and a PhD in sociology. Today he is a professor at Lyon Ecole Normale Supérieure, a member of the UMR Triangle. He has specialised in the diversification of principles of justice in the contemporary world. This question provides the foundation from which he tackles several topical issues: the new forms of the state as an educator; the new organisation of schools and the debates around the notion of leadership; the transition of European states to a post-comprehensive school, etc. Jean-Louis Derouet is chair of the 'Education, Formation, Socialisation' Committee of the International Association of French Sociologists. He is the editor-in-chief of *Education et Sociétés* (Education and Societies) and a member of the editorial board of several European journals: *Mediterranean Journal of Educational Studies; Italian Journal of Sociology of Éducation; Pedagogicky Casopis (Journal of Pedagogy), Université de Trnava (Slovak Republic); Éducation & didactique (Presses Universitaires de Rennes); Revista Lusofona de Educaçao; Revista Brasileira de Educação.*

**Sharon Gewirtz** is Professor of Education and Head of the Department of Education and Professional Studies at King's College London. Her research is in the sociology of education and education policy, with a particular focus on issues of equality and social justice. She is currently researching values and ethics in higher education.

**Magdaléna Hadjiisky** is Senior Lecturer of Political Science at the Institut d'Etudes Politiques, University of Strasbourg, France. She has a doctorate in political sociology from the Institut d'Etudes Politiques of Paris (Sciences Po). Her research deals with post-communist democratic transformations in central European countries. She has published numerous articles and book chapters in French, English and Czech on central European politics and on the reform of the post-communist states, and has co-edited a special issue of the review *Politix* on 'businessmen in politics'. More recently, Magdaléna's research has focused on the role of international organisations in processes of policy transfer in the European space. After having studied civil service reforms from inside central European countries, she has focused on the way international organisations try to assist and/or influence such reform processes from the 'outside'. She has recently coordinated several conference sessions, which will be published in Magdaléna Hadjiisky, Leslie A. Pal, Christopher Walker (eds) *The Micro-Dynamics and Macro-Effects of Policy Transfers: beg, borrow, steal or swallow?* Cheltenham: Edward Elgar, forthcoming 2016.

**John Holford** holds the Robert Peers chair in adult education at the University of Nottingham. A sociologist who has spent his career in adult education, his research has focused on lifelong education's role in the formation of citizens, communities and social movements. His main current work is on policy processes for the education of adults in the European Union, and on the history of universities, adult education and citizenship in Britain. His recent books include: *Adult Education Policy and the European Union: theoretical and methodological perspectives* (editor, with M. Milana, Sense Publishers, 2014) and *Lifelong Learning in Europe: national patterns and challenges* (editor, with E. Saar and O.B. Ure, Edward Elgar, 2013). He is Editor of the *International Journal of Lifelong Education*. Before moving to Nottingham, he taught at the University of Surrey, the University of Hong Kong and the Workers' Educational Association.

**Aniko Horvath** is a researcher at the Centre for Global Higher Education (CGHE) at the UCL Institute of Education and a Visiting Research Fellow at King's College London. Her current research focuses on higher education governance in the UK, Europe and globally, as well as on inequalities, identities and academic values in the higher education sector. Aniko's earlier work focused on issues of identity, nationalism, inequalities and higher education policies in east central Europe. Before coming to CGHE, she worked at King's College London, the University of Bristol, the Hungarian Academy of Sciences and Central European University. She holds a PhD in sociology and social anthropology from the Central European University.

**Niilo Kauppi** is Research Director at the French National Center for Scientific Research (CNRS). He is currently Academy of Finland Distinguished Professor at the University of Jyväskylä and fellow at the University of Strasbourg Institute for Advanced Study. He teaches at the universities of Helsinki and Lausanne. Kauppi is a former president of the Finnish Political Science Association and vice-chair of ECPR (European Consortium for Political Research). Convener with David Swartz (Boston University) of the ECPR Standing Group in Political Sociology, Kauppi is the author and editor of 11 books and over 100 articles in political sociology, European politics, social theory and intellectual history. His current research interests include higher education policies and knowledge governance. Some recent publications are: *'Global Bourdieu'*, *Comparative Sociology* (4/2015, with David Swartz) and 'Knowledge Warfare: Social Scientists as Operators of Global Governance', *International Political Sociology* (8/3/2014). Kauppi is also a senior editor of the *Oxford Research Encyclopedia of Politics* (http://politics.oxfordre.com).

**Paolo Landri** is a senior researcher of the Institute of Research on Population and Social Policies at the National Research Council in Italy (CNR-IRPPS). His main research interests concern educational organisations, professional learning and educational policies. He edited with Tara Fenwick a special issue on 'Materialities, Textures and Pedagogies: Socio-Material Assemblages in Education' in *Pedagogy, Culture and Society* 20(1) March 2012, and recently published 'The Sociomateriality of Education Policy' in *Discourse* 36 (4) November 2014.

**Chris Muellerleile** is a lecturer in economic geography at Swansea University in Wales, UK. He recently completed a Marie Curie post-doctoral research fellowship at the Centre for Globalization, Education and Social Futures at the University of Bristol, where he was studying the political economy of open access publishing and the intersection of the finance industry with the emergent higher education sector. His work on financial markets and financialisation has been published in venues such as the *Journal of Economic Geography* and *Environment and Planning A*.

**Romuald Normand** is Professor of Sociology at the University of Strasbourg, Faculty of Social Sciences, France (Research Unit SAGE: Societies, Actors and Government of Europe). He works on comparative education policies and politics, Europeanisation and lifelong learning, higher education and research. Romuald Normand is convenor of the network 28 'Sociologies of European Education' at the European Educational Research Association. He is a member of the editorial board of the *British Journal of Sociology* *of Education* and co-editor of the Routledge series 'Studies in European Education', 2014, with Martin Lawn, *Shaping of European education. Interdisciplinary Approaches*, Abingdon: Routledge.

**Susan L. Robertson** is Professor of Sociology of Education at the University of Bristol, UK. She is Director of the Centre for Globalisation, Education and Social Futures. She is also founding co-editor of the journal *Globalisation, Societies and Education*. Susan's research is concerned with the changing nature of the relationship between education and the economy, and the role of governance frameworks in this.

**Eric Verdier** is Research Professor (directeur de recherche) at the National Centre for Scientific Research (CNRS), Institute of Labour Economics and Industrial Sociology (LEST), Aix-Marseille University and CNRS. As sociologist and economist, his main topics are vocational education and training policies, sociology of work and employment. Some recent publications are: Verdier, E., 'The social conventions of guidance as a major component of lifelong learning systems. A French-Danish-British comparison' in *History of VET: Cases, Concepts and Challenges* by Esther Berner and Philip Gonon (eds), Peter Lang Verlag (Studies in Vocational and Continuing Education), 2016; Ben Sedrine, S., Ben Yaou, M., El Yacoubi, D. and Verdier, E., 'Les réformes de la formation des jeunes au Maghreb. Entre référentiels internationaux et recherche de cohérence sociétale'. *Revue Tiers Monde* no. 223, 2015, 147–64.

# Chapter 1

# Introduction

*Romuald Normand and Jean-Louis Derouet*

For the past few decades, Europe has been a key focus of policy studies. It has given rise to many contradictory debates and theories on the building of Europe: is it a cumulative process fulfilled by states? Do European institutions, and particularly the European Commission, have sufficient power and autonomy to impose their choices on member states? Is it being just built from a compilation of successive and heterogeneous communications, reports, and recommendations or from a coherent strategy producing convergence and harmonisation? Do researchers assume a Europeanisation of public action or do they postulate that European norms and incentives are divided into fractioned and hybrid elements across national and local policies?

If these discussions are important for political sciences, social inquiry hardly goes beyond institutional discourses and representations reflected in official documents (Saurugger and Mérand 2010). Only a few political or social scientists have opened up the European policy 'black box' to look at the 'bricolage' of categories, ideas, instruments, norms as well as how the actors prepare and legitimise decisions. A French tradition of political sciences has had the merit of studying European actors, their strategies and power relationships, their careers and paths (Georgakakis 2009; Georgakakis and Weisbein 2010; Robert 2010). For the past few years, the sociology of education has also studied the issue of Europeanisation (Nóvoa and Lawn 2002; Dale and Derouet 2012; Lawn and Grek 2012; Lawn and Normand 2014). The genesis of the European space for lifelong learning, the effects of the Lisbon Strategy and the Bologna Process, or the role of international organisations have been proved. However, in the field of education, empirical research remains quite weak on the subject of European actors, their modes of socialisation, their paths and careers, negotiation and compromise processes among policy-makers, experts and stakeholders, the role of certain representatives and public/private institutions in shaping directives and recommendations, etc.

Therefore, this book in gathering political scientists and educational sociologists provides a criss-crossed, critical and reflexive perspective on the forms and contents of European politics, without limiting itself to certain institutional and discursive aspects of policy. It considers politics as the institutionalisation of power relationships based on knowledge frameworks, types of instruments and calculative spaces, but also strategies, interactions and commitments of individual and collective actors stabilising a European order and governing at a distance on behalf of a certain idea of justice and truth.

In this book, the authors share the same postulate: European policy-makers, even if they advocate rational and universalistic decision-making, have to deal with limited cognition and uncertainty. Their discourses take official documents (reports, communications, directives and recommendations) as a reference, thus giving the appearance of a coherent implementation of the European lifelong learning strategy. But, in fact, policy-makers have to take into account arbitrary and contingent relationships found within the commission and general directorates, operational units, member states' representatives, European Parliament members, as well as having to include data and analyses provided by other institutions (Eurostat, OECD) and certain expert networks. Persuasion, negotiation, arrangements, compromise, but also bypassing, strategy, trickery, pressure, threats are mobilised in the political arenas to prepare the decision-making process (Majone 1989).

Even if, since Machiavelli, the mechanisms of politics are well known, few studies have analysed the games of power and influence within European institutions. Marc Abelès has clearly described the organisation of the European Parliament, the life of deputies in the backstage of public sessions and the power of lobbying in statements and positions (Abelès 2006). Chris Shore has shown the identity collusion among the European Commission's civil servants and the mechanisms by which policy-makers and experts were progressively converted to European values and ideals (Shore 2013). It is currently assumed that the European Commission is at the centre of a political network of interactions between officials and experts from Brussels and civil servants from member states who maintain close links and a techno-cratic connivance outside of professional relationships (Majone 1996). The commission can be characterised as a political entrepreneur: it uses a large variety of resources and expertise and it is opportunistic in persuading its interlocutors (member state representatives or European Parliament members) to take the right decision or to vote in favour of certain legislation. It is also confronted by a double process of political competition and fragmentation: competition for power with other institutions such as the European Council and the European Parliament, and fragmentation because European policy is fragmented and it is difficult to capture a global coherence when decisions are subjected to multiple negotiations and pressure. This politics can also be analysed through standardisation.

## Standards and quality politics

The European technocracy, while it has no coercive power over states, uses expertise as a form of authority and power (Radaelli 1999). Since the implementation of the Lisbon Strategy, decision-making has been supported by a large variety of working groups, expert committees, agencies and think tanks (Gornitzka and Sverdrup 2008). Transnational networks produce transferable standards and measurements in time and space. The standardisation process, applied to statistics and other technologies, remains critical for the harmonisation of European policy and the building of a 'calculative space'. The European Commission delegates responsibilities to other actors and accepts the design of standards and measurements based on voluntary commitments. Harmonisation has not created a centralised European government but it is supported by a set of scattered and heterogeneous institutions and agencies such as research centres, expert groups or networks, normalisation committees and ministerial departments.

On this basis, the commission seeks to establish recommendations, targets and benchmarks to provide directions for policy-makers and member states. Based on the definition of Bowker and Star (1999), standardisation can be defined as the process of building uniformities in time and space through agreed rules. Standards make it possible to work at a distance by using measurement tools beyond communities of practices. They are designed by external institutions such as professional organisations, agencies and the state itself. This common representation by standards specifies constraints for actors but also possibilities for action and interaction. Standards and metrological procedures shape the world and can be negotiated and revised according to the conventions and values held by a group or an institution.

As Paolo Landri demonstrates in the book's first chapter, the actor-network theory is particularly useful in characterising the manner in which different actors (scientists, experts, normalisers, etc.) seek to deploy techniques to mobilise other actors and to govern at a distance, beyond local spaces, via calculative devices and translation processes (Fenwick and Edwards 2010). Standards fix a variety of socio-technical assemblages, which technologise and systematise education policies through spaces of commensurability and calculability resulting from the development of governing instruments (Lascoumes and Le Gales 2007; Gorur 2013). They define new agencies between persons and things and they shape new epistemic knowledge by guiding interactions in teaching and learning (Fenwick and Landri 2012; Gorur 2011). However, the actor-network theory also describes power relationships that give an irreversible standardisation to objects and mechanisms supporting politics. It also demonstrates that causality is not direct but mediated by chains of association and translation due to the complexity and uncertainty of travelling policies and knowledge transfer.

Standards support quality politics by serving multiple aims in the Europeanisation process. The design of indicators and the production of data enables comparable education policies to be enacted on a large space and at different scales (Lawn 2011; Gorur 2014). This comparison of standards stimulates competition between countries but it also measures progress in terms of policy convergence with the European agenda. All the areas of the lifelong learning Strategy are concerned (compulsory schooling, higher education, vocational education and training, adult education) while international organisations (World Bank, OECD, UNESCO) multiply reports promising education quality for all. Quality politics travel beyond borders and even beyond Europe while they shape education and training systems despite national and local hybridisations (Ozga and Jones 2006). This transfer is not linear, as Magdaléna Hadjiisky argues in her chapter: it has to be situated in a large international context and via a circulation influenced by international organisations. This import/export interaction corresponds to a new governance in which national policy-makers and experts exchange best practices in search of a new political legitimacy.

Quality politics have also an epistemological legitimacy (Grek 2008; Normand 2008, 2010). They are sustained by the human capital theory, which considers that comparison between education systems is a good means for improving economic productivity and competitiveness. It legitimises new psychometrics, which develop international studies focusing on student and adult skills. PISA (Program for International Student Assessment) is one of the best examples of this new worldwide epistemology circulation and creation of a calculative and common space for States (Grek 2009; Meyer and Benavot 2013). As Luís Miguel Carvalho wrote, PISA is part of a long term movement towards the institutionalisation of comparative knowledge and scripts for knowledge-policy relationships (Carvalho 2014). In his chapter, he shows how international surveys reshape the knowledge tradition of comparative education by building indicators for decision-making. In dealing with its own data, the OECD has acquired capacities in transnational governance for education and provides an expert-based independent framework for monitoring and steering school systems. In doing so, it has woven a chain of mutual-surveillance practices by setting up rules, agendas and initiatives in national contexts.

The building of a European and common space of measurement, like the implementation of global quality politics, corresponds to 'governing by numbers', which transforms the relationship between science and policy. PISA is supported by accountability systems developing student tests and transforming regimes of inspection in Europe (Grek and Ozga 2009; Ozga *et al.* 2011; Grek *et al.* 2013). The role of experts is crucial as they are mobile and used by different organisations for decision-making (Grek 2013). Relatively invisible, even if it is present at different stages of the process, expertise guarantees evidence for policy-making and legitimates knowledge. The OECD has become the boundary organisation in the field of transnational educational governance. With its work on the construction of performance indicators, and more recently with its success in international comparative testing, it has emerged as the central producer of policy-oriented knowledge in the developed world; and it offers not only measureable and comparable data but also – what is considered – reliable guidance for the open method of coordination (Bruno *et al.* 2006).

By describing the epistemic dimensions of expertise, Romuald Normand is studying the building of expert knowledge from the inside, in order better to grasp its genesis and mechanisms, and to complete the work carried out in prior studies on expert networks and epistemic communities (Normand 2010). An analysis of encounters and interactions between experts and policy-makers explains the variety and contingency of expertise within a European group or network. Learning is linked to the socialisation and commitments of different actors through role plays, crossed representations and mutual recognition. There are therefore different institutional and epistemic arrangements defining the shape and the content of policy learning and expertise at the European scale.

## Calculative universities and technologies

Beyond indicators and expertise, quality politics are largely supported and consecrated by the Bologna Process, of which the aim was and is to make the European higher education area a driver for the development of the knowledge economy (Vögtle and Martens 2014). The aim of creating a harmonised space is to make Europe more attractive and competitive in standardising structures of diplomas to facilitate the European mobility of students. The Bologna Process has been pursued by the development of comparable criteria and methodologies for student learning and curriculum. Quality politics led to the European qualifications framework, which sets up different levels of knowledge and skills and structures the evaluation and accreditation systems developed in Europe. The European network for quality assurance in higher education (ENQA) is particularly active in the development of networks and cooperation between national quality insurance agencies. In establishing standards and guidelines, the ENQA has sought not only to promote insurance quality methods and programmes for higher education institutions in Europe but also instruments of measurement (rankings, benchmarks and national performance-measurement exercises).

The definitions of academic quality correspond to the same standards and the building of an international reputation, which has important effects on the governance of higher education institutions (Kauppi and Erkkilä 2011). Rankings have been implemented worldwide and have been extended as 'world-class excellence' measurements. They have led higher education policies to restructure and concentrate resources to give a higher visibility to universities. Niilo Kauppi shows how these rankings are symbolic technologies that reflect and shape transnational convergence/divergence processes based on knowledge production and use. He analyses the links between these tools and the formation of discursive hierarchies and the reproduction/transformation of dominant values in global higher education. In many cases, the search for quality increases competition through economic evaluation and exchanges of goods and services that were not previously considered to be of economic value, thus leading to the constitution of markets or quasi-markets.

Quality insurance is completed by new public management technologies in higher education, which are now common throughout Europe. Budgetary constraints have been tightened through reduced funding, and with new instruments based on indicators and performance, university leaders are now expected to play managerial roles at the expense of collegial power in deliberative, representative bodies. Faculties and departments have to introduce evaluation in the curriculum and the definition of pedagogical objectives as argued by Jean-Emile Charlier and Sarah Croché in their contribution. Indeed, within universities, a myriad of internal tracking, data collection and audit processes are applied to ensure policies and practices are in place and to make sure that performance targets are well managed. As Susan Robertson demonstrates, risk calculations are now found in a widening range of activities within the higher education sector. But, beyond the need to adapt to the market and management policies, the representations of risk also affects academic work and the forging of academics' reputations.

## Virtues, values and sense of justice

Benchmarking plays an important role by proposing standards, which, like rankings, go beyond what the institutions can fix by themselves in terms of objectives and performance targets (Bruno 2009). As Isabelle Bruno shows, benchmarking is a mode of government that promotes initiative, self-evaluation, responsibility, volunteerism and personal commitment. Instead of subjecting people to orders and rules, it leads their involvement and governs their initiatives. Governing by benchmarks fixes numerical targets considered to be indisputable. This use of probing data is currently named evidence-based management or management by facts in business. It has penetrated education systems via positivist epistemology. Educational research is increasingly considered as engineering and problem solving while certain 'entrepreneurs' are penetrating political agendas and international organisations to promote evidence-based research in education (Lingard 2013). This technocratic policy focuses on issues and means of effectiveness, and limits the opportunities for practitioners to produce context-based judgements (Biesta 2007). Gert Biesta challenges the idea that there is a model for professional action as claimed by evidence-based research and practice, in which education is reduced to a treatment or an intervention according to a causal and external model borrowed from natural sciences. Judgements in education are not only factual: they are based on values.

Some of these values are highlighted by Sharon Gewirtz in her chapter. In universities, professional practices are associated with peer regulation in a hierarchical and bureaucratic context. But the strategy of managerialism is to create academics capable of integrating themselves into a new professionalism, a quality approach and to support their students (Derouet and Normand 2008). Some of them are tempted by the ideological components of empowerment, innovation, autonomy and responsibility. As Sharon Gewirtz shows, this new professionalism is translated into an explicit assessment of professional skills, controls and audits, performance targets interpreted as committed, accountable and which generates competitiveness among academics. It is a way of supporting academics with regard to normative values and self-motivation, the language of quality and satisfying student needs, the ideologies of empowerment and team work. It legitimises a discourse of individualisation and competition in which individual performance is linked to academic success or failure.

At the European scale, the new relationship between knowledge and politics has shaped an 'epistemic governance' affecting the beliefs, ideals and desires of actors (Alasuutari and Qadir 2014). Policy-making and decision-making shape knowledge through mechanisms and techniques that are not directly perceptible but define and make the context acceptable to people. This scientific and expert context characterises the ontology of actors, their background understanding, the preconception they have regarding facts and measurements. In this appeal to authority to make reality accountable, science and particularly expertise play an essential role by providing knowledge, facts and numbers considered as relevant, transparent and independent even in the computation of risks. Evidence-based policies are the touchstone of this new ordering of actors' ontology.

The epistemic work also focuses on norms and principles of justice, as has been observed in universities, where an academic is capable of convincing others and making claims for a common good (rationality, equality, freedom, the well-being of students, sustainable development, etc.) that allows or forces them to act in a given situation. It is a morale of reciprocal rights and duties based on explicit or tacit arguments or assumptions. They gain support or conviction for a better world while they are legitimised by an 'objective' evidence, as can be observed in expert groups. The horizon of justice is one of the driving forces of the European construction of education and training. As John Holford writes, different discourses of modernisation and change have supported the implementation of the lifelong learning policies, as was the case earlier for the comprehensive school system (Derouet *et al.* 2015).

A detour through history is particularly enlightening to show how a certain conception of equality of opportunities shifted to the imaginary of equity and effectiveness in abandoning the ambition of non-vocational education for adults. Eric Verdier shows how the lifelong learning policies are made up of a diversity of societal arrangements and compromises, which have been historically forged in European countries according to certain principles of justice and conventions.

These regimes of justice and diversity of goods are important features of the interactions among actors, and they also structure lifelong learning policies. Luc Boltanski and Laurent Thévenot's theory, from their book *On justification. Economies of worth* (Boltanski and Laurent 2006), is useful to specify that evaluation and standardisation and quality relate to different orders of worth: an industrial worth when evaluation is aiming for effectiveness, a market worth when evaluation puts people and resources in competition against each other, a civic worth when evaluation reduces, for example, inequalities, etc. Boltanski and Thevenot's use of the notion of evaluation is substantially different from its usual meaning: they consider modes of valuation in the sense that judgement from standards has to be put into the perspective of a plurality of valuations for the common good. The interesting aspect of standards and quality are that they allow the deployment of different orders of worth in terms of justification. One can invoke standards on behalf of student well-being, on behalf of the increase in performance, on behalf of maintaining a university's prominence, on behalf of equality of opportunities, on behalf of the tradition of curriculum, etc. Standards have therefore drawn up a global political order and they are the result of arrangements and compromises between different actors to emphasise such or such conception of the common good. They also allow several forms of evaluation oriented according to this perspective.

## Lifelong learning politics: what critical stance?

However, in lifelong learning politics, some actors have more resources than others, particularly data and knowledge, and they occupy asymmetrical positions determining power relationships (Kauppi 2010). If a diversity of actors, resources and positions produce standardised knowledge and governing instruments, some standards are predominant. Furthermore, European politics is the sum of representations, discourses and actions supporting a normative, ideological, technical and scientific definition of expertise and decision-making. A diversity of principles of justice and commitments can emerge but there is no guarantee that they will be accepted equally. European politics is based on interactions and knowledge shared by researchers, experts, policy-makers and professionals who give meaning to a certain political reality and seek to make it acceptable to lay people. But it is also a truth-seeking process, based on a certain conception of evidence, and defined by institutional arenas in which participation and deliberation are subjected to normative expectations and frames.

European lifelong learning politics presents a modelled representation of the current reality, while anticipating and translating them into instruments, deploying irreversible and often invisible frames, which do not leave much place for criticism. When criticism does arise via protests and diverse accusations (debates, controversies, polemics), it faces constraints of relevance and acceptability, as shown by the discussions on the PISA survey. Criticism is therefore often included in reformist changes and proposals, and leads to quarrels among experts keeping lay people at a distance. The vision of education is framed by a technical and abstract formulation in which numbers play a key role in breaking with the 'common sense' of lay people and in bringing an 'enlightened' and 'neutral' vision far from 'ideological stances'. This scientific rationalisation, based on technical criteria, tends to ignore the social and cultural dimensions of education as the values and principles of justice guiding the action of individuals.

In the confrontation and public debate about educational reforms, criticism is not only based on the representation of national political interests (for example between trade unions and governments) but on the opposition between the realism 'claimed' by international expertise and the relativism imputed to other proposals, particularly those coming from critical social sciences and anti-globalisation movements. The creation of an 'official truth' is facilitated by certain rituals and ceremonies during meetings between policy-makers and experts in which some indisputable assumptions are claimed, because they are based on 'irrefutable evidence'; while certain data are not accessible to lay people as that would generate a counter-demonstration that does not fit into the time allocated for discussion. Consequently, these proposals have the capacity to restrain the field of criticism and to prevent discourses with their own semantical and hermeneutical coherence.

However, criticism has not disappeared and it has reinvested the field of education policies in challenges against reforms. During the past few years, accusations have been made against the damaging effects of testing and accountability on the teaching profession: stress, burn-out, demotivation and people leaving the profession for good. The gap between professed theories of evidence-based education and the reality of teaching practices has been denounced while the PISA survey is coming up against an increasing number of contradictors. Consequently, there is significant tension between European politics supporting international networks of experts and the practitioners' experiences in the daily life of schools and classrooms.

Given these circumstances, how can a critical stance be affirmed? A research programme for a critical and reflexive sociology of education would establish connections between empirical data coming from European-scale comparative studies, normative assumptions structuring actors' representations, interpretative judgements from common theoretical frameworks and a specific focus on the particular contexts in which lifelong learning policies are implemented. It would require withdrawing from methodological nationalism and landscaping the horizon of education policies beyond national borders. It would study trans-nationalisation, scales of governance and interdependencies between both local and global actors. It would overcome discursive analyses of policy to consider the embeddedness of instruments and technologies that transform the representations of education and are forging new norms and visions. This research programme would investigate asymmetries of power and representation within European institutions and networks and the role of some invisible colleges (think tanks, agencies, foundations, associations, etc.) in defining discourses of truth and new rules of evidence. The challenge would also be to shift from a static stance by introducing temporality into the critical perspective. Sociologists would be able to analyse long-term transformations, dynamics and reconfigurations and to take a step back from narratives conveyed by expertise and international organisation, and short-term visions shared by policy-makers.

This book is a contribution to this emerging field of research. In studying politics from education to lifelong learning, the development of this type of research would relativise the sectorial divides linked to the structuration of European programmes and fragmented studies, and to analyse circulations from one sector to another, the complementarities between different decisions and implementations, the connections at different European scales. It would require us to rethink and redesign comparative education's theoretical and methodological tools, as well as the way in which sociology has focused on a dual opposition between agency and structure. A possible path would be to consider the ontology of European actors and how they transform the European political order by their cultures, ideas and languages, but also by their specific actions in institutional contexts when mobilising cognitive and material resources to influence policy-making. It is also time to study how the subject of European politics is governed by daily narratives, experiences and practices.

## References

Abelès, M. (2006). "Parliament, politics and ritual", in *Rituals in Parliament: political, anthropological and historical perspectives on Europe and the United States*. Berlin: Peter Lang, pp. 19–40.

Alasuutari, P. and Qadir, A. (2014). Epistemic governance: an approach to the politics of policy-making. *European Journal of Cultural and Political Sociology*, 1(1), 67–84.

Biesta, G. (2007). Why "what works" won't work: evidence-based practice and the democratic deficit in educational research. *Educational Theory*, 57(1), 1–22.

Boltanski, L. and Thévenot, L. (2006). *On Justification: economies of worth*. Princeton: Princeton University Press.

Bowker, G.C. and Star, S.L. (1999). *Sorting Things Out: classification and its consequences*. Cambridge, MA: MIT Press.

Bruno, I. (2009). The "indefinite discipline" of competitiveness benchmarking as a neoliberal technology of government. *Minerva*, 47(3), 261–280.

Bruno, I., Jacquot, S. and Mandin, L. (2006). Europeanization through its instrumentation: benchmarking, mainstreaming and the open method of co-ordination... toolbox or Pandora's box? *Journal of European Public Policy*, 13(4), 519–536.

Carvalho, L.M. (2014). 'The attraction of mutual surveillance of performances: PISA as a knowledge-policy instrument' in Fenwick T., Mangez E., Ozga J., (eds). *Governing Knowledge: comparison, knowledge-based technologies and expertise in the regulation of education.* New York: Routledge World Yearbook of Education, pp. 58–72.

Dale, R. and Derouet, J-L. (dir.) (2012). The Europeanisation of education policies. *Globalisation, Societies and Education*, 10(4), 150 pp.

Derouet, J.L. and Normand, R. (2008). French universities at a crossroads between crisis and radical reform: toward a new academic regime? *European Education*, 40(1), 20–34.

Derouet, J.-L., Mangez E. and Benadusi L. (2015). Where is the European comprehensive school project today? *European Educational Research Journal*, 14(3–4), 195–205.

Fenwick, T. and Edwards, R. (2010). *Actor-network*. New York, NY: Routledge.

Fenwick, T. and Landri, P. (2012). Materialities, textures and pedagogies: socio-material assemblages in education. *Pedagogy, Culture & Society*, 20(1), 1–7.

Georgakakis, D. (2009). The historical and political sociology of the European Union: a uniquely French methodological approach and quest. *French Politics*, 7(3), 437–455.

Georgakakis, D. and Weisbein, J. (2010). From above and from below: a political sociology of European actors. *Comparative European Politics*, 8(1), 93–109.

Gornitzka, Å. and Sverdrup, U. (2008). Who consults? The configuration of expert groups in the European Union. *West European Politics*, 31(4), 725–750.

Gorur, R. (2011). Policy as assemblage. *European Educational Research Journal*, 10(4), 611–622.

Gorur, R. (2013). The invisible infrastructure of standards. *Critical Studies in Education*, 54(2), 132–142.

Gorur, R. (2014). Towards a sociology of measurement in education policy. *European Educational Research Journal*, 13(1), 58–72.

Grek, S. (2008). From symbols to numbers: the shifting technologies of education governance in Europe. *European Educational Research Journal*, 7(2), 208–218.

Grek, S. (2009). Governing by numbers: the PISA 'effect' in Europe. *Journal of Education Policy*, 24(1), 23–37.

Grek, S. (2013). Expert moves: international comparative testing and the rise of expertocracy. *Journal of Education Policy*, 28(5), 695–709.

Grek, S. and Ozga, J. (2009). Governing education through data: Scotland, England and the European education policy space. *British Educational Research Journal*, 36(6), 937–952.

Grek, S., Lawn, M., Ozga, J. and Segerholm, C. (2013). Governing by inspection? European inspectorates and the creation of a European education policy space. *Comparative Education*, 49(4), 486–502.

Kauppi, N. (2010). The political ontology of European integration. *Comparative European Politics*, 8(1), 19–36.

Kauppi, N. and Erkkilä, T. (2011). The struggle over global higher educa-tion: actors, institutions, and practices. *International Political Sociology*, 5(3), 314–326.

Lascoumes, P. and Le Gales, P. (2007). Introduction: understanding public policy through its instruments – from the nature of instruments to the sociology of public policy instrumentation. *Governance*, 20(1), 1–21.

Lawn, M. (2011). Standardizing the European education policy space. *European Educational Research Journal*, 10(2), 259–272.

Lawn, M. and Grek, S. (2012). *Europeanizing Education: governing a new policy space*. Oxford: Symposium Books Ltd.

Lawn M. and Normand R. (2014). *Shaping of European Education: interdisciplinary approaches*, Abingdon: Routledge.

Lingard, B. (2013). The impact of research on education policy in an era of evidence-based policy. *Critical Studies in Education*, 54(2), 113–131.

Majone, G. (1989). *Evidence, Argument, and Persuasion in the Policy Process*. New Haven: Yale University Press.

Majone, G. (1996). *Regulating Europe*. Abingdon: Routledge.

Meyer, H. and Benavot, A. (2013). *PISA, Power, and Policy: the emergence of global educational governance*. Oxford: Symposium Books.

Normand, R. (2008). School effectiveness or the horizon of the world as a laboratory. *British Journal of Sociology of Education*, 29(6), 665–676.

Normand, R. (2010). Expertise, networks and indicators: the construction of the European strategy in education. *European Educational Research Journal*, 9(3), 407–421.

Nóvoa, A. and Lawn, M. (2002). *Fabricating Europe: the formation of an education space*. London: Kluwer.

Ozga, J. and Jones, R. (2006). Travelling and embedded policy: the case of knowl-edge transfer. *Journal of Education Policy*, 21(1), 1–17.

Ozga, J., Dahler-Larsen, P., Segerholm, C. and Simola, H. (eds). (2011) *Fabricating quality in education: data and governance in Europe*. Abingdon: Routledge.

Radaelli, C.M. (1999). The public policy of the European Union: whither politics of expertise? *Journal of European Public Policy*, 6(5), 757–774.

Robert, C. (2010). Who are the European experts: profiles, trajectories and expert 'careers' of the European Commission. *French Politics*, 8(3), 248–274.

Saurugger, S. and Mérand, F. (2010). Does European integration theory need soci-ology and quest? *Comparative European Politics*, 8(1), 1–18.

Shore, C. (2013). *Building Europe: the cultural politics of European integration*. Abingdon: Routledge.

Vögtle, E. and Martens, K. (2014). The Bologna Process as a template for transna-tional policy coordination. *Policy Studies*, 35(3), 246–263.

# Chapter 2

# Standards and standardisation in European politics of education

*Paolo Landri*

## Introduction

Standards are playing a key role in the complex transformation of the educational landscape. The increasing investment in standards and standardisation is revealing of the effort to change education governance and practice, by clarifying educational objectives, means and practices, reaching 'optimal' or 'good' performance levels and establishing the best conditions for the many elements of the ecology of education practice. The attention to standards suggests a tendency towards the objectification of education practice, i.e. a shift towards what is measurable in education practice, and translation of the many aspects of education practice often considered 'tacit', or left as 'implicit' in scientific evidence to support policy-making in the field. Schools and educational organisations are expected to be more accountable and to comply with 'best practice', or to increase their capacity to meet predefined educational goals.

Standard-based reforms are evident worldwide. In Europe, the construction of a European education space is taking place through the introduction of standards intended to govern a panoply of educational differences still under national legislation (at least in principle). In this case, standardisation concerns the use of common benchmarks and indicators (from the Lisbon Strategy); the development of infrastructure, such as ECTS (European credit transfer system) in higher education, or the EQF (European qualification framework) aimed at enhancing the transparency, portability and mobility of knowledge and competences in the EU; the adoption of platforms in the field of new educational technologies (Lawn 2011).

As investment in standards is almost a 'universal belief' several questions can be raised. In particular, we are interested in understanding: (a) How does this 'indisputable truth' emerge? How does the focus on standards and standardisation of education practice come to be the dominant trend in education policy-making, and inspired education reform? (b) What aspects of education practice are the current trends of standardisation in European education policy focused on? To provide some answers to these questions, the chapter draws on sociomaterial approaches to education (Fenwick *et al.* 2011; Fenwick and Edwards 2010; Fenwick and Landri 2012) and considers education standards as epistemic objects. In particular I will: (a) trace back some of the theoretical thinking supporting the standardisation of education practice and reflected in policy documents triggering standard based reform, and (b) try to analyse the dominant circuits of knowledge and expertise supporting the black-boxing of standards in European education. While standards in the making are assemblages of dispersed and partly heterogeneous trasnational associations of networks, they are frequently enacted and viewed as technical objects for producing ecologies of predictable and transparent educational practice. In the following pages, I will first present some conceptual reflections on educational standards by claryfing some definitions, in order to position the theoretical framework of the chapter. I will then discuss the recent history of the construction of European space of education in terms of the fabrication of an infrastructure of education, and an installation of a regime of performativity. I will consider how this space emerges as a web of discourses, technologies and circuits of expertise. In particular, I will show how the investment in standards from the adoption of the Lisbon Strategy on has been a significant shift in the Europeanisation of education since it made visible what appeared opaque and hidden before.

## Standards as epistemic objects

In this chapter I will consider standards as epistemic objects (Mulcahy 2011). By following a sociomaterial approach to education policy (Fenwick 2011; Fenwick and Edwards 2010; Fenwick and Landri 2012), the 'incompleteness' of educational standards is underlined. While they usually appear as technical objects in contemporary educational discourses (that is, as fixed, stable, ready to hand, transparent, etc.), a closer investigation into the ontology of standards reveals the lack of precise definitions, their multiple instantiations and ambiguities, i.e. their capacity being indefinite unfolding, question-generating and complexity. A literature review of standards and standardisation in organisation studies highlights that (a) there is struggle to define standards, albeit, as it is suggested, they are carriers of a specific sense of normativity, and (b) most of the contributions underestimate the dynamics of standards and standardisation, that is to say, the fluidity of standards by emphasising the stability and the uniformity of standards in organisational and institutional settings (Brunsson *et al.* 2012). In following this argumentation, it is noted how standards may concern any aspect of the ecology of education practice, i.e. from the 'inputs' (for example, teachers, learners, school buildings, etc.), to the 'processes' (planning, evaluation, the delivery of the education provision, etc.), to the 'outputs' of the educational practices. They contribute, to some extent, to the construction of the infrastructure of education (Gorur 2012).

However, standard and standardisation are often considered negative terms in educational discourses. It appears to introduce a logic of uniformity that is at odds with the unpredictability of the educational events. Opponents suggest that standards enclosing the ecology of education practices in an unnecessary uniformity risk devaluing the teaching professionality and significance of learning for students in schools and elsewhere. Of course, it is a 'non-sense' to be 'either or not' standardisation in education, yet in being the infrastructure of what education relies on, i.e. the set of technologies, protocols and spaces for education, a given form of standardisation is not neutral. As a matter of fact, the infrastructure may orient educational agencies in a significant way, and affect the very conditions of education as practice. In some cases, education reforms or specific education policies are oriented to modify certain aspects of this infrastructure, by influencing in a more or less direct way educational work. Changing the infrastructure, therefore, is expected to change the shape of the spaces of education. The dominant critics' standards in education, however, are related mostly to the efforts at standardising educational outcomes that are the core of the standard-based reform. Even in this case, and despite the efforts of their proponents, standards are less stable than expected as they come to be associated with many legitimating discourses (Waldow 2014; Lundahl and Waldow 2009).

## Waves of standardisation

It is beyond the scope of this chapter to discuss the history of educational standards. Nevertheless, it is possible to note the increasing attention towards standardisation in education. The attention to standards and, in particular, standard-based reform is related to the history of mass schooling and the construction of industrial society (Aldrich 2000). In 1862, with the introduction of the revised code in elementary schools in England, standards of proficiency were identified that permitted classifying children according to their performance in examinations. Accordingly, standards came to be defined as the expected levels of achievement for all the children of a particular age. Advocates of the benefits of setting educational standards may be found first at the end of the nineteenth century and then during the early twentieth century in the social efficiency movement in the United States. The social efficiency movement in North America was part of the progressive movement aimed at developing reforms to cope with the emerging problems of the first industrialisation. This movement was heavily influenced by Taylorism, whose success in industrial production led to the application of the principles of scientific management to the development of the curriculum and the organisation of schooling. In an explicit way, several authors tried to establish some guidelines to raise school efficiency and set a number of basic principles for educational planning, through predefining objectives and educational aims (i.e. the 'Tyler rationale'). Here, the application of scientific management in schools was part of a general effort to standardise several aspects of the high school curriculum and college policies in the United States. J.F. Bobbitt was one of the authors who expressed in the clearest way interest in making schooling more efficient, by focusing on school outputs. In his treatise (Bobbitt 1913) he attributed a relevant role to educational standards. Schools have to decide very much like a factory on the desidered product, and standardise it in order to become efficient. Standards, however, are to be defined by the customer, and not by the students, or by the internal school subjects. Therefore, educational standards should emerge from a careful survey of the community needs (the 'customer' in his argumentation). Community needs were translated into educational standards that defined the specific requirements of each occupational group, and the objectives of the curriculum. This translation implied the construction of forms of testing to determine whether the educational standards had been met and to what extent. At that time, tests developed by psychometricians like Thorndike permitted measuring performance, and evaluating the progress of individuals, as well as the performance of teachers, schools, or school districts in accomplishing educational standards. It may be noted then how educational standards have their origins outside schools, and here, in particular, the community, or societal needs represent the point of reference for considering the level of efficiency of the system of instruction. Also, educational standards imply forms of evaluation, or a better standardised way of assessment, whereby it is possible to assess the achievement of an expected outcome. Standards and evaluation play a central role in making clear the social expectations about school performance, and how to evaluate individual and school positions with respect to a hierarchy of achievements. In this respect, they are 'normative specifications for the steering of educational systems' (Waldow 2014), While Taylorism, and, more generally, the parallel with corporate enterprise is hardly appropriate for supporting educational standards, the logic for rational curriculum-making, and modernising school organisation soon become, in particular with Tyler's work, a 'taken for granted' shared repertoire of pedagogy. The emphasis on predefined educational purposes, the selection of educational experiences and their evaluation constituted as a matter of fact the building blocks of the discipline that resemble closely the procedure suggested by Bobbit for defining educational standards.

The attention to standards emerged again: (a) with the publication of the famous book *A Nation at Risk* (ANAR) (Gardner 1983) and (b) emphasis worldwide on accountability during the last two decades. The publication of ANAR, a report by the US Commission of Excellence, had a notable impact in the United States and elsewhere. It was a dramatic description of the state of education, and an attempt at defending federal governance of education in a time when the states had, and still have, the powers of regulation in educational policy-making, and President Reagan sought to eliminate the federal Department of Education. It raised the issue of the possible decline of the United States in the marketplace, and of the threat of losing the Cold War. The report recommended the introduction of measurable standards in order to raise academic performances and to fill the achievement gap. Here, the attention to standards was part of the strategy to regain the position of the United States in economic and military terms, and it meant also the definition of external reference for education policy. As a matter of fact, education was not important per se, but instrumental for an economy and for securing the United States' position in the world. Standards were means of transforming an educational issue into a matter of national defence making possible the development of a strong argument in favour of federal intervention. ANAR convinced the United States government to place pressure on OECD to invest more in collecting and analysing data to pave the way for programmes like PISA (Program for International Student Assessment). Furthermore, it ushered in several reforms that tended to consolidate the standard-based reform, like the introduction of standards in teaching mathematics.

Standard-based reforms were recently supported by the rhetorics of accountability in public service, and the discourse of new public management. In this respect, the No Child Left Behind Act 2002 was a decisive move for standard-based reforms in the present age of accountability and gained support in the United States from conservatives and republicans. Generally, in the last few decades, we have witnessed in Europe and all over the world, the development of apparatuses of accountability of educational systems. The policy epidemic envisages both the construction of a devolved environment and the consolidation of school autonomy, as well as the setting-up of dispositifs of standard-based assessment (Levin 1998). Some authors underline how educational standards are ingredients of the neoliberal agenda (Ball 1998; Klees 2008), introducing logics of performativity in education by drawing on the measurability of the learning outcomes and mechanisms of competition among schools and social and individual agencies to such an extent as to conflate education and learning (Biesta 2008). More generally, the measurability of the learning outcomes are to be understood as increasing attention to the economic role of knowledge in the generation of wealth and innovation (Piketty 2014). Contemporary capitalism favours the creation of a knowledge economy (Powell and Snellman 2004), in which investments in knowledge should enhance the competitiveness of economic systems.[1] However, the development of knowledge has different trajectories in societal and organisational sectors (David and Foray 2003; Foray 2001) according to an economistic approach to innovation. Schools and universities would display limited improvements in the knowledge-base of causal dynamics of teaching and learning (Foray 2001). The underdevelopment of the knowledge base would inevitably lead to the so-called 'Baumol-disease', i.e. the increase of the overall costs, without significant gains in terms of productivity rate, such as those occurring in other manufacturing sectors. The 'disease' would result from (a) the relationship between science and technology in education; (b) the low level of codification of professional knowledge; and (c) the lack of incentives for the diffusion of innovation in education practice (Foray 2001; Nelson 2003). To cure the 'disease' it is suggested investing in the objectualisation of teaching and learning, and shifting educational research to evidence-based perspectives, thus privileging the search for representational objectivity. In other words, a 'right cure' would be to develop a new regime of visibility, to place emphasis on the explicit, measurable and standardised aspects of education. This strategy would help in improving the quality, efficacy and efficiency of the educational sectors by facing complex dilemmas between increasing spending by accepting low productivity and privatising some aspects or the whole sector with negative effects in terms of social equity (Baumol 2012; Hill and Roza 2010). To some extent, this proposes moving from loosely coupled systems to tighter educational systems, by translating them into variable-centred relationships among contexts, processes and outcomes. At the forefont of this shift in policy knowledge about education and in the search for educational standards are the intergovernmental organisations (IGOs); a prominent role is played by the World Bank, OECD and UNESCO. Overall, they are contributing to diffusing educational ideologies, and, in particular, to expanding the neoliberal agenda in global education, by promoting a 'soft' convergence of educational policies. While they are not able to affect directly national education agendas, they shape global education spaces: (a) by soft laws, (b) through grants and loans (especially in the case of poor countries), (c) via the elaboration of the knowledge base for educational policies and (d) by promoting complex exercises of evaluation of educational policies at the global level (Rutkowski 2007). Of particular interest is their key role at the global level in shaping the data infrastructure of education and their ability to assemble a network of expertise in measuring and evaluating educational policies recognised as an obligatory point of passage for national education policy constituencies. As regards the data infrastructure, they have over time constitued a space of commensuration. In 1970, UNESCO created the international standard classification of education (ISCED), which was updated in 1997 with the new realease of ISCED 97, with the aim of providing a statistical framework for collecting and reporting international comparable education statistics. ISCED97 is now used by IGOs to provide comparable educational indicators from different countries. As a matter of fact, OECD, Eurostat and UNESCO collect and distribute all national comparable educational indicators, by constructing a 'structured oligopoly' in that field. The investment in educational indicators has led to a huge accumulation of comparative data from international surveys carried out by IGOs and by their specific programmes. PISA is one of the most successful programmes from OECD, and concerns, as is well known, international standard assessments jointly developed by participating countries. Administered every 3 years to 15-year-old students, and promoted by OECD as real assessment, it is focused on mathematics, literacy and science. However, it promises to provide information about the capacity to face real life problems. It was initially designed for OECD countries, although there is now a growing participation of non-OECD countries. Accordingly, the outcomes from these countries seem to have low validity because students are not adequately measured by PISA (or at least not the majority). PISA success then transforms the programme as a point of reference, as a benchmark for measuring and assessing learning outcomes so that OECD contributes to defining what is to be evaluated, raising issues from which national agendas may be influenced. In this way, PISA becomes a prominent standard, or, in a more appropriate way, it reinforces large-scale survey assessment, as a standard for educational evaluation, and OECD is in turn recognised as popularising PISA as an expert in evaluation. Of course, participating countries have reacted in many different ways by either incorporating or not incorporating it in their national standards and policies. We will return in the next section to the dynamics of incompleteness of standards with reference to the history of the construction of a European space of education, which can be understood as an example of soft convergence with notable investment in standardisation. In this history, OECD plays an important role as an agency of Europeanisation. EU institutions are reinforcing the Europeanisation of education from the perspective of increasing collaboration with international and globalising organisations, which is revealed to be detrimental in the creation of a new education policy space (Lawn and Grek 2012). We will see how the materialisation of this space occurred via the institution of standards of equivalence and performance standards.

## The fabrication of the European space of education

The fabrication of a European space of education developed in the long history of EU cooperation in education and training (Pépin 2007). The emergence of this space was not a straightforward process; it was a complex and unexpected trajectory that started from a condition of impossibility, and led to the emergence of a new topology of education: the European space of education.

By following Pepin's (2007) reconstruction of history of cooperation in education and training in the EU, it is possible to distinguish four stages: (1) 1957–1971: pre-history – education and training have different starting points; (2) 1971–1992: the foundation years for cooperation in education – towards recognition in the Maastricht Treaty; (3) 1992–2000: the emergence of the concepts of lifelong learning and knowledge-based society – cooperation in education and training become closer; (4) 2000–2006: the Lisbon Strategy for 2010 and lifelong learning – from rhetoric to implementation. This history describes a shift from a condition of incommensuration to an increasing investment in standardisation and, in particular, developing forms of commensuration of educational systems (Espeland and Stevens 1998; Espeland and Stevens 2008).

Initially, education systems of member states were thought to be incommensurable. Education was intended to be a national competence, a classic locus of nation-state sovereignty, a place for national regulation closely related to the discourse of cultural identities. It was then a politically sensitive topic in international cooperation. Education policy-making is thought to be regulated at the national level linked to the formation of national identities, and as such is not comparable or equivalent. In fact, education was not at the centre of the fabrication of Europe. While there was much hope for the reconciliation of the peoples of Europe after the destruction of the Second War World, education was a 'taboo' subject for 20 years at the European Community level, and indeed the cooperation among European countries was limited and informed by a logic of pragmatism. The Treaty of Rome signed in 1957 involved only six member states, and concerned only economic integration and agricultural policy. The dominant approach was to develop European cooperation step by step, by privileging economy first, because 'politics will follow' (Jean Monnet). A preserved heterogeneity was the point of departure of the Europeanisation of education. Cooperation started to develop in the field of vocational training, which was explicitly mentioned in the Treaty of Rome (article 128), and concerned those aspects of learning mostly related to the needs and opportunities of economic cooperation at the community level. However, vocational training remained peripheral in political agendas, and while the treaty included the need for a 'common policy framework in vocational training', little was done at the beginning in this field. Education and cultural cooperation was instead the responsibility of the Council of Europe, an intergovernmental locus that was considered most suitable for sensitive topics. Ministers of education met for the first time in November 1971, and agreed on a first resolution in 1976, a non-legally binding document that, nevertheless, represented an opportunity for cooperation because it recognised the need to work together in the field of vocational training and to supplement this effort through joint initiatives in education. The document reaffirmed the diversity of education systems and excluded any harmonisation. However, it allowed for the design and implementation of the first community action. At this stage (i.e. the second step in Pepin's chronology), the cooperation in education lacked a legal basis. Until 1992, there was no clear institutional framework: (a) by 1981, commission services in education were integrated to directorate general XII responsible for research, and vocational training was the responsibility of directorate general V working on social affairs; (b) the work done in the first community action programme in education (research, joint programme, study visits, etc.) developed in parallel with the initiative in the field of vocational training. In 1985, importantly, the European Court of Justice gave a broad interpretation of the Treaty of Rome, and, in particular, article 128, so that it was possible to enlarge European cooperation to include higher education. Between 1985 and 1992 several European programmes (Erasmus, Petra, Lingua, etc.) were launched, and the overall budget was increased. These programmes facilitated the creation of transnational action nets, by enhancing collaboration and mobilities mostly in the field of vocational training and higher education albeit implemented in a separate way. Finally, the Maastricht Treaty in 1992 ended disputes among member states and the commission over the legal basis of cooperation in education. The treaty clearly recognised education as a locus for collaboration, but left the member states with the task of defining the content and organisational structure of education. Nonetheless, it considered community action as a support and supplement of national policies both in education and vocational training. In this text, the domains of education and vocational training were still kept separate. However, a European space of education consisting of networks of collaboration was emerging, and a legal infrastructure supported its developments. The 1990s was characterised by the expansion and rationalisation of existing European programmes (Socrates, Leonardo Da Vinci) in an attempt to integrate the different initiatives. Also, the period witnessed a change in educational discourses leading to the above-mentioned rhetorics of knowledge economy. The publication of Jacques Delors' White Paper and the document of the European Community on the learning society solicited a transformation in education and vocational training to face the challenges of the knowing capitalism (Thrift 2005), and to maintain the competitiveness of the EU in line with the traditions of the member states. Those documents reshaped for the first time the boundaries between education and vocational training, and proposed the adoption of perspectives on Lifelong Learning at the European level to recognise the need for 'giving value' in the experiences of knowing and learning in work, education and everyday life. They supported a set of related initiatives: the work of validation of non-formal competencies, youth voluntary services, second chance schools, etc. aimed at valourising knowledge and learning in the multiple spheres of activities. Lifelong Learning became fundamental in the 1997 Amsterdam Treaty, because it represented a key objective of an integrated European strategy on economy and employment. Member states committed themselves to elaborating policies raising knowledge of their populations by widening access to education, and ensuring ongoing improvements in their skills and competencies. Finally, the decade ended with the Sorbonne Declaration that initiated the so-called Bologna Process a year later, i.e. the committment to a common restructuring of European higher education systems to make them comparable and compatible, by incorporating the principle of lifelong learning. The Bologna Process was a significant event in the history of the European higher education system that was preceded by the successful Erasmus programmes and the networks developed over time by the most important European higher education institutions. It promoted the convergence of the systems of higher education by means of a standard framework (the two cycles structure of bachelor and masters degrees) and a standard platform (European credit transfer system) of recognition that regulated and made possible the mobilities of students in a space of equivalence. Yet, a notable turn in the field of education, and indeed in the development of a more integrated policy framework, was the Lisbon Strategy at the beginning of the millennium. The Lisbon Strategy defined a 10-year EU economic and social strategy that called for the modernisation of the educational system, and affirmed the relevance of knowledge and lifelong learning as key strategies for economic competitiveness, social innovation and equity. The Lisbon agenda promoted even more community collaboration in the field of education and training. It did so by providing a set of objectives and a method of work, i.e. the open method of coordination. In addition, the Lisbon Strategy promoted the unfolding of a space of commensuration; common metrics (here 'performance standards') made comparable what in the past were meant to be incommensurables. Through the open method of coordination ministers of education agreed on common objectives, and translated these goals into performance standards for educational systems, i.e. benchmarks to be met. Standards were made operational via educational indicators concerning three broad areas: the quality and efficiency of educational systems, their access to all and their openess to the world. They concerned: early school leaving (2010 EU goal: average of no more than 10 per cent); low achievers in reading (2010 EU goal: 20 per cent decrease in the number of 15-year-old low achievers); completion rate of upper secondary school (2010 EU goal: 85 per cent of 22-year-old students); graduates in maths, science and technology and gender balance (2010 EU goal: 15 per cent increase in the number of graduates); lifelong learning (at least 12.5 per cent of the adult working age population are expected to participate). The machinery of the open method of coordination envisages the availability of data infrastructure that frames the confrontation, the exchanges and the discussion. Also, it provides a framework to monitor the progress in achieving the objectives, and identifying policies or practices most effective for meeting the agreed benchmarks. Yet, the Lisbon Strategy was relevant for the development of a common framework to identify the key competencies for lifelong learning. In 2006, the council and European parliament defined a European qualifications framework; some general principles for the validation of non-formal and informal competences, and quality assurance in the field of vocational training and lifelong learning. In this respect, it further contributed to creating a European space of equivalence and mobilities around education, knowledge and learning.

The fabrication of a European space of education implies the creation and the mobilisation of standards aimed at making possible comparisons and equivalences. Of course, the implementation of the objectives of the Lisbon Strategy is far from realised, and they have been updated in the actual conditions of economic crisis to consider the wider horizons of 2020. Nonetheless, the Lisbon Strategy has proved to be a 'quantum leap' in the Europeanisation of education (Grek and Lawn 2009), and it is important to pay attention to what has made possible the decisive move towards commensuration. A relevant role here has been played by the circuits of expertise and knowledge mobilised by the Directorate General for Education and Culture to support the open method of coordination in shaping and black-boxing educational standards. Knowledge and expertise in the datafication of education have been mobilised to influence the policy-makers of member states that, notwithstanding the recognition of the Maastricht Treaty and the need to develop a more integrated approach, still control their national education and training systems. Expertise and knowledge were constructed in a complex assemblage of networks developed over time by interfacing OECD, European institutions (Eurostat, directorates, etc.) and experts (Normand 2010). In this history, as we have already stated, OECD became an obligatory point of passage. The datafication was a long process as up to the late 1970s there were no comparable statistics from countries, no reliable educational indicators and benchmarks. In the mid-1980s an important development was the international indicators and evaluation of education systems project (INES), which was carried out by the OECD's Centre for Educational Research and Innovation. The project assembled three international networks: (1) a network led by the United States, which was interested in international survey assessments, and joined later on by PISA; (2) a network led by Sweden, which mobilised representantives from the European Commission and the European Centre for Vocational Training, and produced educational indicators for education at a glance for a similar Eurostat data collection; (3) a network led by the Netherlands, which mobilised officials from UNESCO to construct educational indicators for school inputs, processes and outputs. These works were completed at the end of the 1980s and led to the OECD's publication *Education at a Glance*, whose first edition was at the beginning of the 1990s. The publication received very positive comments from policy makers, and the networks were relaunched to produce guidelines about how to collect comparable education data. The analysis of the networks of expertise permits understanding the circuits of knowledge mobilised to enact the European space of education as a space of commensuration (Normand 2010). In the first circuit, school effectiveness research suggesting evaluation of schools through diverse variables concerning inputs, processes and outputs, teaching and management are the main independent variables (Luyten *et al.* 2005). A second international circuit was more closely related to the OECD's position on education and drew on human capital theory. Here, it is assumed that the measurement of cognitive skills is a good indicator of the quality of an education system, and of the success of individuals in the labour market. Models of variables are expected to link educational inputs to learning outcomes. This circuit includes economists who pay particular attention to how human capital contributes to innovation and the production of wealth (Hanushek and Wössmann 2007). Finally, the third circuit concerned experts in international large-scale assessments, and developed from the publication of the already cited ANAR in 1983. It included experts from OECD, the US educational testing agency, etc., and promoted the expansion of the international association for the evaluation of the educational achievement that supported the development of large-scale assessments, like PIRLS, trends in international mathematics and science study, PISA and international adult literacy studies, now considered authoritative sources of policy knowledge. The Directorate General for Education and Culture drew largely on the INES' project work, and made connection with the third circuits to build comparable data on European education, and to develop quality indicators of educational systems. In this way, the data infrastructure of the Lisbon Strategy was largely shaped by the search for common metrics elaborated in these transnational networks of knowledge and expertise and, in particular, by their theoretical frameworks and assumptions. While presented as objective and neutral, datafication is not, because the translation from the complexities of education practice to complicated numbers implies normative choices. First, it draws on a mathematical model that privileges the logic of the correlation between variables, and incorporates education practice within a causal-like reasoning. Second, it reflects assumptions from theoretical frameworks that support the commensuration. In this case, it reveals the perspective of human capital theory. For instance, the decision to concentrate on educational indicators, like preschool education, early school leavers, or the rate of completion of upper secondary school, highlights an interest in the conditions to improve the productivity of youth. Similarly, the attention to the participation of adults in the lifelong learning initiative is oriented towards understanding the extent to which the knowledge stock of the population is updated. Therefore, while the member states are still responsible for the content and organisation of their education systems, they are, nonetheless, influenced by educational standards that are shaped in/by complex assemblages of expertise at the European and global level. It might be argued that the difficult road of constructing a European identity was replaced by the development of a space of commensuration.

In considering the EU standards, however, we are not dealing with once-and-for-all defined objects, rather, their fluidity and incompleteness may be observed. Educational standards, accordingly, are not static, and come to be refined through discussion and negotiation both at the design stage and also through the process of monitoring. The education and training 2010 work programme (ET 2010) containing educational indicators and benchmarks was approved in 2002 by the European Council and by the European Commission. The final list was refined from several previous passages. The initial list contained 33 indicators, which was then reduced to 29 thanks to the standing group on indicators and benchmarks, and the work of nine working groups that included representatives from the different European countries. Furthermore, in the changing conditions of contemporary societies, the difficulties in meeting the objectives called for a reconsideration of the performance standards. Data showed the lack of reforms at the national level, and solicited repeated recommendations from the commission aimed at improving the capacity to meet the agreed upon objectives. The 'Kok report' highlighted the little achievements in realising the Lisbon Strategy in education and training, and in devising policies to improve the performance of educational indicators. On the basis of this report, the commission reconsidered the strategy of 2002, by restricting its broader focus and concentrating on the economic effects of the investment in human capital, i.e. the relation between education and employment (European Commission, 2005). A simplified version of an open method of coordination from now on will ease the work of reporting from member states. Also, the space of commensuration is moving according to the monitoring process, and the challenges in policy discourses are changing. The economic crisis of 2008 impacted the Eurozone, and brought to the forefront the issue of employment, in particular youth employment, to such an extent that there emerged a need for a revised strategy for education and training. The education and training work programme 2010 (ET 2010) was in fact replaced by the education and training strategy (ET 2020), by reflecting the passage from the Lisbon Strategy to the Europe 2020 strategy. A closer look at the list of benchmarks reveals continuity, but also difference. The differences in terms of novelties are concerned with: (a) the increase of benchmarks (eight from 2012); (b) and some revisions of the benchmarks already in the list of ET 2010. As to the increase, they are related to benchmarks for early childhood, tertiary attainment, learning mobility (adopted from 2011), employability of young graduates (from 2012) and language teaching (from 2012). Revisions regard the benchmarks for early school leaving, low achievers and lifelong participation that has been broadened. Finally, the completion rate of upper secondary school is no longer on the list. Two benchmarks are among the five headline targets for Europe 2020, namely, early school leaving and tertiary attaintment. ET 2020 is divided into a series of cycles; as a matter of fact, the results of the ongoing evaluation process are included in the next cycle by defining priority areas. In other words, the strategy envisages a flexibility mechanism to improve the capacity for meeting the standards. When it comes to the process of monitoring progress, in addition to the joint reports, a new education and monitor has been designed to improve the overall accountability of the ET 2020. Education and monitor is 'an annual series that reports on the evolution of education and training systems across Europe, bringing together the latest quantitative and qualitative data, recent technical reports and studies, plus policy documents and developments'. It includes a full report on the state of the educational systems of member states, 28 countries reports and a visualisation tool (http://ec.europa.eu/education/dashboard/index_en.htm).

The latter tool permits the visualisation of the European space of education as a space of commensuration. For each benchmark of ET 2020, it is possible to get coloured displays that have the standard form of a geographical map useful for obtaining a general picture of the EU28 situation, and of each member state in meeting the targets. Displays are also used to retrieve and highlight the dynamics of progress over time at the national and EU level. Colours allow understanding the position of each member state with respect to the agreed benchmarks. The visualisation is supplemented by additional statistics and links, which can be easily accessed on the Internet. Moreover, the full report of the education and training monitor contains figures and graphics (histograms, etc.), in which educational systems are visualised and compared against the benchmarks. Overall, this assemblage creates a new surface and, accordingly, a new topology of European education space, that intersects with the ecologies of education practice. The fabrication of this space of commensuration needed more than 40 years after the first meeting between the ministers of education in Europe. Finally, the convergence and agreed upon educational standards made visible what was thought to be incommensurable in terms of cultural identities. While this contributed to the multiplication of representations of European education space, it was, nonetheless, oriented strategically towards the common metrics of educational standards by virtue of its performative effects.

## Conclusion

The chapter focused on current trends in education standards and standardisation. It explored some reasons why standard-based reforms are a dominant trend, and increasingly an indisputable truth for supporting educational changes at a global level. Moreover, it traced the history of the fabrication of the European space of education in terms of the construction of a space of commensuration, whereby equivalence and normative specifications for steering education systems in Europe are established, which has the effect of making educational outcomes and processes more accountable to societal sectors and interests. Below, I recapitulate the main points of this study to pave the way for further investigations in this field.

Firstly, I discussed the history of standards and standardisation in education that specifically relates to the consolidation and the development of contemporary modern education systems since the beginning of industrial society. While the tendency towards objectualisation of education practice is a long-term process, a first wave of standardisation may be traced back to the end of the nineteenth century, which was made explicit by the rise and consolidation of mass schooling. In particular, the success of Taylorism, and of the principles of scientific management in industrial production, extended the logic of standards to education to cope with the emergent problems of the first phase of industrialisation. Setting education standards is considered a way to improve school efficiency, by reshaping educational planning and outcomes. Several scholars, like Bobbit and Tyler, supported this development, and described different ways to introduce educational standards. In an explicit sense, the factory is a model to imitate; schools are expected to define, in collaboration with the community, the desired outcomes, and to state clearly the educational standards to meet. In a similar way, the setting of standards implies pressure to introduce standardised devices to understand the extent to which school outcomes have met the expected educational standards, and, accordingly, notable attention to the measurability of educational performance paving the way for the development of psychometric knowledge. Two subsequent waves of standardisation occurred at the time of the publication of *A Nation at a Risk* in the 1980s, during the Cold War, in an attempt to focus attention on the achievement gap in the United States and to reinforce through standard-based reform a federal role in education policy-making. More recently, renewed attention globally has been on school accountability in the last two decades. In this non-linear history, standards and standardisation are supported by many legitimating discourses (Waldow 2014). However, it is possible to see a relevant shift in current times with increasing investment in the datafication of education. Standard-based reforms then have reached a global level, and we are witnessing the emergence of global spaces of commensuration fabricated by the 'structured oligopoly' of the OECD, Eurostat and UNESCO. Loosely coupled systems are absorbed into a sphere of metrics, i.e. variable-centre relationships among contexts, processes and outcomes.

The chapter described how the Europeanisation of education can be read as a standardisation process, and, in particular, as the enactment of space of commensuration made possible by standards of equivalence and performance. Initially, European education systems were thought to be incommensurable. It was even impossible to view education policy at a European level, and education was considered a taboo subject for 20 years by the member states of the emerging European Union. In particular, education was intended to be a locus of national sovereignty, and a national competence related strongly to national identities. The chapter reconstructed the many stages of the fabrication of this new topology: (a) the reshaping of the institutional framework, i.e. a modification of the legal basis of cooperation that occurred in a particular way in the passage from the Treaty of Rome to the Maastricht Treaty; (b) the creation of a transnational network as a result of the sequence of European programmes in education (Erasmus, etc.); (c) the definition of standards of equivalence (like ECTS and EQF), and the introduction of performance standards. In particular, a 'quantum leap' occurred with the introduction of the Lisbon Strategy. The Europeanisation of education was connected to the increasing datafication of education, and the consolidation of the 'structured oligopoly' of OECD, Eurostat and UNESCO. Three circuits of expertise supported the emergence of the European space of education as a space of commensuration (Normand 2010; Normand 2009): (1) school effectiveness research; (2) human capital theory that relates school outcomes to the dynamics of economy, and is concerned with the efficiency and the quality of education systems; (3) international large-scale assessments. These circuits mobilise knowledge for the construction of educational standards and indicators, and help in black-boxing education standards as neutral and objective tools in education policy.

Is the creation of this space of commensuration leading to the depoliticisation of European education policy-making? Is this an ultimate space of commensuration? The history of the waves of standardisation, the literature review and the documents from the European Commission seem to suggest the incompleteness of standards. While they are frequently presented as objective, neutral and evidence based, they appear in practice more fluid. In some ways, they are constantly objects of dispute, negotiation and contestation, although these discussions are rarely visible to the wider public. Sometimes they are presented as technical or academic problems, while as the chapter has tried to highlight, they are political questions with political implications. There is a need then for further investigation of the likely effects of standardisation regarding: (a) the transformation of the normativity of education policy and (b) the modification of education policy and practice. While for some it will lead to increasing the uniformity of education systems and practice, for others it will not suppress the many possible enactments of standards in practice, and in some cases, the sophisticated strategies to resist and to reintroduce a political dimension in the apparently cold and neutral discourse of standardisation. In other words, the actual space of commensuration of European education is only one among the many possible enactments of the Europeanisation of education.

## Note

1 In a similar vein, Thrift conceptualised this stage as knowing capitalism, in order to underline the importance of data infrastructure for contemporary economies.

## References

Aldrich, R. (2000). Educational standards in historical perspective. *Proceedings of the British Academy*, 102, 39–67.

Ball, S.J. (1998). Big policies/small world: an introduction to international perspectives in education policy. *Comparative Education*, 34(2), 119–130.

Baumol, W.J. (2012). *The Cost Disease: why computers get cheaper and health care doesn't*. New York and London: Yale University Press.

Biesta, G. (2008). Good education in an age of measurement: on the need to reconnect with the question of purpose in education. *Educational Assessment Evaluation and Accountability*, 21(1), 33–46.

Bobbitt, J.F. (1913). *Some General Principles of Management Applied to the Problems of City-School Systems*. Bloomington, IN: National Society for the Study of Education.

Brunsson, N., Rasche, A. and Seidl, D. (2012). The dynamics of standardization: three perspectives on standards in organization studies. *Organization Studies*, 33(5–6), 613–632. Available at: http://oss.sagepub.com/cgi/content/long/33/5–6/613 [Accessed 16 December 2013].

David, P.A. and Foray, D. (2003). Economic fundamentals of the knowledge society. *Policy Futures in Education*, 1(1), 20–49.

Espeland, W.N. and Stevens, M.L. (1998). Commensuration as a social process. *Annual Review of Sociology*, 24(1), 313–343.

Espeland, W.N. and Stevens, M.L. (2008). A sociology of quantification. *European Journal of Sociology*, 49(03), 401.

Fenwick, T. (2011). Reading educational reform through actor network theory: fluid space, ambivalences, otherings. *Educational Philosophy and Theory*, 43(1), 114–134.

Fenwick, T. and Edwards, R. (2010). *Actor-Network Theory and Education*. Abingdon: Routledge.

Fenwick, T. and Landri, P. (2012). Materialities, textures and pedagogies: socio-material assemblages in education. *Pedagogy, Culture & Society*, 20(1), 1–7.

Fenwick, T., Edwards, R. and Sawchuck, P. (2011). *Emerging Approaches to Educational Research Tracing the Socio-Material*. Abingdon: Routledge.

Foray, D. (2001). Facing the problem of unbalanced development of knowledge across sectors and fields: the case of the knowledge base in primary education. *Research Policy*, 30(9), 1553–1561. Available at: http://linkinghub.elsevier.com/retrieve/pii/S0048733301001676.

Gardner, D.P., *et al*. (1983). *A Nation at Risk: the imperative for educational reform. An open letter to the American People*. Washington, DC: National Commission on Excellence in Education, USA. Available at: http://files.eric.ed.gov/fulltext/ED226006.pdf.

Gorur, R. (2012). The invisible infrastructure of standards. *Critical Studies in Education*, 54(2), 132–142.

Grek, S. and Lawn, M. (2009) A short history of Europeanizing education. *European Education*, 41(1), 32–54.

Hanushek, E.A. and Wössmann, L. (2007). *Education Quality and Economic Growth*. Washington, DC: The International Bank for Reconstruction and Development, pp. 1–39. Available at: www.worldbank.org.

Hill, P. and Roza, M. (2010). *Curing Baumol's Disease: in search of productivity gains in K-12 schooling*, Seattle, WA: Center on Reinventing Public Education, University of Washington Bothell.

Klees, S.J. (2008). A quarter century of neoliberal thinking in education: misleading analyses and failed policies. *Globalisation, Societies and Education*, 6(4), 311–348.

Lawn, M. (2011). Standardizing the European education policy space. *European Educational Research Journal*, 10(2), 259. Available at: http://www.wwwords.co.uk/rss/abstract.asp?j=eerj&aid=4602&doi=1.

Lawn, M. and Grek, S. (2012). *Europeanizing Education: governing a new policy space*. Oxford: Symposium Books.

Levin, B. (1998). An epidemic of education policy: (what) can we learn from each other? *Comparative Education*, 34(2), 131–141.

Lundahl, C. and Waldow, F. (2009). Standardisation and "quick languages": the shape-shifting of standardised measurement of pupil achievement in Sweden and Germany. *Comparative Education*, 45(3), 365–385. Available at: http://www. tandfonline.com/doi/abs/10.1080/03050060903184940 [Accessed 21 January 2014].

Luyten, J.W. *et al.*, (2005). School factors related to quality and equity. *Educational Psychologist*, 45(3), 185–202. Available at: http://www.oecd-ilibrary.org/education/school-factors-related-to-quality-and-equity_9789264008199-en.

Mulcahy, D. (2011). Assembling the "accomplished" teacher: the performativity and the politics of professional teaching standards. *Educational Philosophy and Theory*, 43(S1), 94–113.

Nelson, R.R. (2003). On the uneven evolution of human know-how. *Research Policy*, 32(6), 909–922. Available at: http://linkinghub.elsevier.com/retrieve/pii/S0048733302000938.

Normand, R. (2009). La mesure de l'école: une arithmétique politique des inégalités. In J.-L. Derouet and M.-C. Besson, eds. *Repenser la justice dans l'éducation et la formation*. Berlin: Peter Lang.

Normand, R. (2010). Expertise, networks and indicators. *European Educational Research Journal*, 9(3), 407–421.

Pépin, L. (2007). The history of EU cooperation in the field of education and training: how lifelong learning became a strategic objective. *European Journal of Education*, 42(1), 121–132.

Piketty, T. (2014). *Il capitale del XXI secolo*, Milano: Bompiani.

Powell, W.W. and Snellman, K. (2004). The knowledge economy. *Annual Review of Sociology*, 30(1), 199–220.

Rutkowski, D.J. (2007). Converging us softly: how intergovernmental organizations promote neoliberal educational policy. *Critical Studies in Education*, 48(2), 229–247.

Thrift, N. (2005). Knowing capitalism. *Growth and Change*, 37, 640–643. Available at: http://doi.wiley.com/10.1111/j.1468–2257.2006.00344_2.x.

Waldow, F. (2014). From Taylor to Tyler to no child left behind: legitimating educational standards. *Prospects*, 45(1), 49–62. Available at: http://link.springer.com/10.1007/s11125-014-9334-x.

# Chapter 3

# Policy transfers in Europe

## The European Union and beyond

*Magdaléna Hadjiisky*

*Translated from French by Jean-Yves Bart**

Since the 1990s, the dissemination of policy models has become a particularly salient phenomenon in the European space. Europe is characterised by the density of its institutional web, organised around the European Union's actors and norms. It is thus tempting to present 'Europeanisation' as a progressive convergence stemming from a coherent European source (of inspiration, of norms, of action). It has been shown, however, that policy transfers are complex processes, which cannot be reduced to a unidirectional link between a 'sender' and a 'receiver' (Dolowitz and Marsh 1996, 2000; Delpeuch 2008). This type of top-down focus has been criticised in the literature on Europeanisation because it tends to underestimate the role of domestic actors and frames (Caporaso *et al.* 2001; Palier and Surel 2007).

However, the convergence narrative can also be criticised from the 'top' side. To what extent are the European Union's (EU) actors isolated and autonomous when 'European' policies are considered? It seems necessary here to leave the 'EU-isation' focus behind and to situate the European Union within its wider international context. This is particularly important when addressing areas that do not fall within the European Union's legal prerogatives and in which the European Commission (EC) has not developed a specific expertise yet (human rights, governance, education...). In these areas, many important developments at the European level originate in other international organisations (IOs), which have dealt with these issues longer than the EU and with which the EC can find an interest in collaborating.

Instead of the concept of transfer, which entails the intentional adoption of a univocal message transmitted by a sender to a receiver, I suggest exploring the role of community actors as participants in an international circulation process, a non-linear and equivocal phenomenon of which they are not necessarily the main initiators. In this chapter, this phenomenon is addressed through the study of the interactions linking the EU, the OECD (Organisation for Economic Co-operation and Development) and some national governments on the 'better regulation' issue. Based on interviews with national and international civil servants and on a process-tracing study, this research highlights the importance of the inter-institutional circulation of ideas between the EC and the OECD in the emergence and progressive use of the initially contentious notion of 'regulation policy' in the European Union.

The relationship between the EU (and previously the EEC) and the OECD has some peculiar features. It dates back to 1960, when the Organisation for European Economic Cooperation, which played a central role in implementing the Marshall Plan, gave birth to the OECD.[1] As outlined in the official site of the EU delegation, 'the participation of the EU goes well beyond simple observership. In legal terms, the EU has a status of a quasi-member. The EU is committed to cooperating fully in the achievement of OECD fundamental objectives',[2] which means, in practical terms, that the agents of the EC can participate in all the committees and working parties of the organisation.

To go beyond the threshold of the institutions and analyse the mutual influences that can develop there, the analysis must move past the IOs' institutional boundaries as well as the monographic temptation of much international relations research.[3] This is necessary first to study these relationships in practice, delving beyond the official ties forged between two organisations that originated in western Europe. Only by leaving behind legal nominalism can we account for what is really at stake in these relationships, which generally depend as much on the practical logics of the bureaucracies involved in them as on the official positions of the institutions. On the other hand, this is also necessary to account for the interest and strategies of the European actors in fields of shared competence, in which the national delegations of EU member states have even more opportunity for action.

Adopting this multilateral outlook will allow us to investigate the mechanisms of influence and power at the international level. The collaboration between OECD and EU on sensitive areas like good administration, education and social policies calls into question the EU's autonomy in sectors considered to fall under democratic sovereignty or to reflect a European social 'model'. Yet, in the literature, the OECD is described as an 'identity-defining international organisation' (Porter and Webb 2008: 44), which 'defines standards of appropriate behaviour for states that seek to identify themselves as modern, liberal, market-friendly, and efficient' (March and Olsen 1998: 961). Because of its 'liberalising vocation' and of the importance of economics in the inner hierarchy of the organisation, 'the OECD advice often takes the form of applying liberal economic theory to policy problems' (Porter and Webb 2008: 45).

To what extent and in which ways has the EC's regular participation in the OECD's work influenced the contents and form of European policies? In many areas, the circulation of public policy instruments and models between Paris (home to the OECD's headquarters) and Brussels (EC) is apparent. How are we to interpret this phenomenon? Does it take the form of transfers between IOs, in which the proximity between international bureaucrats plays a key role? Do national delegates play an active role; with which means and through which channels?

## Europeanisation or internationalisation? The EC's 'better regulation' agenda

The phrase 'better regulation' refers to a reform strategy aiming whenever possible and useful to reduce the body of legal norms governing social activities. One of the underlying assumptions of this strategy is that the number, contents and/or form (complex, illegible...) of legislative norms are hindrances to the development of private initiatives. The procedures and instruments bearing the label 'better regulation' are intended to introduce systematic evaluation of projected and existing legal norms. This evaluation takes place on two levels: on the one hand, the contents of law, regulations and implementing acts are assessed according to specific criteria; on the other hand, the appropriateness of the legal framework is assessed in comparison with other forms of organisation of economic and social relationships.

The literature presents the 'better regulation' movement as a European-wide process. This interpretation is justified to a certain extent, as after the Lisbon European Council, this strategy openly became one of the EC's priorities, and this was reasserted at the time of its relaunch by the Barroso Commission in 2005. As per the conclusions (14) of the Lisbon European Council of 23 and 24 March 2000:

> The competitiveness and dynamism of businesses are directly dependent on a regulatory climate conducive to investment, innovation, and entrepreneurship. Further efforts are required to lower the costs of doing business and remove unnecessary red tape, both of which are particularly burdensome for SMEs. The European institutions, national governments and regional and local authorities must continue to pay particular attention to the impact and compliance costs of proposed regulations, and should pursue their dialogue with business and citizens with this aim in mind.

After the European Council of Lisbon and in the context of the preparation of the White Paper on governance,[4] the EC adopted a range of regulatory reform measures in 2002, including guidelines on impact assessment.[5] Following a communication from the new Barroso Commission in March 2005,[6] these guidelines were revised in 2005[7] and updated again in 2006.[8] Impact assessment is required for all regulatory proposals on the commission's work programme (Wiener 2006: 447). In addition, the commission is pushing for the simplification of existing laws (through consolidation, codification and repeal), the reduction of administrative costs ('cutting red tape'), and consultation with those affected by regulatory policies (Wiener 2006: 448).

More broadly, specialists consider that the institutional design of the EU secretes in itself some of the main features of a 'regulatory state' (Majone 1996).

The smoothed-over institutional narrative focusing on the EC depicts national initiatives in favour of better regulation as a result of the EC's influence. The EC itself gives credence to such interpretations by releasing lists of the good and bad European countries in that field.[9] However, some member state governments, on the one hand, and the uses that some of them have made of their double membership (EU/OECD), on the other, have played an important role in the agenda setting of 'better regulation' at the European level. The institutional approach underestimates the cleavages and cross-influences that developed in the late 1990s and early 2000s at the time when 'better regulation' became a part of the EU's agenda.

As in other areas of public administration and policy, in Europe the first initiatives that aimed to 'assess and monitor regulations'[10] were taken in the United Kingdom. The regulation issue had been an explicit theme of government action in the United Kingdom since the establishment of an enterprise and deregulation unit in 1986.[11] It is thus not surprising that one of the origins of regulation as an item on the EU's agenda dates back to the 1992 Edinburgh summit under the British presidency. The conclusions of the summit 'expressed concern about the quality of legislation and the tide of rules coming from Brussels' (Radaelli 2007: 192). At that time, 'compliance cost assessment' was the tool used by the UK government to evaluate the likely impact of legislative proposals on business (see Froud *et al.* 1998).

Still, between 1992 and 2002, better regulation had relatively little impact within European circles. Admittedly some member states and employers' interest groups promoted 'simplification' and good regulation,[12] directorate general XXIII (enterprise, tourism, social economy) launched initiatives to that effect, like the 'impact assessment', but they did not succeed in making it a European priority (Radaelli 2007: 192).

Despite what the official narrative of its introduction at European level would have one believe, the promoters of regulatory policy were initially not received very warmly by the EC, although they did have the support of directorate general XXIII. According to a civil servant of a member state who worked on that policy:

> You should know that in the European Commission, at the end of the 1990s, they were totally against regulatory reform. They were thinking that introducing tools like RIA (Regulatory Impact Assessment) or even consultation was somehow giving Member states a tool to interfere into

the EC affairs, into their policies. Because it was giving transparency, accountability, more participation from outside.

'Better regulation' tools were often interpreted as hindrances to the EC's autonomy regarding in its main competency in the European institutions – legislative initiative. That one of the first European promoters of better regulation came from one of the member states that most resisted the EU's regulatory intervention could only reinforce their fears.

Far from being merely technical, in Europe debates on 'better regulation' relate to the question of the division of competencies between the EU and the member states, as well as to the thorny issue of the implementation of European directives by national administrations.[13]

Furthermore, the American roots of the programmes launched under the 'better regulation' label inspired reluctance in the EC and in some member state administrations. It was indeed in the United States and Canada in the 1970s that the regulatory impact assessment (RIA) began to be used systematically ex-ante to assess the economic consequences of bills, with a view towards alleviating the legal and administrative burden on private initiatives. The 1990s witnessed a number of trade disputes between the EU and the USA (most famously concerning hormone-treated beef), causing the EU to defend and attempt to export the 'precautionary principle', particularly in the fields of environment and public health (Löfstedt 2004). The precautionary principle was denounced by opponents as yet another tool to justify the EC's regulatory interference to the detriment of the freedom of economic and trade relations and exchanges.[14] At the European level, the introduction of managerial tools under the 'better regulation' label is far from a politically (and economically) neutral subject.

It was precisely during that decade that the OECD began pushing 'better regulation' extensively, including through the promotion of the RIA. The OECD's public management committee (PUMA) developed arguments and implementation methods in the early 1990s; these were negotiated within the framework of the public governance committee, whose members comprised member states delegates specialised in public administration (senior civil servants of national reform units in the ministries of the interior, administration and decentralisation, chancelleries, etc.). The promotion of regulation was at the time part of a broader strategy developed by PUMA that consisted in restoring the efficiency and legitimacy of public administration by introducing managerial tools and methods in its functioning.

PUMA's work on 'regulation' was officialised for the first time in 1995 by the OECD, which issued a 'recommendation' through its governing body, the council. The OECD's website has some proud words about the OECD *Recommendation of the Council on Improving the Quality of Government*

*Regulation* (C(95)21/FINAL): 'In 1995 the first-ever international statement of regulatory principles common to member countries was published by the Council.'

'Regulation' would then become a full-time area of activity for PUMA, to the extent that it justified the creation of an OECD-GOV working party on regulatory governance and reform (in 1999), which was bumped up in 2009 to official committee status (becoming the regulatory policy committee). The OECD's output reflects the organisation's intense investment on the issue. It took the form of synthetic reports like the ambitious analytical reports *Regulatory Policies in OECD countries: from interventionism to regulatory governance* (2002) or *Regulatory Policy Outlook 2015*, of (many) reports focused on better regulation's central instrument, the RIA, documenting the regular updating and extension of OECD principles and recommendations in these matters – examples include the *OECD Guiding Principles for Regulatory Quality and Performance* (2005) and the *Recommendation of the Council of the OECD on Regulatory Policy and Governance* (2012) – and finally of practical tools and guides for practitioners (*Ten Good Practices in the Design and Implementation of RIA*, 1997; *Indicators of Regulatory Management System*, 2009).[15]

The EU very largely drew on this managerial and regulatory arsenal to build its better regulation agenda in 2000–2001. The Mandelkern group report released on 13 November 2001 is widely cited by specialists as an important step in the progressive setting of better regulation on the European agenda. It is thus interesting to note that the OECD is the only organisation cited (and quite extensively at that) in the report.[16] Appendix A even fully reproduces the *OECD Reference Checklist for Regulatory Decision-making* (1995). The latter document is frequently cited in the main text, particularly the measures it suggests to achieve 'simplification' or the effective structures for the implementation of regulatory policy (final report, p. 50). In some areas, OECD recommendations are used as yardsticks: section 8.3.2.1 'Content and quality of European legislation' begins by citing the OECD: 'The OECD has set up criteria for the quality of legislation in general. These criteria are lawfulness, administrability and enforceability, effectiveness and efficiency, subsidiarity and proportionality, mutual harmonisation, simplicity, clarity and accessibility' (p. 70). Likewise, concerning the RIA: 'A RIA should be based on coherent guidelines across all policy areas within the administration, should follow OECD guidance' (p. 25).

More generally the EC relied on the OECD to assess member states' progress on regulation. In 2008, the OECD was commissioned and funded by the EC to publish annual better regulation in Europe reports including 'country reviews' on 15 EU member states. The OECD also evaluates the EC in that area (*Sustainability in Impact Assessments: a review of impact assessment systems in selected OECD countries and the European Commission*, 2012). In a more indirect yet no less effective way, the EC confirms the credit it gives to

OECD expertise in the administrative field by suggesting member states that they use its services.[17] Likewise, when a member state does not have sufficient funds to finance an OECD review, it often happens that the EU pays for it (interviews with OECD administrators).

The cooperation between the two organisations is based not only on long-time inter-institutional links, but also on a relative interdependence that has developed over time. The EC tends to rely on the OECD to provide expertise that it is unable (particularly for reasons of personnel) to produce in-house; in addition, the OECD's recognition and non-partisan image can facilitate the dissemination of certain principles and tools in member states. This relationship is also a strategic one for the OECD. Fruitful cooperation gives credit and exposure to the validity and usefulness of its output. Furthermore, the EU is an important contributor to the OECD's activities. While the EC does not put funds into the OECD's general budget, it helps fund the activities of OECD directorates through numerous 'voluntary contributions', which have become indispensible to the development of those directorates. In their analysis of the OECD, Tim Balint and Christoph Knill (Balint and Knill 2007) rightly emphasise that only 7.3 per cent of the OECD's budget comes from its own funds (resulting in part from the sales of publications); also, since 1996,[18] the recurring budget allotted by member states has stagnated, which further increases the strategic importance of voluntary contributions. The EU's voluntary contributions reached 35–45 million euros in 2012–2014 (in 2014, the OECD's general budget was 357 million euros) (interview, Delegation of the European Union to the OECD and UNESCO, 18/12/2014). In addition to these voluntary contributions, the EU almost single-handedly funds one of the OECD's programmes, SIGMA, whose mandate is to provide targeted assistance in the institutional and administrative fields to candidate and neighbouring countries.[19] SIGMA was, for instance, the source of the study on regulatory reforms in the new member states that joined the EU in 2007.[20]

Should we then conclude that the EU is under the OECD's influence both in theoretical (arguments, strategic lines) and practical (guides, toolbox…) terms due to its dependence on OECD expertise? Has it as a result adopted a framing and solutions devised outside of the EU framework by an organisation whose mandate and scope of action differ from its own?

An element in support of this thesis is that in parallel to the development of cooperation between the EU and the OECD changes have occurred in the forms of evaluation of European legislation. The original – and still largely dominant – approach to the evaluation of the pertinence of EU legislative intervention is based on legal criteria of good law-making: democratic legitimacy, subsidiarity, proportionality, the transparency of the legislative process, legal certainty. The early 2000s saw the addition of factual criteria, which examine the capacity of the law to act on facts on the basis of pre-set objectives (evaluation of effectiveness and efficiency through impact assessment).[21]

Does this reflect a phenomenon of borrowing/transaction between an expert and a policy organisation?

## The European Union under the influence?

Comparison with education policies sheds some light on this question. In this domain, Sotiria Grek very convincingly describes the special relationship of competition and collaboration that the EC and the OECD have developed since the early 2000s (Grek 2014).

She shows that 'the OECD became a dominant education policy actor as a result of its deliberate and systematic mobilization by the EC, which found in the OECD not only a great resource of data to govern (which it did not have before) but also a player who would be pushing the Commission's own policy agenda forward, albeit leaving the old subsidiarity rule intact' (Grek 2014: 267). Her study described the specific form of interdependence that has emerged in both organisations. The OECD provides expertise on subjects partially predefined by the EC (see interview excerpt in Grek 2014: 277) when the latter does not have that expertise; the EC pays for the costs resulting from these studies, directly through voluntary contributions or by funding studies on member states. Much as in the case of 'better regulation', the EC ends up funding a significant part of the OECD's output on education policy (interview excerpts in Grek 2014: 274–275).

At the same time, European education policy has become progressively dominated by international comparison and quantitative indicators,[22] resulting in 'the alignment in approaches to measurement and category construction' (Grek 2014: 270) and the systematic underestimation of non-measurable qualitative criteria. Grek observes a historical concomitance between the OECD and the World Bank's participation in European education policy and the European project's shift from a 'rather idealistic project of cultural cohesion' towards a 'much sharper contemporary competitive reality' based on (and enabled by) the 'international comparative testing' performed by these organisations (Grek 2014: 270). In other words, the intervention of these IOs has influenced the European trajectory towards the standardisation (and economisation) of its goals and policy instruments.

In the field of better regulation, there was a debate regarding the criteria used for assessing legislation. Does ' "better regulation" lead to more socially and environmentally aware regulation or is it part of a deregulative agenda?' (Torriti 2007: 249; see also Radaelli 2007). Jacopo Torriti considers that better regulation is a nominal rhetorical mask of a deregulative agenda (Torriti 2007: 257). Is this agenda a consequence of the OECD's influence? Where better regulation is concerned, this must be nuanced: the 'red tape' and 'promise to build a bonfire of regulation' of the then president of the commission Barroso, reflecting a quantitative approach to legislative 'simplification', had much more to do with the member states and the EU's trajectories than with the OECD. While the OECD has systematised the tools of better regulation, it also emphasises the fact that better regulation must be a global policy that goes beyond a set of management instruments – in the process erasing the possibility of quantitative standardisation in the field. It is also worth noting that the EC shares to a large extent the rationalist ideal that is manifested in the planning according to ends and means of impact assessments and evaluations of legislative performance.[23] The use of the label 'regulatory policy' masks underlying disputes, but the latter exist both in the EU and the OECD, even if the dividing lines are not exactly similar.

According to Grek, in the field of education, the EC and the OECD share the same objective of internationalisation in the context of strong resistance from national education systems. The two organisations may have their differences, but these differences are approached first and foremost in terms of a competition between experts on the same market: 'most large international research organizations strive to secure the limited and diminishing funding available from national governments for the conduct of these studies' (Grek 2014: 275). Although my research supports this observation to some degree, it must be nuanced. The 'better regulation' case calls into question the apolitical and a-national character of these inter-institutional relationships. In the 'European education governance' case, Sotira Grek analyses the relation between the EU and the OECD as an exchange between a 'policy' and an 'expert' organisation (sometimes in competition when the EU tries to produce its own expertise), with no or very little interference of the national delegations. For its part, the 'better regulation' case requires putting the national actors back in the analysis, in a triangular relationship between the EC, OECD and some member states' national delegates. Among the 34 OECD member states (as of 2015), 21 are also EU member states. Insofar as the OECD has no political competency and does not pose a threat to national governments, its arenas can under certain conditions be places for more fruitful exchanges, mutual persuasion and pre-negotiation than in the EU's context.

Despite what research centred only on expertise production suggests, politics in the most classic sense of the term – pertaining to national and European elections and to the governments' geopolitical choices – influences IOs' orientations and productions. If the EU is under the influence of the OECD's expertise, this may be because a coalition of national actors wished it to be so.

## Political strategies in action

In the better regulation case, member state governments have played an active part in the promotion of 'better regulation' in Europe. Their initiatives have generally preceded those of the EC, which is not the driving force in this policy.

The UK's role has already been pointed out. The British were also involved in the formation of a coalition of four of the rotating six-month presidencies of the European Union on the same issue in 2004. The presidencies of Ireland, the Netherlands, Luxembourg and the UK issued a joint statement of their intention to pursue better regulation efforts during their upcoming presidencies.[24] In this statement, emphasis was placed essentially on the European institutions (not at the member state level): 'we need further to enhance the quality of impact assessments and ensure that their analysis actually influences decision-making by the Commission, the Council and the European Parliament' (p. 2). This letter played an important role in spurring the EC to update and strengthen its impace assessment guidelines (Wiener 2006: 448).

Since the early 1990s, the UK has been joined by other members. The Netherlands, in particular, began developing their own standard cost model (SCM) in 2002 to measure administrative costs, with a goal of 25 per cent reduction of the administrative burden. The Dutch SCM in turn served as a model in other European countries such as Germany and Austria. In 2003, an informal network of exchange and promotion of this model, the SCM network, was set up; Scandinavian countries were particularly active in this network.[25] In September 2004, the OECD's working party for regulatory management and reform decided to give priority in its 2005–2006 programme of work to activities on administrative simplification.[26] Therefore, the OECD launched the 'red tape scoreboard' project. In order to measure administrative burdens across OECD countries an adapted version of the SCM was used. A manual was prepared, and over a dozen countries participated in a steering group; eight countries carried out the measurements.[27] It was only in May 2006 that the EC launched its own programme for reducing administrative costs. Citing the Dutch case as an example, Vice President Günter Verheugen announced the EU's own 25 per cent target to reduce administrative costs, to be achieved in partnership with the member states' own cost reduction programmes.[28] As in other parts of the 'better regulation' agenda, the EC is not in the lead when it comes to 'cutting red tape'.

The resulting convergence was only partial, in the sense that each state had its own use of the instrument adopted in common (at least on paper). This diversity in the meanings and uses ascribed to international models has been rightly pointed out by studies on the reception of international policy transfers (Hood 1998; Caporaso *et al.* 2001; Radaelli 2005). The paucity of such studies at the international level implicitly suggests that national actors only have influence on transfers once the model has 'arrived' in their jurisdiction. Crossing the threshold of IOs (here, the OECD and the EU) alerts us to the artificiality of a static presentation of the elaboration and circulation of 'international models'. A similar diversity of conceptions and uses can be found in the 'international' phase of the transfer process. National actors who take initiative in given public policy areas – and who as a result may under certain conditions have an influence on international programmes – are generally moved by the bureaucratic and/or political agenda of their main space of activity (state, local authorities, administration). In doing so they introduce a variety of strategies and uses into the process that must be accounted for.

An illustration of this is the Mandelkern group, whose action plan served as a basis (at least rhetorically) for all subsequent initiatives. In the post-Lisbon context, the group was created not by the EC, but by member states. The high level (Mandelkern) advisory group was formed by a resolution of the ministers of public administration at Strasbourg, which gave it the 'mandate to develop a coherent approach to this topic and to submit proposals to the ministers, including the definition of a common method of evaluating the quality of regulation'.[29] Presided over by the French senior official Dieudonné Mandelkern, the group was composed of 28 senior officials from member states and the EC. Following the Mandelkern report, the ministers of public administration created the group of directors and experts of better regulation to monitor the implementation of its action plan. Members of the Mandelkern group were encouraged to participate to ensure continuity.[30] In the eyes of the ministers, the Mandelkern initiative was not meant to be shelved.

According to one of the Italian delegation members, that a Frenchman was head of the group should not make us overlook that the UK was behind the initiative of creating this group, supported by Italy. The European strategy devised by Tony Blair, whose political objectives included having his country join the Eurozone, involved bringing the EC's 'way of regulating' (interview with the author) closer to that of the UK. This political interest explains the high hierarchical level of the British representatives within the group (Colin Church, senior official of the Department of Energy and Climate Change in the Better Regulation Executive, formerly director of the Regulatory Innovation Unit, and Phil Wynn Owen, then Director of the Regulatory Impact Unit at the Cabinet Office). It also sheds light on the choice of a british commissioner at the vice-presidency of the Prodi Commission (1999–2004), namely Neil Kinnock, in charge of administrative reform (Kinnock was responsible for introducing new staff regulations for EU officials after the dismissal of the Santer Commission).

> This high level member of the Italian delegation recounts that the British: found in us [Italians] an unexpected partner from an old style civil law country. We somehow connected our efforts and put in the middle France, which was not that pushing, but the minister for PA of France was Michel Sapin 99–00. We had several bilateral meetings with minister Bassanini. We said 'Hey, come on! We want to reform, so why don't we reform the EC too with the OECD principles?'
>
> (Interview with the author)

France had to be involved in the initiative in part because at the time it presided over the EU Council (second semester of 2000). This also explains the choice of a French high representative as president of the group (beyond that, affinities developed that resulted in the renewal of Mandelkern's mandate after the French presidency).

The Italian representatives were then pursuing a domestic policy dynamic that shed light on their strong commitment to this policy in the OECD and EC. A professor of constitutional law and centre-left politician, Franco Bassanini, as minister for the civil service in the Olive Tree coalition government (1996–2001), conducted the major reforms of civil service and administrative procedures that have transformed the Italian administration since (with 80 per cent of state agents now employed under private sector contracts on a voluntary basis, administrative simplification, the decentralisation of formerly government-managed functions...). Known for his relentlessness (he gave his name to a series of laws on state reform called *Leggi Bassanini*), Franco Bassanini drew on the OECD's expertise and legitimacy to further his position at the national level. According to the Italian negotiator:

> the best use you can do of OECD is when you want to build reform in your country and you have resistance, from bureaucracies, from all the powers. To win then you need an external support, from an international organization very strong, very credible, autorevole [spoken in Italian: 'authoritative']. The best experience for Italy was to take advantage from the OECD work.

Indeed, after having introduced some of the features of 'better regulation' in the Italian legislation (Law 50, 1999), Italy commissioned an OECD review on regulation policy (OECD Reviews of Regulatory Reform: Regulatory Reform in Italy, 2001), whose conclusions were favourable – inspiring this comment by the interviewee: 'we would have liked to have recommendations to strengthen even more our position [by justifying some more reforms]'.

Worth noting is that previously, during the Lisbon European Council, Prime Minister Amato was flanked by his adviser, Pier Carlo Padoan, a professor of economics and close friend of Bassanini and of one member of the Mandelkern group, Luigi Carbone. Employed by the International Monetary Fund from 2001 to 2005, Pier Carlo Padoan then worked at the OECD as deputy secretary general (2007) and chief economist (2009).[31] An Italian member of the Mandelkern group explains that this connection allowed Bassanini and him to pressure the Italian delegation into making explicit mention of the regulation in the European Council conclusions – which was done in the aforementioned paragraph 14.

The involvement of national actors highly active in their respective countries explains that diverse political orientations can be inferred from the inflections given to policies gathered under the same label of 'better regulation'.

The Italian and British initiative was facilitated – if not enabled – by the partisan ties between Tony Blair, Franco Bassanini, Michel Sapin and, not least, Romano Prodi. It proposed a partial redefinition of regulation policy with a less economics-oriented approach than that advocated by the preceding conservative governments. In the UK, where the deregulation initiative was launched after the election of the Conservative government in 1979, the new Labour cabinet reorganised the British regulatory bodies just after its election in 1997: the Better Regulation Unit replaced the Deregulation Unit in March 1997 under the supervision of the Better Regulation Executive.[32] As Claudio Radaelli perceptively notes, this reorganisation was a way to put an 'explicit emphasis on consultation, transparency, and regulatory quality (as opposed to the deregulation agenda, based on 'quantity'). The old compliance cost assessment turned gradually into a more comprehensive appraisal of proposed legislation, based on the analysis of a wide range of benefits and costs affecting different stakeholders – not just the business community, but also citizens, civil society organizations, and public administration' (Radaelli 2007: 192).

Pushed by centre-left politicians and senior civil servants, the initiative in favour of introducing 'better regulation' in Europe did not look like an ideological manoeuvre, but rather a 'common sense' step forward (our Italian interviewee used the phrase 'common sense' on several occasions during our interview) to deal with the 'excessive' complexity of European regulation.

The Mandelkern report appears to strike a balance between the different parties. The executive summary insists:

> better regulation is not about unthinking removal of such regulation. Rather, it is about ensuring that regulation is only used when appropriate, and about ensuring that the regulation that is used is high quality. Improving the quality of regulation is a public good in itself, enhancing the credibility of the governance process and contributing to the welfare of citizens, business and other stakeholders alike.
>
> (Final Report, p. 1)

In the early 2000s, this broad definition of better regulation greatly facilitated its incorporation in the European agenda. In its 2002 communication on impact assessment, the EC emphasised the fact that the RIA had to take into account the three priorities of the Lisbon Strategy: economic competitiveness, sustainable development and social cohesion (Commission, Communication on Impact Assessment, COM (276) Final 5 June 2002). The context was also marked by the preparation of the White Paper on European Governance (published in 2001), in which the EC put forward the involvement of 'civil society' in the EU's decision-making process.

As majorities changed in many European countries, however, better regulation began in the mid-2000s to be interpreted from an economic angle (competitiveness, private initiative, growth) and a quantitative angle (deregulation, 'cutting the red tape', 'one regulation in, one out' initiative of the British cabinet in 2005). The initiatives of the SCM network multiplied at the time, working alongside the high level group of independent stakeholders on administrative burden reduction, then presided over by the member of the German Christian Social Union, Edmund Stoiber.

At the EU level, the commission, headed by Portuguese conservative Jose Manuel Barroso 'has provided a redefinition of the Lisbon agenda based on simplification, the removal of administrative burdens, and economic competitiveness (Commission, 2005b)' (Radaelli 2007: 199). At the OECD level, the guidelines published in 2005 explicitly cite economic competitiveness as the sole objective of 'better regulation', as per the introduction:

> Better regulation and structural reforms are necessary complements to sound fiscal and macroeconomic policies. (...) [Regulatory policy is] a coherent, whole-of-government approach to create a regulatory environment favourable to the creation and growth of firms, productivity gains, competition, investment and international trade.

## Internationalisation through impregnation

The classic geopolitical interpretation of international relations scholars, wherein member states are those who have genuine decision-making power and instrumentalise international bureaucracies so that they follow their domestic agendas, is too simple here. There are more complex interactions at work, and the segmentation of national and international public authorities must be taken into account. The intense activity of IOs in the field of public governance since the early 1990s has produced its own effects. National civil servants are particularly affected by its outcomes and potential effects on their professional statuses and practices. Some, however, focus their interests on other issues and spaces and neglect it or attend international meetings passively. Others have intermittent but lasting investments in international arenas. In the latter case, the experiences and exchanges resulting from these investments frequently influence the national actors' perceptions of situations and strategies – to various extents depending on the more or less centralised character of the national administrations concerned. This means that emphasising the sometimes strategic role played by coalitions of national actors in IOs does not mean embracing a strictly strategist interpretation that neglects the socialising effects of international arenas.[33] The political and bureaucratic agendas of national actors are indeed often informed by the IOs' outputs and experiments conducted at the international level.

The way the OECD operates is a clear illustration of this phenomenon. As it lacks the legal and financial means to enforce conditionality in member states, the OECD has to demonstrate the usefulness and validity of its expertise and co-opt national representatives as much as possible.[34] Thus, in practice, the OECD's activities have the distinguishing feature of embracing the active participation of member states delegates. In the field of better regulation and in others, in addition to the usual political activity aimed at ministers,[35] the OECD has set up various types of arenas, instruments and networks aimed at facilitating the member states' appropriation of reform instruments. No fewer than 12 workshops on the RIA have for instance been organised between January 2008 and June 2015.

Having this context in mind, it is worth noting that some of the senior members in the Mandelkern group were active in the OECD's committees on governance, specifically on the RIA and regulation quality. Admittedly, the group included many members who were specialists in the field and had never worked with the OECD. This particularly applies to the British members, both highly specialised and not manifestly connected to the OECD (possibly because they have never needed to). However, at least five of the group's senior members have been invested in better regulation for a long time (and therefore using it to further their career) and active in the OECD's networks. Adam Wolf, from Denmark, was then head of the public management department of the Ministry of the Interior and at the same time chaired the OECD's public governance committee – from 1998 to 2002 – at a time when better regulation became a prevalent issue. The Greek Panagiotis Karkatsoulis, a professor of public administration and adviser to the Greek Minister of the Interior (public administration and decentralisation department) began actively working with the OECD in the late 1990s; in the early 2000s he led the OECD regulatory governance initiative in south east Europe. Also worth noting is the case of Luigi Carbone (Italy), then vice-coordinator of the unit on regulatory simplification and about to be appointed liaison officer with the vice president of the European Convention Giuliano Amato (2002–2004), who presided over the OECD-GOV's working party on regulatory governance and reform from its creation in 1999 to 2002. The participation of these high-ranking officials in the OECD committees and working groups may have influenced their perception and framing of their country's national interest inside the European Union.

Overall, 17 of the 21 states that are both EU and OECD member states were subjected on several occasions to the OECD's regulatory policy review process. Far from being formalities, peer reviews require the active participation of member state governments and administrations, generally for 1–2 years. The secretariat and government of the member state concerned first negotiate the scope and objective of the review. Once this has been done, the secretariat conducts an investigation into the country's administrations and its partners to produce a detailed study, complete with reasoned and precise recommendations. The entire investigation process is also monitored by peer reviewers who are senior civil servants in other member states. This peer reviewing process is one of the OECD's core methods in its work with member states. In the primary sense, the term refers to an informed review conducted by fellow specialists of a given domain. In the OECD's practice, it has come to refer to multiple evaluation practices and to justify the extensive use of inter-country comparisons.

The OECD's standards, aimed at serving as yardsticks for inter-country comparison, are discussed within the OECD committees and working groups, which conduct expertise and discussions between the secretariat and the national delegates (and their hierarchy). Once they have been established, the common guidelines and recommendations are endowed with a consensual legitimacy that becomes difficult for delegates to question unless they have strong (governmental) political support. This process of definition of the criteria for 'good' conduct in given areas of governmental action generally entails the diffusion of a detailed questionnaire in the member states' ministerial departments. Borrowing from the register of evidence-based policy, the secretariat justifies the recurrent recourse to these questionnaires by the crucial need to have the committee's work based not only on formal rules but also on administrative practices. While the questionnaires are also instruments used to gauge the progress of member states, they seem to have an indirect effect that is just as important. My interviews with national public governance committee and regulatory policy committee delegates appear to indicate than in certain contexts, the questionnaires result in forms of self-assessment, self-naming and shaming that extend far beyond their supposed role of neutrally providing factual information, causing them to orient the perceptions and actions of civil servants. One of the national delegates I interviewed describes this realisation in the following manner:

> I was chief of the legislative office of this government in 1998. It was the time when the OECD launched the first real country review on regulatory reform. Using the questionnaires that they were circulating to produce the indicators of the use of regulatory tools, I, as a young and full of hopes officer, I was realizing that many times we had to answer 'no'. Do you use consultation? – no – 'impact analysis' – no. So, in 98, I came back to my minister [of Public Administration]. Because I had a direct link to my minister. And I said, 'hey, we have this huge potential to reform our way of regulating'. And actually we produced one bill with all the OECD tool-kit and then it became a law (…) It was a sort of an abstract of all the OECD recommendations.

This is a borderline case: the conditions for such direct influence between the definition of the OECD's standard and legislative initiative are rarely met.[36] Nevertheless, the OECD's national delegates frequently discuss the elaboration and implementation of these questionnaires in terms of reputation and realisation.

## Conclusion

Now institutionalised under the 'smart regulation' label, the regulation of European legislative acts has specificities that relate to the distinctive way of operating of EU institutions. The setting of regulatory policy on the European agenda, however, does not appear to be the result of a top-down EU-wide dynamic. This chapter has attempted to show that this 'Europeanisation' is the outcome of a triangular international dynamic resulting from the many-sided interactions between the OECD, some EU member states that are also OECD members and the EC. More generally, the trend away from classic Weberian bureaucracies towards more market-oriented principles and structures does not appear to be the result of the expert or political domination of one IO – whether we think of the EU or the OECD – but instead derives from the convergence of interests and perceptions between various groups of actors, among which the national ones are not the least influential.

## Notes

\* This chapter received support from the Excellence Initiative of the University of Strasbourg, funded by the French government's Future Investments program.

1 In the additional protocol no. 1, annexed to the Convention of the Organisation for Economic Cooperation and Development (1960), signatory countries decided that the European Community, through the European Commission, would 'take part in the work of the OECD'.

2 http://eeas.europa.eu/delegations, consulted on 20/10/2015.

3 Vincent Gayon takes a similar approach (Gayon 2013: in particular p. 49), as does Sotiria Grek: her research about the OECD's role in the governance of the European educational policy moves 'beyond top-down accounts of the mere and one-directional transfer of policy from the international to the national, towards more attention to the interaction and mediation across 'levels' and actors' (Grek 2014: 267).

4 European Commission, 'European Governance: A White Paper', COM(2001) 428.

5 European Commission, Communication from the Commission on Impact Assessment, COM(2002) 276, 5 June 2002.

6 European Commission, Communication from the Commission to the Council and the European Parliament, 'Better Regulation for Growth and Jobs in the European Union', COM(2005) 97, SEC(2005) 175, 16 March 2005.

7 European Commission, Impact Assessment Guidelines, SEC(2005) 791, 15 June 2005.

8 European Commission, Impact Assessment Guidelines, SEC(2005) 791, 15 June 2005, with 15 March 2006 update.

9 To cite an example given by Wiener (2006: 448), the Communication of 16 March 2005 (COM(2005)97) included a colourful chart of relative progress on better regulation among the member states. Highest marks went to Denmark, the UK and Poland; lowest marks went to France, Portugal and Cyprus.

10 'Deregulation Initiative. Memorandum from the Cabinet Office', 1998. UK Archive document. http://webarchive.nationalarchives.gov.uk/20050202182438/http://cabinetoffice.gov.uk/regulation/docs/general/doc075.pdf.

11 The enterprise and deregulation unit was established in the Cabinet Office but moved swiftly to the Department of Employement, to coordinate the deregulation initiative. 'Deregulation Initiative. Memorandum...' op. cit.

12 In 1995, the UNICE (Union of Industrial and Employers' Confederations of Europe) issued for example a reportintitled *Releasing Europe's Potential through Targeted Regulatory Reform*. (The Unice Regulatory Report, Bruxelles: Unice, 1995).

13 Two examples – one that opposes 'better regulation' and one that supports it – corroborate this hypothesis. In their report *Better regulation: A critical assessment* (ETUI Report 113, 2010). Vogel and Van der Abeele cite a debate that took place during a Coreper working group meeting in preparation of the Competitiveness Council of 4 December 2009. During that debate, 'Germany, backed by the United Kingdom, the Netherlands and Denmark, tried to get a requirement that impact assessments be conducted for all Commission proposals, including non-legislative acts, written into the Conclusions. It took determined action by the Commission, Belgium, Luxembourg and France to impress the terms of the 2003 Interinstitutional Agreement on them'. Eventually the compromise extended the recourse to impact assessments, which can also be requested for non-legislative acts (communications, recommendations, guidelines...) under the condition that they are 'important'. According to Vogel and Van den Abeele the intention of Germany and its allies was to 'screen the output of new EU rules in order to control and try and reduce legislation' (Van den Abeele and Vogel 2010).On the other hand, the conclusions of the OECD's pro-'better regulation' study *Better regulation in Europe* read: 'the regulatory interface between member states and the European Union needs to be managed carefully. A strongly recurring theme across all the OECD reviews of the EU15 was that countries do not feel that they control the situation effectively. *General context* – An increasing proportion of national regulations originate at European Union (EU) level. Member States estimate, that around half of all of their domestic regulations have their roots directly in the EU legislation causing circa 50% of the overall regulatory burdens. *Negotiating EU regulations* – European countries want to find ways of exerting stronger influence on the development of EU legislation. This is important in order to avoid creating policy problems (and burdens) for the implementation of EU directives into national law. But countries often find this process frustratingly hard.' (Power Point presentation of the study 'Better Regulation in the EU 15 countries', signed by Rolf Alter and Daniel Trnka, OECD, undated. ec.europa. eu/smart-regulation/refit/admin_burden/docs/111207_better_regulation_in_ the_eu_15_countries_final_en.ppt (consulted 27/10/2015).

14 On the precaution principles as related to the 'regulation' agenda, see Löfstedt 2004.

15 On the role of the OECD in the international diffusion of RIA, see de Francesco 2013.

16 No other IO is cited in the report (I verified this for the IMF, the World Bank, the WTO and the ILO).

17 For instance, Poland turned to the OECD for expertise on the 'good governance indicators' required for securing European structural funds. *Poland: Developing good governance indicators for programmes funded by the European Union*, OECD, Paris, 2013.

18 Following the 1996 ministerial council meeting, then newly appointed Secretary General Donald J. Johnston had been tasked with modernising and reforming the secretariat and its working methods. He had to deal with the steady decrease of the recurrent budget, which continued until 1999. He introduced internal reforms that led to a 21% drop in operational costs between 1996 and 2003 (*OECD. Getting to Grips with Globalisation: The OECD in a Changing World*, 2004: 31).

19 The pre-existing ties between the two organisations facilitated the construction of the original institutional architecture of the SIGMA programme, hosted by the OECD and funded by the EU. Having neither the required expertise, nor the institutional ability to perform its mission of assistance autonomously, the team of the EC's PHARE programme turned to the OECD in 1991. Its members were looking for an international partner liable to take charge of institutional and administrative assistance in central and eastern European countries (interviews with Bob Bonwitt and Karen Fogg). This resulted in the birth of SIGMA in 1992.

20 Report *Regulatory management capacities of member states of the European Union that joined the union on 1 May 2004*, Sigma paper no. 42, 2007, GOV/SIGMA(2007)6.

21 On the distinction between legal and factual criteria – to which drafting quality should be added – see Alexandre Fleckinger 2008: 14–15.

22 Concerning the OECD, besides the well-known PISA (programme for international student assessment), we can cite the 'Education at a glance' annual reports, the international adult literacy survey or the teaching and learning international survey.

23 As Fleckinger rightly points out, 'by defining effectiveness as the capacity of the law to achieve the objectives initially set, we focus on an ideal situation that is rarely attained in practice where precise and non-contradictory objectives exist' (Fleckinger 2008: 23).

24 Joint initiative on regulatory reform, 26 January 2004. http://oldwww.finance.gov.ie/documents/pressreleases/2004/janmcc12462.pdf.

25 The network comprised up to nineteen participating states. http://www.administrative-burdens.com, consulted 22 October 2015.

26 Unclassified GOV/PGC/RD(2004)9 GOV/PGC/RD(2004).

27 Unclassified GOV/PGC/RD(2006)2 GOV/PGC/RD(2006).

28 10 May 2006, SPEECH/06/287, available at http://ec.europa.eu/commission_barroso/verheugen/speeches/speeches_en.htm_, cited by Wiener 2006: 499.

29 Meeting of Ministers of Public Administration on 6 and 7 November 2000 in Strasbourg. Mandelkern report, p. 8.

30 La Rioja conclusions of the meeting of the Ministers of Public Administration, May 2002.

31 Known for having criticised the budget cutbacks in the Eurozone's weakest economies, he was until 2014 the OECD's G20 finance deputy, leading the initiatives 'strategic response', 'green growth' and 'innovation'. In February 2014, he became Italy's new finance minister of the government of Matteo Renzi.

32 The Better Regulation Executive is a part of the British Department for Business, Innovation and Skills. It is in charge of regulatory reform across the British government.

33 The 'realistic' and 'constructivist' approaches in international relations studies are frequently opposed in a clearcut way. According to the first one, national actors are merely the delegates of clearly defined national goals; according to the second, they are internationally socialised members of global expert networks. In our view, this opposition is often sterile, as both logics are clearly combined in the social reality of international arenas.

34 For an analysis of the consequences of this status on the way the OECD operates, see Martens and Jakobi 2010.

35 See for example the 1997 OECD report to ministers, which sets up a comprehensive plan for action on regulatory reform.

36 In the case at hand, two important conditions arguably facilitated the adoption of OECD tools at national level: the interviewee's high hierarchical position and ties with the minister, and the Olive Tree coalition's political emphasis on administrative reform.

## References

Balint T. and Knill C. (2007). The limits of legitimacy pressure as a source of organizational change: the reform of human resource management in the OECD, in Bauer M.W. and Knill C. (eds). *Management Reforms in International Organizations*. Baden-Baden: Nomos, pp. 117–131.

Caporaso, J., Cowles, M. and Risse, T. (2001). *Transforming Europe: Europeanisation and domestic change*. Ithaca: Cornell University Press.

de Francesco, F. (2013). *Transnational Policy Innovation: the OECD and diffusion of regulatory impact analysis*. Colchester: ECPR Press.

Delpeuch T. (2008). L'analyse des transferts internationaux de politiques publiques: un état de l'art. *Question de recherches du CERI*, 27.

Dolowitz, D.P. and Marsh, D. (1996). Who learns what from whom: a review of the policy transfer literature. *Political Studies*, 44(2), 343–357.

Dolowitz, D.P. and Marsh, D. (2000). Learning from abroad: the role of policy transfer in contemporary policy-making. *Governance*, 13(1), 5–25.

Fleckinger, A. (2008). Qu'est-ce que 'mieux légiférer'?: enjeux et instrumentalisation de la notion de qualité législative, in Flueckiger A. *et al.*, *Guider les parlements et les gouvernements pour mieux légiférer: le rôle des guides de légistique*. Genève: Schulthess, pp. 11–32.

Froud, J., Boden, R., Ogus A. and Stubbs, P. (1998). *Controlling the Regulators*. London: Macmillan.

Gayon, V. (2013).Homologie et conductivité internationales. L'etat social aux prises avec l'OCDE, l'UE et les gouvernements. *Critique Internationale*, 2013/2, 47–67.

Grek, S. (2014). OECD as a site of coproduction: European education governance and the new politics of 'policy mobilization'. *Critical Policy Studies*, 8(3), 266–281.

Hood, C. (1998). Individualized contracts. *Governance*, (4), 443–462.

Löfstedt, R.E. (2004). The swing of the regulatory pendulum in Europe: from precautionary principle to (regulatory) impact analysis. *Journal of Risk and Uncertainty*, 28, 237–260.

Majone, G. (1996). *Regulating Europe*. Abingdon: Routledge.

March, J G. and Olsen, J P. (1998). The institutional dynamics of international political orders. *International Organization*, 52(4), 943–969.

Martens, K. and Jakobi, A.P. (eds) (2010). *Mechanisms of OECD Governance: international incentives for national policy-making?* Oxford: Oxford University Press.

Palier, B. and Surel, Y. (eds) (2007). *L'Europe en action, l'européanisation dans une perspective comparée*. Paris: L'harmattan.

Porter, T. and Webb, M. (2008). Role of the OECD in the orchestration of global knowledge networks, in Mahon R. and McBride S. (eds). *The OECD and Transnational Governance*. Vancouver: UBC Press.

Radaelli, C. (2005). Diffusion without convergence: how political context shapes the adoption of regulatory impact assessment. *Journal of European Public Policy*, 12(5), 924–943.

Radaelli, C. (2007). Whither better regulation for the Lisbon agenda? *Journal of European Public Policy*, 14(2), 190–207.

Torriti, J. (2007). Impact assessment in the EU: a tool for better regulation, less regulation or less bad regulation? *Journal of Risk research*, 10(2), 239–276.

Van den Abeele, E. and Vogel, L. (2010). *Better regulation: perspectives critiques.* Brussels: Institut Syndical Européen, Rapport 113.

Wiener, J.B. (2006). Better regulation in Europe. *Current Legal Problems*, 59, 447–518.

## Institutional sources

European Commission (2001). *European Governance: A White Paper*, COM 428.

European Commission (2002). Communication from the Commission on Impact Assessment, COM 276, 5 June 2002.

European Commission (2002). Communication on Impact Assessment, COM (276) Final 5 June 2002.

European Commission (2005). Communication from the Commission to the Council and the European Parliament, 'Better Regulation for Growth and Jobs in the European Union', COM 97, SEC (2005) 175, 16 March 2005.

European Commission (2005). Communication of 16 March 2005, COM 97.

European Commission (2005–2006). Impact Assessment Guidelines, SEC 791, 15 June 2005, with 15 March 2006 update.

European Council in Edinburgh (1992). Conclusions of the Presidency, 12 December 1992 (SN456/92 E).

European Council in Lisbon (2000). Presidency conclusions, 23–24 March 2000.

Mandelkern Group on Better Regulation Final Report (2001). Available at: http://ec.europa.eu/smart-regulation/better_regulation/documents/mandelkern_report.pdf.

OECD (1960). *Convention of the Organisation for Economic Cooperation and Development*, OECD, Paris.

OECD (1995). *Recommendation of the Council on Improving the Quality of Government Regulation* (C(95)21/FINAL), OECD, Paris.

OECD (1995). *Reference Checklist for Regulatory Decision-making* (1995), OECD, Paris.

OECD (1997). *Ten good practices in the design and implementation of RIA*, OECD, Paris.

OECD (2002). *Regulatory Policies in OECD countries: from interventionism to regulatory governance*, OECD, Paris.

OECD (2004). *Getting to Grips with Globalisation: the OECD in a changing world*, OECD, Paris.

OECD (2005). *Guiding Principles for Regulatory Quality and Performance*, OECD, Paris.

OECD (2009). *Indicators of Regulatory Management System*, OECD, Paris.

OECD (2012). *Recommendation of the Council of the OECD on Regulatory Policy and Governance*, OECD, Paris.

OECD (2012). *Sustainability in Impact Assessments: a review of impact assessment systems in selected OECD countries and the European Commission*, OECD, Paris.

OECD (2013). *Poland: Developing good governance indicators for programmes funded by the European Union*. OECD, Paris.

OECD (2015). *OECD Regulatory Policy Outlook 2015*. OECD Publishing, Paris.

OECD-GOV (2004). Meeting summary of the working party on regulatory reform, 27–28 September 2004, Unclassified GOV/PGC/RD(2004)9.

OECD-GOV (2006). Activity report 2005–2006. Public Governance Committee Working Parties and Networks, Unclassified GOV/PGC/RD(2006)2.

OECD-SIGMA (2007). *Regulatory management capacities of member states of the European Union that joined the union on 1 May 2004*. Sigma paper no. 42, 2007, GOV/SIGMA(2007)6.

UK Government (1998). Deregulation Initiative. Memorandum from the Cabinet Office, 1998. UK Archive document. Available at: http://webarchive.national-archives.gov.uk/20050202182438/http://cabinetoffice.gov.uk/regulation.

UNICE (Union of Industrial and Employers' Confederations of Europe) (1995). *Releasing Europe's Potential through Targeted Regulatory Reform*. (The Unice Regulatory Report). Brussels: Unice.

Chapter 4

# The praise of mutual surveillance in Europe

*Luís Miguel Carvalho and Estela Costa*

## Introduction

In 2002, on introducing the book *Fabricating Europe*, Nóvoa and Lawn (2002: 1) referred to the emergence of a 'European educational space' resulting from crossing a variety of discourses and practices of a plurality of actors and actants – 'national state collaboration, European Union guidelines and products, academic networks, social movements, business links and sites, city 'states', virtual connections' – in short, as a result of a diffuse and polycentric movement. After more than a decade, the programme for international student assessment (PISA) – the international performance comparison of educational systems prepared since the mid-nineties (and launched at the turn of the century) by the Organisation for Economic Co-operation and Development (OECD) – could well be included in this bundle of discourses, practices, actors and objects that structure and that restructure European education space. Currently, this larger scale international comparative assessment, and the comparability that it promotes, seems to pervade multiple European policy and politics contexts: to galvanise disputes or to legitimise policies; to set targets; to build assessment tools at a national level; only to mention a few significant applications.

This chapter addresses the uses and effects of PISA in the imagination and the scrutiny of educational problems and solutions in Europe and, concomitantly, its participation in the creation of a European policy space in education (Lawn and Grek 2012). It builds on previous work that shows PISA as a knowledge-policy instrument (Carvalho 2012); that is, as a tool that combines sophisticated comparative assessment techniques with a set of representations about education and a philosophy of (transnational and national) regulation of education policies and practices. In addition, the descriptions and analysis developed in this chapter draw on previous literature that depicts comparability as a mode of European governance (Nóvoa 2002, 2012), and the OECD as an indirect strong agent of the Europeanisation in education (Lawn and Grek 2012; Grek 2014). We summarise these inputs in the following paragraphs.

PISA, the OECD's self-portrayed quality monitoring tool, is here understood as a device that embraces and conveys different ways of imagining (and doing) education and the governing of education and that – simultaneously – plays a part in the coordination of education policies and public action (Carvalho 2012: 173). Moreover, PISA is envisaged as a knowledge-based and knowledge-oriented regulation instrument (Van Zanten 2011: 33): it draws on knowledge 'but also produce[s] and diffuse[s] knowledge in order to shape the behaviour of actors in a given policy domain'. Therefore, PISA exemplifies the presence, in the contemporary policy processes, of soft forms of regulation that favour information and persuasion (and acting through the actors' reflexivity) instead of command and control (Lascoumes and Le Galès 2007).

Comparability was one of the 'main tenets' of the European educational policy emerging since the mid-1990s (Nóvoa 2002). Also, the comparability associated to the dissemination of best practices, and the boosting of activities aimed at the creation and adoption of indicators and benchmarks that are likely to be monitored still is a main tenet of European education policy, as the ET 2020 programme relies deeply on the rationale followed in its 'predecessor' – ET 2010 (Nóvoa 2012). The four action verbs that circumscribe the intervention of the European Commission (EC) characterise this form of soft regulation that has been set in motion: 'identifying (common goals); spreading (good practices); measuring (the results); comparing (the developments and policies)' (Nóvoa et al. 2014: 275).

Parallel to the importance of comparability comes the close collaboration with the OECD, developed over the past 10 years (Grek 2014). Put in different terms, the monopoly of competence developed by the OECD on the competencies of literacy has found a favourable ecology at the European Commission (EC). It can therefore be seen as an expression of the 'expansions' of PISA over the past decade: amplifications of the geopolitical scope, the objects assessed (number and focus of the surveys), and the partnerships involved (Carvalho 2012); enlarging the scope (broadening the set of skills and competencies) and the scale (covering more countries, systems and schools), and improving the explanatory power of the assessment (Sellar and Lingard 2014). This is an expansion that involves the construction of a 'social matrix of interrelated governing actors' (Grek 2010: 401). The important thing, though, for the present text is that the interdependence between the EU and the OECD fosters the creation of the European education space as a governable space of comparison and commensurability (Nóvoa and Lawn 2002; Lawn and Grek 2012; Normand and Derouet 2016).

Drawing on the outlined contributions, this chapter focuses on the active reception and the political uses of PISA data/information/knowledge, at national and supranational arenas, in order to enrich our understanding about the role of knowledge-based and knowledge-oriented regulation instruments in constructing the European policy space. Overall, the chapter depicts the fabrication of chains of 'mutual surveillance practices': the development at a national and European level of policies regulated by a comparative logic, and supported by data resulting from a particular larger scale international comparative assessment.

The chapter proceeds in the following manner. The first section is based on a review of the literature on PISA receptions and effects in European contexts, more precisely of papers on the national receptions and effects of PISA in European countries, published in English language academic journals between 2000 and 2014. The text highlights and discusses two concomitant features of PISA participation in the contemporary policy process: the different uses and interpretations of PISA; the attraction it transversely achieves in diverse social worlds (policy-makers, experts, high administration agencies and media) with diverse interests and perspectives. In short, the section emphasises the 'the aggregation effect' (Lascoumes and Le Galès 2007) that PISA accomplishes in European countries. The second section of the chapter describes and analyses the densification of the relations between EC/the Directorate General for Education and Culture (DGEAC) and OECD/PISA and the reception of PISA results at the EU level, and the agenda-setting, rule-setting and rule-following initiatives built upon it. These initiatives are observed as part of the reinforcement of vertical processes deployed in the social and cognitive construction of a European education space and a European policy space in education.

## PISA active reception and effects on educational policies

Over the past decade several studies, ranging from a single country analysis to a multiple countries analysis, have examined the active receptions and the effects of PISA texts and objects at national and supranational policy-making levels. Those studies say much about the diverse uses of PISA in public policies and in other social worlds of education: the multiple purposes assigned and the wide range of policies connected to PISA, the selection and (re)contextualisation of data/information/knowledge provided by PISA and the social, cultural and political factors related to the plurality of active uses and responses. But they also depict a transversal phenomena – or 'crossing effects' – associated with the use of PISA for the imagination, scrutiny and steering of educational systems, policies and practices. In the next pages we identify, describe and discuss these major trends.

### With multiple purposes, in multiple policies

The extent, the intensity and the depth of PISA reception varies between countries and within each country over time. Even more, the reception is characterised by the assignation of multiple purposes to PISA texts and objects, particularly of legitimation, information and idealisation.

Thus, PISA is associated with the legitimisation of ongoing or new, sometimes potentially controversial, reforms (Afonso and Costa 2009; Berényi and Neumann 2009; Bonal and Tarabini 2013; Ertl 2006; Greger 2012; Grek 2009; Pons 2012; Rautalin and Alasuutari 2007; Sellar and Lingard 2013), as well as with the legitimisation of knowledge-based regulatory instruments previously developed by national authorities (Grek *et al.* 2009). Distinctly, PISA is seen as a primary, or a supplementary, source of information for the steering of educational systems, by compensating the lack of national sources, adding or reassuring the existing ones (Afonso and Costa 2009; Berényi and Neumann 2009; Bieber and Martens 2011). Finally, PISA is understood to be supporting the construction of diverse educational ideals, projections or narratives, about education and educational reform (Afonso and Costa 2009; Berényi and Neumann 2009; Dobbins and Martens 2012; Grek 2012; Grek *et al.* 2009; Mons and Pons 2009; Neumann *et al.* 2012; Pettersson 2014); and nurturing new advocacy coalitions (see Dobbins and Martens 2012; Ertl 2006).

The variety of policies held with reference to PISA is also noticeable. Curriculum is the more conspicuous area, from the syllabuses to the organisational structures, from the focus on competences to changes in school schedules (Afonso and Costa 2009; Berényi and Neumann 2009; Bieber and Martens 2011; Ertl 2006; Mangez and Cattonar 2009; Dobbins and Martens 2012). Then, it is possible to display a large list of policy areas where PISA is invoked: student assessments' rationales and instruments (Berényi and Neumann 2009); quality standards and national assurance measures (Bieber and Martens 2011; Ertl 2006); priority action programmes targeting inequality and segregation issues (Afonso and Costa 2009; Berényi and Neumann 2009; Ertl 2006); initial and in-service teacher education curricula (Afonso and Costa 2009; Ertl 2006; Mangez and Cattonar 2009; Ringarp and Rothland 2010); school management and school evaluation policies (Bonal and Tarabini 2013; Mangez and Cattonar 2009; Ringarp and Rothland 2010; Dobbins and Martens 2012) and national school network restructuring (Berényi and Neumann 2009). Finally, and perhaps more importantly, specific programmes have been undertaken to promote better literacy levels in PISA assessed competences (Bonal and Tarabini 2013; Ertl 2006; Afonso and Costa 2009).

### Context-specific and transnational dynamics

Several authors point out the selective processes involved in these prolific mobilisations of PISA data. For instance, it seems clear that only some of all the policy domains addressed by PISA 'recommendations' – equity, national school structures and standards, teacher training, quality assurance, school autonomy, educational research and statistics (Bieber and Martens 2011) – are taken into account. Moreover, when an intense mobilisation of PISA occurs, only some domains are considered and, what is most significant, others are completely ignored (Bonal and Tarabini 2013; Greger 2012; Grek 2009; Neumann *et al.* 2012; Ringarp and Rothland 2010). Finally, the knowledge/information/data actually mobilised in public debates or by policy measures is reduced and it is often transformed into a limited number of simplified statements (Mangez and Hilgers 2012). Apart from selection, ideas such as appropriation, re-contextualisation and translation are recurrently put forward in the literature to emphasise the active reception of PISA. Some authors refer to the appropriation and re-politicisation of knowledge in line with pre-existing agendas (Afonso and Costa 2009; Bonal and Tarabini 2013). Other authors identify the translation of circulating texts into local terminologies and problems (Neumann *et al.* 2012), and others the creation, under certain circumstances, of specific bodies of knowledge for policy, by combining scientific, technical and political ingredients with specific explanations about PISA results (Mons and Pons 2009; Pons 2012).

The social, cultural and political factors related to the plurality of active uses and responses to PISA is one of the most open to discussion issues concerning the analysis of PISA reception. Nonetheless, it is possible to identify in the literature some major factors, like the path and the trends of national education systems, the present cultural and political features of the reception contexts and the characteristics of the assessment and the credibility of the OECD. The existence of previous reform efforts is largely documented as a very important element (Berényi and Neumann 2009; Bieber and Martens 2011; Steiner-Khamsi 2003), but other characteristics are recognised. Some, of structural nature – for instance, the degree of centralisation/decentralisation and homogeneity/heterogeneity of each educational system (Bieber and Martens 2011), or the socioeconomic position of the country in the EU (Bonal and Tarabini 2013) – others, of a cultural nature, like the educational evaluation and assessment traditions, in the academy, in high-level state bureaucracy or in the professions of education (Carvalho 2012; Dobbins and Martens 2012; Grek 2009; Mons and Pons 2009; Pons 2012), the attitudes towards international comparisons as (valid) resources for the administration of education systems, and the orientation of policy-makers and their staff concerning evidence-based policies (see Afonso and Costa 2009; Berényi and Neumann 2009; Dobbins and Martens 2012; Pons 2012). Studies also point out the dynamics of national politics (Grek *et al.* 2009; Dobbins and Martens 2012; Pons 2012; Sellar and Lingard 2013) and the contingent needs to revitalise or to block problems/solutions carried by PISA results, as well as to the degree of 'mediatisation' of PISA results, thus stressing the issues of the 'resonance' of PISA data at the ongoing national debates, and the resulting legitimation needs (see Bieber and Martens 2011; Steiner-Khamsi 2003; Greger 2012; Mangez and Cattonar 2009). Finally, individual agency may also be emphasised: the 'capacity' of policy actors and systems to transform external pressures into concrete processes of reform (Dobbins and Martens 2012); the agency of policy brokers, namely the PISA national representatives and experts (Neumann *et al.*, 2012), or other mediators (Bonal and Tarabini 2013). PISA-related factors are also relevant. The impact of PISA results is recognised per se, their variations along the cycles, and the sense of crisis induced by the results (Dobbins and Martens 2012; Greger 2012; Ringarp and Rothland 2010; Waldow *et al.* 2014), as well as the importance of specific characteristics of PISA (when compared with other international comparative assessments), like its regularity, geopolitical scope and the singularity of the object of inquiry (Carvalho 2012, following Bottani 2006), and the deep-rooted 'centrality', for the school systems, of the subjects examined (Steiner-Khamsi 2003). Finally, the OECD status and strategies should also be considered: its credibility as a purveyor of expert independent knowledge (Bieber and Martens, 2011; Carvalho, 2012; Grek *et al.* 2009; Rautalin and Alasuutari 2009) and the 'impetus' of OECD interventions (Bieber and Martens 2011), particularly the OECD strategies of communication in the media (Mangez and Cattonar 2009; Mons and Pons 2009).

As evidenced in the preceding paragraphs PISA objects/texts are re-interpreted, made acceptable and efficient for specific sociocognitive contexts, and each context may exhibit different abilities and knowledge resources and circumstances in which to do so. However, along with such a multiplicity of uses, a few commonalities are also patent in PISA reception, such as the fabrication/legitimation of new governing modes, the naturalisation of mutual surveillance as a way of governing, and the redefinition of reference societies. We address these issues in the next section.

### 'Crossing effects' and 'new geographies'

Associated with PISA texts and objects diffusion/reception is the fabrication and legitimisation of new governing modes: the adoption of evidence-based approaches (Afonso and Costa 2009; Berényi and Neumann 2009; Dobbins and Martens 2012), even if 'only' a phony adoption (Greger 2012; Pons 2012) or a kind of a 'categorical' script for policy-making (Mangez and Cattonar 2009); the use of international comparisons as external legitimation resources (Bonal and Tarabini 2013; Mons and Pons 2009; Dobbins and Martens 2012; Grek 2009) and an increased engagement in policy learning and policy borrowing approache (Dobbins and Martens 2012; Ertl 2006), although sometimes within incomplete borrowing and superficial learning processes (Ringarp and Rothland 2010), and not necessarily conducting to a deeper rationalisation of policy-making processes (Mangez and Cattonar 2009; Mangez and Hilgers 2012; Pons 2012); the creation of new assessment structures and the reshaping of the pre-existing balances between centralised and decentralised administration (Ertl 2006; Grek 2009); the introduction

and the development of instruments for the monitoring of education systems, either on a national scale (Berényi and Neumann 2009; Bieber and
Martens 2011; Ertl 2006; Neumann *et al.* 2012), or on a supranational level
(Grek 2010); the emergence, in the media and public sphere, of international comparative assessments as a 'third evaluator' between the state and
the civil society, as a source to scrutinise the 'evaluative state' on behalf of
the public interest (Mangez and Cattonar 2009). These manifestations may
be related to deep changes in national evaluative cultures (Neumann *et al.*
2012) but more broadly they are part of the institutionalisation of governing
modes based and oriented to data/information/knowledge production, thus
strengthening the hypothesis that new forms of governing are connected
with new ways of knowing (Nóvoa and Yariv-Mashal 2003; Ozga 2008).

Despite the persistent existence of critical voices, PISA is usually perceived by political actors as capable of raising public awareness about education systems, and capable of helping to identify problems and provide good
examples, and as accurately portraying the performance of education systems, their weaknesses and strengths. As recently argued, PISA is a kind of
meta-policy: 'a policy that frames the possibilities and expectations of, and set
limits to, what can count as policy' (Dale and Robertson 2014: 220). Thus,
PISA data and analysis open and close routes and establish a set of possibilities for policies, and its power lies in keeping actors referring to it or using
it for the imagination and/or the scrutiny of educational systems, policies
and practices. Ultimately, the reported uses of PISA legitimate the centrality
of the knowledge for policy generated by the OECD (Carvalho 2012; Grek
2009, 2012).

International comparative assessments are driving new practices of relation
with the 'other' and of guiding policies through relating with the 'other'
in the making of educational policies (Nóvoa *et al.* 2014; Steiner-Khamsi
2012). A particular way of seeing these injunctions is exposed in papers that
address and discuss the use of PISA in the continual process of governing
through the country's location in a competitive world space, and the reconfiguration of reference societies (e.g. Bonal and Tarabini 2013; Carvalho
and Costa 2014; Grek *et al.* 2009; Ringarp and Rothland 2010; Sellar and
Lingard 2013; Waldow *et al.* 2014).

In a recent paper, based on empirical data from six case studies on the
reception of PISA in six European countries, we have noticed that the specificities of the reception contexts are still important for understanding the
diversity of 'reference societies' invoked in domestic debates about educational systems in each PISA cycle (Carvalho and Costa 2014). Yet, one might
have to consider seriously the existence of more direct PISA effects regarding
the societies taken as reference points for the reflection on education systems.
This direct effect has multiple expressions: the 'other' that ranks the top of
the league tables; the 'other' that is taken into account because they made
progress; the 'other' taken as a role-models of seriousness in the way they

handled the PISA results; the 'other' who is seen as sharing the same educational problems (as evidenced by PISA categories and indicators).

From what has been said, we suggest that around PISA occurs an updating of the reference societies. Moreover, in the six European cases examined, these re-updates are made generally by invoking European countries (and exceptions often result from a rhetorical dramatisation that is the invocation of countries with non-equivalent positions – and therefore incomparable – in the world). This trend, albeit tenuous, supported by studies, allows us to speculate that we are facing the imaginary activation of a common space.

## PISA active reception and effects at the European level

What happens if we change our observation from individual countries to the reception of PISA at an EU level? That is what we deal with in the next section, focused on the relationship that is being built between the EU and the OECD and on the mobilisation and/or integration of PISA in the EU political processes. Firstly, we will try to clear up and identify the main ideas that are conveyed in data that highlight the intensification of relations between the OECD and the EU. Secondly, we will proceed to an interpretative analysis in the European documents of references to the OECD and PISA.

### The densification of relations between the EC and the OECD

We capture the densification of relations in a wide range of sources: the European legislation (Official Journal of the European Union) and other EU documents (memorandums, press releases, executive summaries and disseminating brochures); public speeches from members of the DGEAC; reports published by the EC (elaborated within the framework of the ET 2020 monitoring procedures, and those resulting from the European policy networks and working group); and in new European instruments and initiatives documentation/websites. The data provided consolidated the idea that the intensification of ties between the two bodies (EU/OECD) is a growing reality, which can be seen from two key aspects: the adoption of the framework of literacy to discuss education in Europe and the use of PISA (rationale or data) as a source for new European monitoring devices. We will, then, analyse each of the referred aspects.

### Adopting the literacy framework to discuss education in Europe

The literacy framework plays a primary role in the European debate on education and in the establishment of European targets. The highest expression of this are the targets set for the European education and training 2020 framework, with PISA influencing the formulation of the European standards related with low achievement in reading, maths and science (European Commission/DGEAC 2013: 1).

In addition to supporting the Europe 2020 targets, the importance attributed to PISA literacy turns out to be reflected in different aspects of the European policy, as evidenced in the EC adoption of (PISA's) literacy as an area of concern. In fact, the 'problem' of literacy leads to the creation, within the EU, of a working group on literacy, which developed a multilayer approach to literacy, related to numeracy and other competences 'in broad terms to levels defined in the OECD's PISA' (European Commission 2012b: 13). Similarly to the process of enlarging the scope of literacy by widening the skills and competencies observed at the OECD level (Sellar and Lingard 2014) different literacies emerge in the context of Europe, such as the digital literacy, the entrepreneurial literacy (whose data were collected for the first time in PISA, 2015) and adult literacy. The latter, and as already examined by Grek (2010), discloses an assembly of interdependence between the two entities, and became part of the European agenda, to the point of imagining the development of literacy programmes at work by employers and other 'social partners' (European Commission 2012a: 12).

The adoption of (OECD's) literacy as a 'problem' may be seen as an example of a policy alignment between the EU and OECD. For some, PISA may only be present as a proof of the quality of the EC policies – 'The report is consistent with the Commission's policy: increasing the quality of education and raising skills levels is a smart investment and a powerful way of combatting inequalities in our societies' (EC Press Release 2014); however, the EC alignment with the OECD is repeated successively at different moments and places, and disclosed by the same commissioner in the Erasmus+ launch conference, when legitimising the launching of Erasmus+ with PISA data:

> Together with our Member States we have agreed that early school leaving is an urgent priority; therefore Erasmus+ will share the best solutions from across Europe. We have identified poor reading skills as a serious problem; Erasmus+ will fund new cross-border projects to tackle it. (…). We know that we need to open up education to new technologies; Erasmus+ will support better use of ICT for learners and teachers. Our vocational training systems are too often failing our young people; Erasmus+ will help to modernise them (…).
>
> (European Conference 2014)

The alignment on education and training policies is also visible in widely published documents An example is the brochure 'Preparing for life – How the European Commission supported education, youth, culture and sport (2010–2014)', which is exemplary in the way it shows how the EU intends to reinforce collaboration with the various member countries and the OECD:

> Over the last 5 years we have deepened pan-European cooperation in higher education and vocational training, making it easier for students

and teachers to compare courses and qualifications; created new tools for measuring progress and promoting transparency; extended cooperation with the OECD so that we better analyse education outcomes; and delivered policy strategies on early childhood education and care, early school leaving, vocational training, rethinking skills and open education resources.

(European Commission/DGEAC 2014b: 5)

Moreover, to prove the pooling of efforts between the EC and the OECD, the PISA 2012 results were, for the first time, officially presented in a joint EC/OECD event, in Brussels, as it has happened with the launch of the results of the Survey of Adult Skills (PIAAC), a building block of the two institutions' enhanced cooperation (European Commission/DGEAC 2013: 2).

### PISA as a source for monitoring instruments

The densification of the relationship between the OECD and the EU can also be observed through the relevance that PISA (rational and/or data) has in European monitoring processes. For instance, under the 'European semester' initiative, the EU's annual cycle of economic policy guidance and surveillance, PISA is presented as:

an important component of the strategic framework for European cooperation in education and training (ET 2020) and a prominent source of information for the Europe 2020 strategy and the European Semester, where it is widely used in fields as literacy, mathematics, early leavers from education and training, low achievers and ICT skills.

(European Commission/DGEAC 2013: 2)

The importance and dependence on comparability find themselves strengthened since the EC has intensified and sophisticated the practices of rule-following. At present times, the education and training monitor is perhaps the most relevant monitoring strategy/device in use by the EC for the sector of education, and is a good example of this intensification of the EC's participation in monitoring the national policies (see Nóvoa 2012). In this coordination and control instrument, where data and figures, benchmarks and targets – generated by diverse organisations – mix and complement each other, PISA and the OECD's other international surveys and comparisons (like TALIS and PIACC) have a relevant presence. As reminded by the European Director-General for Education and Culture in the forward to its third edition, the device is as an example of the 'close cooperation' with the OECD through several programmes (European Commission/DGEAC 2014a: 3).

Furthermore, PISA and PIAAC are being used as a legitimising source of the European initiatives 'rethinking education', the 'Entrepreneurship360 project', both focused on developing entrepreneurial education, and both deploying monitoring processes. 'Rethinking education' (COM 2012) is a country-monitoring initiative set up in 2012 to monitor the progress of institutions. It was carried out with the OECD, in the area of skills policies, 'to guide and advance the development of entrepreneurial education institutions at all levels including schools and vocational education and training' (COM 2012: 4). In 2013, the EC launched the public portal 'education and skills online assessment' in order to allow 'individuals and enterprises, through the PIAAC methodology, to benchmark skills against other survey users' (COM 2012: 16). As for the 'Entrepreneurship360 project', it is a new 'self-assessment' tool created with the OECD, in 2014, with the aim of nurturing entrepreneurship as a key competence in schools and technical and vocational institutions (European Commission/DGEAC 2014c: 51).

## References to the OECD in EU documents and events

In this part of the chapter, we held an interpretative analysis of the references to the OECD/PISA in European documents. Following the methodological approach developed by Alasuutari (2009), we discovered three major trends regarding the presence of the OECD and PISA: the comparability between the OECD and the EU; the presentation of the OECD as a body of expertise; and the diffusion and endorsement of OECD models and recommendations.

### Comparability between the OECD/EU

The OECD has an assiduous presence in EU documents, frequently being referenced on a comparative basis to analyse results and legitimise statements. This comparative atmosphere that dominates the tone of the European narratives on education is deeply present in very diverse places, such as press releases, memorandums, official speeches, reports and in published documents, and is used mainly to analyse the performance of the member states and is very much associated with the ET 2020 and the EU indicators:

> The latest PISA (...) found that, among EU countries, 22.1% are low achievers in maths, 17.8% in reading and 16.6% in science. Although these figures represent a slight improvement on previous years, the EU average masks significant differences between Member States. For example, the share of low achievers in maths is over 40% in Bulgaria, Romania and Cyprus, compared with only 10.5% in Estonia, 12.3% in Finland and 14.4% in Poland.
>
> (EC Memo 2014)

Sometimes the analysis takes on a diachronic dimension, relating to member countries and non-European countries, and expanding beyond the European context, thereby spreading the exercise of comparability:

> The findings reveal that ten Member States (BG, CZ, DE, EE, IE, HR, LV, AT, PL and RO) have achieved significant progress in diminishing their share of low achievers across all three basic skills since 2009. But five EU countries (EL, HU, SK, FI, SE) have seen an increase in the number of low achievers. Other Member States achieved mixed results (see table). Overall, EU performance is slightly better than the United States, but both lag behind Japan.
>
> (EC Press Release 2013)

However, the OECD is also used for feeding the monitoring processes, as exemplified by the following quote, which uses data from two PISA cycles (2003 and 2009) to describe the trajectory of a specific issue: the size of schools.

> In comparison with PISA 2003 (...), in half of the countries studied, the mean size of schools increased by 50 to 100 students, while a decrease of more than 70 students per school can be seen in Belgium (German-speaking Community), Austria, Poland. A greater decline was recorded in Latvia where the mean school size fell by 30% (205 students). As a general tendency, between 2003 and 2009 student numbers in the larger schools in Europe fell slightly.
>
> (EACEA 2012: 36)

It is under the 'European education and training 2020 framework' (2009/C 119/02) that comparison is used most to fuel statements and political discourse by the European authorities, specifically those related to the ET 2020 benchmarks:

> PISA shows that four of Europe's Member States (EE, FI, PL and NL) are among the top 7 performing countries in the world in mathematics. These countries are already below the EU benchmark of 15%. The proportion of low achievers across the EU is lower than that found in the USA (26%). (...) Another encouraging finding is that the EU as a whole is on its way to reaching the EU-wide benchmark of having fewer than 15% low achievers in reading and science by 2020.
>
> (EC Speech 2013)

Furthermore, this type of comparison is used in press releases to render account and monitor the performances in the main literacies. The following example regards the EU performances in reading in the 2006 and

2009 PISA cycles in comparison to 2012 and the ET 2020 15 per cent benchmark:

> Reading: The percentage of low achievers in reading has declined from 23.1% in 2006 and 19.7% in 2009 to 17.8% in 2012. If this trend continues, the 15% benchmark may be achievable by 2020. So far, only seven EU countries have reached this benchmark (EE, IE, PL, FI, NL, DE and DK). Notable progress has been achieved by CZ, DE, EE, IE, HR, LT, LU, AT, PL and RO.
>
> (EC Press Release 2013)

### The OECD as a body of expertise

A recurring widespread idea is that policies need to have a reliable and rational basis. Indeed, the evidence-based narrative is widely disseminated, like a hallmark and it is steeped in most institutional and formal documents of the EU, as in the case of the framework of ET 2020, which highlights the importance of 'evidence and data from all relevant European agencies, European networks, and international organisations' (Official Journal of the European Union 2009).

The evidence-based trend of the EU nourishes (and is nourished by) the OECD's image as a knowledge provider. This can be directly observed in public speeches of the members of the DGEAC:

> PISA is an example of the kind of partnership we need if we want to combine expertise, knowledge and resources for the benefit of all Member States and to improve the contribution of education to bringing our societies back to a path of growth and jobs.
>
> (EC Speech 2013)

A more indirect way of doing this is to consider that the content of the OECD report meets European policy, as one might observe in the launch of PISA 2012 – 'PISA results strengthen the knowledge base of the Commission and, given the prominence and credibility of the international survey, give the Commission's own policy messages more visibility' (European Commission/DGEAC 2013: 2) – or at the launch of the OECD's *Education at a Glance*: 'This report is a major source of knowledge and evidence for policy-makers; it contributes to increasing our understanding of the challenges we face' (EC Press Release 2014).

However, PISA and the OECD are also repeatedly mentioned within European networks and within concrete intervention devices where they are widely propagated, as exemplified in KeyCoNet (a European policy network focused on identifying and analysing initiatives on the implementation of key competences in primary and secondary school education):

When such an evidence-based approach is used, what are the outcomes and where evaluations exist what do we learn from them? The intention is to analyse international influences, such as how the latest PISA student data has impacted on various countries' formulation of key competence policy, also looking closely at a very pertinent OECD working paper (…) concerning how diverse stakeholders at various levels are involved in curriculum innovations in different countries.

(Arjomand *et al.* 2013: 3)

Necessarily, the credibility of the OECD and PISA is fostered in monitoring processes where the mobilisation of data from multiple sources is recurrent, but especially the OECD and its devices. This is the case with *Key Data on Education in Europe*:

Based on data collected through the Eurydice network, Eurostat and the PISA international (…). We hope that this body of data and information will serve as a valuable source for decision makers in the field of education, helping them in reviewing and reforming their educational policies and institutions (…).

(EACEA 2012: 8)

In sum, the way the EC references the OECD is related, mainly, to the assignment to the agency of an image of credibility, objectivity and expertise. In fact, this idea of a data provider is the one that subsists more clearly and helps to strengthen the EC's 'appetite' for evidence-based policies.

### OECD models and recommendations

In the EC universe of action, there are many references to the lessons that the PISA data provide. The texts always tend to follow an 'evidence–consequence sequence' with evidence being examined in a logic of the implications and repercussions on education policy. Moreover, analyses are developed as 'learned lessons'. The repeated scheme goes as follows: (a) the diagnosis given by statistics allows 'to take lessons' and 'learn something', i.e. PISA data enable the EC to verify 'the necessity of…'; and (b) the 'existence' of such learning process (and learned lessons) makes it possible to make recommendations to member states.

The idea underneath that OECD (PISA) data allow the realisation of something, to find out something and learn about that, is part of a narrative that occupies the speeches of European high officials:

PISA 2012 found that the difference in mathematics performances within countries is generally even greater than that between countries

(...) This observation points to the need to address inequalities between different regions and schools within the same country. Lessons learned from certain high-performing regions within a country may then provide valuable pointers for successful policy interventions (...).

(EC Speech 2013)

The evidence–consequence sequence is found in very different moments and places, such as under the 'education semester' monitoring processes:

The average share of low achieving students in maths in Member States has essentially remained the same in PISA 2012 (22.1%) in comparison to PISA 2009 (22.3%), which means that EU countries should considerably step up their efforts towards reducing the share of low achievement in mathematics.

(European Commission/DGEAC 2014c: 42)

Or in the launch of PISA 2012:

Six main findings from PISA 2012 can be summarised from a preliminary analysis, each with its own implications for education and training policies. 1. When it comes to progress towards the 2020 benchmark of at most 15% low achievers, the EU as a whole is seriously lagging behind in the area of mathematics. Significant policy reform will be required in order to break with this stagnation.

(European Commission/DGEAC 2013: 1)

The importance of PISA in the construction of the content of recommendations to the member states also appears abundantly, in subtle ways, in the form of best practices indicated by PISA and that member states should follow, as put forward in the *Education and Training Monitor 2014*, regarding several domains: teachers training and careers, students at risk, curriculum, student behavioural management; parental engagement, allocation of resources (European Commission/DGEAC 2013: 6–7). However, it may also appear more roughly recently in the form of 'country-specific recommendation in policy areas related to PISA', concerning early school leaving and basic skills, disadvantaged groups and the teaching profession (European Commission/DGEAC 2013: 16).

## Conclusion

Together with the OECD, we will carry out further analysis of the data in order to help Member States better understand how to improve their

education systems. We need to ensure that future editions of PISA provide us with an opportunity to monitor progress.

(EC Speech 2013)

It is surely significant that PISA-based performance targets or indicators have been set in the EC's strategic framework ET 2020; and by several
countries, as recently declared by representatives from Belgium communities, Denmark, Finland, France, Hungary, Ireland, the Netherlands, Poland,
Slovenia, Slovak Republic and Wales–UK, with diverse expressions: rank
of the country in international performance; specific national PISA score;
increases in the number of high performers or decreases in lower performers;
equity goals (see Breakspear 2012).

Operating at the level of 'principles of action' and 'representations',
PISA can be perceived as a promoter and as a resource of a 'cognitive
Europeanisation' (Hassenteufel 2008: 262) of education: it defines an educational 'cooperative-competitive' space, and the ongoing demand for better
results and progresses around a common subject (literacy); naturalises mutual
surveillance as a specific way of doing policy and politics; fosters the commitment to data-based policies.

As shown in the first section of the chapter, this instrument, characteristic of
OECD's soft regulation modalities, has been receiving different uses and contrasting interpretations at the national level. But the attraction for/from PISA
intensifies the practices of mutual surveillance as a way of governing. We can
say that comparing with the 'other' becomes a practice that means to show
the best and the worst vis-á-vis an international standard and, through this,
to animate the belief and hope in 'betterment' or 'reform'. Such imagination
of 'equivalents' and 'differences' does not only strengthen the legitimacy of
choices and measures to be taken; it also helps to trace old/new identities and
even to imagine and set a (new) positioning 'in the European space'.

These PISA effects have intensified through its recurring mobilisation and
reactivation by the EC. As we showed in the second section of the text,
these traits are noticeable in the choices and the EC processes of intervention – clearly, on the adoption of literacy as a central category to problematise
education in Europe, and in the use of PISA as a source for new European
monitoring devices, and can be perceived as contributing to the strengthening of vertical processes deployed in the social and cognitive construction
of a European space policy in education. The use of PISA and other OECD
instruments are associated with the intensification of collaboration between
both organisations – an intensification that, as regards the EC and following
the terms of Grek (2014: 267) has been fostered to obtain 'data to govern' and obtain a supplementary support to push 'the commission's own
policy agendas forward, albeit leaving the old subsidiarity rule intact. Yet
this strategic resource to PISA is partnering with two other phenomena. On
one hand, it arises whether associated with the injunction, in each country,

of 'translation politics' – the translation of priorities and recommendations of the EC, either to hard forms of regulation, linked to the award (or not) and the management of incentives or financial supports (Nóvoa *et al.* 2014). On the other hand, the systematic use of PISA reinforces some of the OECD dicta about governing processes: the primacy of the rational and 'data-based' model, opposed to ideological and/or opinion-based coordination; the 'free acquiescence' of decision-makers to be involved and support expert-based mutual surveillance as an effective practice; the perception of system-atic assessment of literacy – generated by an organisation that performs as an independent expert knowledge provider – as a useful and trustworthy resource for the steering of educational systems.

## References

Afonso, N. and Costa, E. (2009). The influence of PISA on policy decision in Portugal. *Sísifo*, 10, 53–64.

Alasuutari, P. (2009). Use of the OECD in justifying policy reforms. *Journal of Power*, 2(1), 89–109.

Arjomand, G., Erstad, O., Gilje, O., Gordon, J., Kallunki, V., Kearney, C., Rey, O., Siewiorek, A., Vivitsou, M. and von Reis Saari, J. (2013). *KeyCoNet 2013 Literature Review: key competence development in school education in Europe.* Available at: http://keyconet.eun.org/c/document_library/get_file?uuid=060f39a1-bd86-4941-a6ca-8b2a3ba8548e&groupId=11028.

Berényi, E. and Neumann, E. (2009). Grappling with PISA: reception and translation in the Hungarian policy discourse. *Sísifo*, 10, 41–52.

Bieber, T. and Martens, K. (2011). The OECD PISA study as a soft power in educa-tion? Lessons from Switzerland and the US. *European Journal of Education*, 46(1), 101–116.

Bonal, X. and Tarabini, A. (2013). The role of PISA in shaping hegemonic educa-tional discourses, policies and practices: the case of Spain. *Research in Comparative and International Education*, 8(3), 335–341.

Bottani, N. (2006). La más bella del reino: el mundo de la educación en alerta con la llegada de un príncipe encantador. *Revista de Educación, extraordinario*, 75–90.

Breakspear, S. (2012). The policy impact of PISA. *OECD Education Working Papers*, 71. Available at: http://dx.doi.org/10.1787/5k9fdfqffr28-en.

Carvalho, L.M. (2012). The fabrications and travels of a knowledge-policy instru-ment. *European Educational Research Journal*, 11(2), 172–188.

Carvalho, L.M. and Costa, E. (2014). Seeing education with one's own eyes and through PISA lenses. *Discourse: Studies in the Cultural Politics of Education*, 36(4), 1–9.

COM (2012). 669 final European Commission (Strasbourg 20.11.2012). *Rethinking Education: investing in skills for better socio-economic outcomes.* Communication from the commission to the European parliament, the council, the European eco-nomic and social committee and the committee of the regions. Available at: http://eur-lex.europa.eu/legal-content/EN/TXT/PDF/?uri=CELEX:52012DC0669a ndfrom=EN.

Dale, R. and Robertson, S. (2014). Global education policies, in N. Yeates (ed.) *Understanding Global Social Policy*, 2nd edn. Bristol: Policy Press, pp. 209–235.

Dobbins, M. and Martens, K. (2012). Towards an education approach à la *finlandaise*? French education policy after PISA. *Journal of Education Policy*, 27(1), 23–43.

EACEA (2012). *Key Data on Education in Europe*. Brussels: Eurydice.

EC Memo (2014). EU Education Council, 24 February. Available at: http://europa.eu/rapid/press-release_MEMO-14-125_en.htm.

EC Press Release (2013). EU school report: some improvement in science and reading, but poor in maths, 3 December. Available at: http://europa.eu/rapid/press-release_IP-13-1198_en.htm.

EC Press Release (2014). Commission says OECD findings confirm importance of investment in education for EU growth and jobs, 9 September. Available at: http://europa.eu/rapid/press-release_IP-14-979_en.htm.

EC Speech (2013). Launch of OECD PISA 2012 results. Speech by Jan Truszczynski, Director General, DG Education and Culture, European Commission, 3 December. Available at: http://ec.europa.eu/archives/commission_2010–2014/vassiliou/headlines/press-releases/docs/20131204-oecd-pisa-2012-results.pdf.

Ertl, H. (2006). Educational standards and the changing discourse on education: the reception and consequences of the PISA study in Germany. *Oxford Review of Education*, 32(5), 619–634.

European Commission (2012a). *EU high level group of experts on literacy Executive summary*. Luxembourg: Publications Office of the European Union.

European Commission (2012b). *EU high level group of experts on literacy Final report*. Luxembourg: Publications Office of the European Union.

European Commission/DGEAC (2013). *PISA 2012: EU performance and first inferences regarding education and training policies in Europe. Executive summary*.

European Commission/DGEAC (2014a). *Education and Training Monitor 2014*. Available at: http://ec.europa.eu/education.

European Commission/DGEAC (2014b). *Preparing for life – How the European Commission supported education, youth, culture and sport (2010–2014)*. Luxembourg: Publications Office of the European Union.

European Commission/DGEAC (2014c). *Education and Training Monitor 2013*. Luxembourg: Publications Office of the European Union.

European Commission/DGEAC (2014d). *Education and Training Monitor 2014*. Luxembourg: Publications Office of the European Union.

European Conference (2014) Erasmus+ – a new partnership between education and the world of work, Bucharest, 11 March. Available at: http://europa.eu/rapid/press-release_SPEECH-14-196_en.htm.

Greger, D. (2012). When PISA does not matter? The case of the Czech Republic and Germany. *Human Affairs*, 22(1), 31–42.

Grek, S. (2009). Governing by numbers: the PISA effect. *Journal of Education Policy*, 24(1), 23–37.

Grek, S. (2010). International organisations and the shared construction of policy "problems". *European Educational Research Journal*, 9(3), 396–406.

Grek, S. (2012). Learning from meetings and comparison: a critical examination of the policy tools of transnationals, in Steiner-Khamsi G., Waldow, F. (eds). *World*

*Yearbook of Education 2012 – Policy Borrowing and Lending*. Abingdon: Routledge. pp. 41–61.

Grek, S. (2014). OECD as a site of coproduction: European education governance and the new politics of "policy mobilization". *Critical Policy Studies*, 8(3), 266–281.

Grek, S., Lawn, M. and Ozga, J. (2009). PISA and the policy debate in Scotland. *Sísifo*, 10, 73–84.

Hassenteufel, P. (2008). *Sociologie Politique: l'action publique*. Paris: Armand Colin.

Lascoumes, P, and Le Galès, P. (2007). Understanding public policy through its instruments. *Governance*, 20(1), 1–21.

Lawn, M. and Grek, S. (2012). *Europeanizing Education*. Oxford: Symposium Books.

Mangez, E. and Cattonar, B. (2009). The status of PISA in the relationship between civil society and the educational sector in French-speaking Belgium. *Sísifo*, 10, 15–26.

Mangez, E. and Hilgers, M. (2012). The field of knowledge and the policy field in education. *European Educational Research Journal*, 11(2), 189–205.

Mons, N. and Pons, X. (2009). The reception of PISA in France: a cognitive approach of institutional debate (2001–2008). *Sísifo*, 10, 27–40.

Neumann, E., Kiss, A., Fejes, I., Bajomi, I., Berényi, E., Biró, Z. and Vida, J. (2012). The hard work of interpretation: the national politics of PISA reception in Hungary and Romania. *European Educational Research Journal*, 11(2), 227–242.

Normand, R. and Derouet, J-L. (2016). Introduction, in *A European Politics of Education: Perspectives from sociology, policy studies and politics*. Abingdon: Routledge.

Nóvoa, A. (2002). Ways of thinking about education in Europe, in A. Nóvoa and M. Lawn (eds). *Fabricating Europe: the formation of an education space*. Dordrecht: Kluwer Academic Publishers, pp. 131–155.

Nóvoa, A. (2012). The blindness of Europe. *Sisyphus – Journal of Education*, 1(1), 104–123.

Nóvoa, A. and Lawn, M. (2002). Fabricating Europe, in A. Nóvoa and M. Lawn (eds). *Fabricating Europe: the formation of an education space*. Dordrecht: Kluwer Academic Publishers, pp. 1–13.

Nóvoa, A. and Yariv-Mashal, T. (2003). Comparative research in education: a mode of governance or a historical journey. *Comparative Education*, 39(4), 423–438.

Nóvoa, A., Carvalho, L.M. and Yanes, C. (2014). La comparaison comme politique. *Revue Suisse des Sciences de l'Éducation*, 36(2), 265–282.

Official Journal of the European Union (2009). *Council conclusions of 12 May 2009 on a strategic framework for European cooperation in education and training*, C 119/02. Available at: http://eur-lex.europa.eu/legal-content/EN/TXT/PDF/?uri=CELEX:52009XG0528%2801%29&from=EN.

Ozga, J. (2008). Governing knowledge: research steering and research quality. *European Educational Research Journal*, 7(3), 261–272.

Pettersson, D. (2014). Three narratives: national interpretations of PISA. *Knowledge Cultures*, 2(4), 172–191.

Pons, X. (2012). Going beyond the 'PISA shock' discourse: an analysis of the cognitive reception of PISA in six European countries, 2001–2008.*European Educational Research Journal*, 11(2), 206–226.

Rautalin, M. and Alasuutari, P. (2007). The curse of success: the impact of the OECD's PISA on the discourses of the teaching profession in Finland. *European Educational Research Journal*, 6(4), 348–63.

Rautalin, M. and Alasuutari, P. (2009). The uses of the national PISA results by Finnish officials in central government. *Journal of Education Policy*, 24(5), 539–556.

Ringarp, J. and Rothland, M. (2010). Is the grass always greener? The effect of the PISA results on education debates in Sweden and Germany. *European Educational Research Journal*, 9(3), 422–430.

Sellar, S. and Lingard, B. (2013). Looking East: Shanghai, PISA 2009, and the reconstitution of reference societies in the global education policy field. *Comparative Education*, 49, 464–485.

Sellar, S. and Lingard, B. (2014). The OECD and the expansion of PISA. *British Educational Research Journal*, 40(6), 917–936.

Steiner-Khamsi, G. (2003). The politics of league tables. *Journal of Social Science Education*, 1. Available at: www.jsse.org/index.php/jsse/article/view/470.

Steiner-Khamsi, G. (2012). Understanding policy borrowing and lending, in G. Steiner-Khamsi and F. Waldow (eds). *World Yearbook of Education 2012: Policy borrowing and lending in education*. London: Routledge, pp. 3–17.

Van Zanten, A. (2011). Knowledge-oriented instruments and the regulation of educational systems, in H. Ramsdal and A. van Zanten (eds). *Knowledge Based Regulation Tools in Education and Health*. KNOW and POL Integrative report. Available at: www.knowandpol.eu.

Waldow, F., Takayama, K. and Sung, Y.-K. (2014). Rethinking the pattern of external policy referencing: media discourses over the "Asian Tigers" PISA success in Australia, Germany and South Korea. *Comparative Education*, 50(3), 302–321.

Chapter 5

# Policy learning and expertise in European education

*Romuald Normand*

## Introduction

Much research has affirmed the role of knowledge in the shaping of education policies and the implement of reforms at national and global scales (Lawn and Normand 2014; Fenwick *et al.* 2014). The European Commission has the capacity to mobilise expert networks and groups to address its recommendations to member states. European technocracy, instead of having a coercive power on states, uses expertise as a form of authority and power (Radaelli 1999a, 1999b). Since the implementation of the Lisbon Strategy, decisions taken by European institutions have been supported by a wide variety of working groups, committees, agencies and think tanks (Gornitzka 2013). The production of knowledge does not just belong to scientists: it is distributed among heterogeneous experts with a central position to give advice and to guide policy-makers.

In terms of the production of knowledge and expertise, European policy-makers have a regulatory power. Through mechanisms of discussion and negotiation, they try to base their decisions on rational and scientific examinations presented in different instances (Lawn and Grek 2012). The latter are places of compromises of consensuses reducing the direct political fight and open debates (Majone 1996). Meanwhile, the commission faces a double process of competition and fragmentation: competition with other institutions such as the European Council and parliament with whom it competes for power, without forgetting the many conflicts in the relationships between general directorates and units; fragmentation in the sense that European policy is decomposed into functional areas with its general directorates, its expert committees, its parliamentary groups, its interest coalitions. It is therefore difficult to grasp the whole coherence while different sectorial arenas are subjected to multiple negotiations and pressures.

In the vein of Claudio Radaelli (2008), I shall show in this chapter how expertise shapes European policies in the field of education by borrowing concepts from political sciences and studies on expert groups. Policy learning related to expertise and knowledge production will be illustrated. Some arguments from different situations from my experience as an expert in several European networks will be used. My perspective is from that of the 'insider' or 'embedded' researcher who socialises in different expert groups and produced expertise while maintaining his reflexivity, critical distance and categories of judgement as a social scientist. In studying the epistemic dimensions of expertise, my objective is to comprehend better the building of expert knowledge from the inside, to understand its genesis and mechanisms, to complete my previous studies on expert networks and different epistemic communities (Normand 2010).

Expertise is a specific activity of knowledge production participating in a process of negotiation and orientation of public policy (Ozga 2011). This knowledge is technical and comes from professionals working in administrations, international organisations, universities and other higher education institutions, agencies, think tanks or interest groups (Weible 2008). Thousands of expert groups and networks work for the European Commission even if they are not always fully visible (Gornitzka and Sverdrup 2008; Robert 2010). They serve to prepare initiatives for the commission, which creates, frames and funds them. Other entities are shaped by their participation in the commission's funded programmes in response to calls. Others are created as influence and pressure groups to orientate the European strategy and decision-making. Up to now, there has been little work on the expertise produced in these groups and networks in education, their activities, their place within knowledge production and decision-making. However, experts play a determining role in the guidance of European education policies, the dialogue with national and international representatives and the political work within the European institutions.

From these considerations, some links can be established between technocracy, expertise and politicisation (Radaelli 1999b). Indeed, European technocrats, as political entrepreneurs, as experts, as producers of knowledge, shape interpretations and disseminate information to overcome the traditional obstacles of political negotiation according to reciprocal learning. This articulation depends on the degree of certainty and visibility of the political action. When European decision-making is based on certainty in terms of knowledge and strong public visibility in terms of impact, the bureaucratic process predominates the use of expertise. When uncertainty on information and knowledge is high but public visibility is low, technocracy predominates and expertise becomes endogenous in European institutions. When there are politicised stakes on the public scene and low uncertainty, the use of expertise is quite impossible and the process of politicisation dominates. But when decision-making depends on high uncertainty with regard to available information and knowledge, and visibility is high, the use of epistemic communities and exogenous political entrepreneurs becomes the key factor.

Beyond the distinction between endogenous and exogenous expertise, the role of experts in policy learning has become a subject of investigation for researchers interested in how European policies are built. Policy learning gives rise to multiple definitions but it also shows the increasing strong intertwinement between expertise and different institutions (governments, networks, think tanks, agencies) and the variety of processes and modes of technical and scientific knowledge. Radaelli defines policy learning as 'a process of updating beliefs about key components of policy (such as problem definition, results achieved at home or abroad, goals, but also actors' strategies and paradigms)' (Radaelli 2008). Policy learning corresponds to an instrumental approach, which transform policies, programmes and organisations (Bennett and Howlett 1992; Bomberg 2007). It is made up of key actors who, alongside experts, generate processes of knowledge production, cognitive changes, shape new beliefs and ideas, and transformations of rationality (May 1992; Radaelli 2008).

By following in the footsteps of Dunlop and Radaelli (2013), we will explore, in this chapter, four main categories of policy learning that we will illustrate via case studies related to our empirical observations: reflexive learning, epistemic community, social interaction and learning in the shadow of hierarchy.

In reflexive learning, power is polycentric and it opens up a space for deliberation. Changes arise via a process of communicational rationality and knowledge is shared without a priori by experts and lay people. What is at stake is to disseminate knowledge in the community or via a network while learning is supported by a structure of governance facilitating coordination and dissemination. The process of learning relies on an endogenous social interaction that shapes politics. Actors control the means and contents of learning even if objectives can be externally fixed. Reflexivity fails if they do not reach a minimal agreement on common principles.

In the epistemic community, experts have a mandate and a certification for participating in collective learning. Policy-makers call on expertise to reduce uncertainty in information and knowledge and decision-making. Experts are controlled because it is policy-makers who make the decisions regarding the modalities of dissemination and the use of knowledge. Experts have to respect precise specifications defining the modalities of reciprocal learning and knowledge production.

In social interaction, the conditions of learning correspond to a political negotiation with a weak separation between experts and policy-makers. The negotiation focuses on objectives as procedures and instruments. These 'clever' encounters are achieved under certain conditions and in a loosely structured way.

For learning in the shadow of the hierarchy, the relation is less defined by expertise or science than by the content of institutional rules. Actors have to respect certain rules and roles in their interactions but the logic of exploration is relatively free. The first type corresponds to an instrumental learning with some improvements in the tools of governance and instruments of public action. Another mode of learning is the production, dissemination and use of knowledge through a chain of tasks delegation. A last case is highly constrained learning in its contents and objectives through specific institutional procedures.

## The making of story telling by a think tank

The expertise work of think tanks is well known (Medvetz 2012; Stone and Denham 2004; Rich 2005). At the European scale, their actions with member states have been studied for more than a decade (Sherrington 2000; Ullrich 2004). According to Medvetz's classification, experts working for think tanks have various characteristics. Some are academics producing expertise from their research. Others have a role of assistance in participating in the definition of norms and recommendations for policy-making. Experts have the capacity to anticipate emerging political issues from their previous political and administrative experience. Others specialise in entrepreneurship and look to place their claims on the market of ideas for policy-makers, interest groups, foundations, funders, sponsors and advocacy coalitions. Experts also play an important role in the communication of research findings to different audiences. They strive to have a direct impact on the media and specific targets by adopting a clear, concise and understandable language while using the media devices at their disposal (blogs, Facebook, Twitter, etc.).

The Veritas think tank, for which we worked as experts, has different features. It is a reformist and leftist institution producing recommendations in the field of public policies (the economy, welfare, Europe, education, research, justice, etc.). It liaises with other think tanks from the European reformist left. Veritas includes about a thousand experts coming from national and local government, business and associations. It regularly publishes briefs that have generated significant media interest while regularly organising cycles of conferences for a large audience. Think tanks are mainly funded by major companies. Through their expertise and their claims they propose concrete solutions for policy-makers while getting inspiration from the best practices of their European partners and generating public debate.

The working group was quickly set up while a first meeting was organised. I was the only academic and the group included, among the active members, a high-ranking trade unionist, a high-ranking and retired administrative executive and general inspector, a general inspector with close links to the minister's cabinet, two principals, a high-ranking administrator in the training of executives, and two inspectors of primary and secondary education. Mr A, the Veritas representative, explained to us that the think tank had to establish a consensus on education beyond the traditional left and right divide. The objective was to make mid-term proposals that could influence the public debate before the presidential elections, and that it was necessary to work in cross-functional ways with other working groups. The work would be carried out at distance, with few meetings, and the objective was to write a 15/20-page report with precise recommendations.

During the first meeting, a discussion was initiated on the need for a systemic reflection in terms of governance, the preparation of recommendations and the programmatic agenda for the minister and his cabinet, while at the same time we had to communicate the meaning of reforms to the general public. The content of the report could be free but it would not commit the minister who, nevertheless, was persuaded that it was necessary to implement structural reforms in the territorial governance of education. This work was part of a series of reflexions before the state's summit on decentralisation, of which the aim was to go beyond stereotypes and formulate some challenging proposals without forgetting such non-negotiable left-wing values as justice and social mix.

As these initial discussions showed, a working group's tasks within a think tank are similar to shaping narratives to empower a large audience, via the media, but also convincing politicians and policy-makers. Some rational arguments regarding the implementation of reforms had to be mixed with ideological ones related to the ideas shared by the members of the think tank, political friends and members of the cabinet. Shaping the contents of discourse is often called 'story telling', an activity in which think tanks specialise.

Very quickly the papers produced by the experts in the working group appeared extremely heterogeneous even though the work was carried out at distance with rare moments of coordination. Some of them, like the principals, were concerned about the daily experience and problems they faced while they had imaginary representations about the possibilities of making changes, which they shared with the Veritas representative who was also a principal. High-ranking civil servants had a technocratic vision inspired by reflections developed in reformist circles but they were also eager to convince members of parliament and bureaucrats to design a bill. These differences are accentuated by the tension between centralisers and de-centralisers in the administration as in political parties from top to bottom. Some experts had a political and systemic vision because they had important responsibilities in governance, while others were more focused on devices and rules in context, particularly among the principals. The trade unionists and the Veritas representative had quite an ideological discourse. I, as an academic, tried to deliver a message inspired by some evidence from international research. Papers were therefore compiled without establishing guidelines and it gave the impression of an incoherent and unreadable patchwork.

This problem of readability alerted Mr A who judged that the report should not adopt a technocratic vision but remain understandable to lay people attached to reforms. This is why he phoned me because I was, due to my position as an academic and after having read my contribution, able to write a harmonised and consensual report after removing its technocratic vulgate and reformist common sense. He explained that I had to use simple language, which the minister himself could understand, to whom it was necessary to talk to him as a parent. During the discussion, some elements of discourse were reflected on and they had to be written in the report and transformed into reformist proposals understandable to all. I was then invited to participate in a meeting with the ministry to finalise the report and to adjust recommendations better to the minister's desiderata.

Several weeks later, a meeting was organised at the ministry, in the minister's office, with the head of the think tank and a high-ranking retired civil servant close to the leftist party and highly influencial within Veritas. As a general inspector, he had worked in ministerial circles and he supervised all the education working groups in the think tank. The minister welcomed us and proposed that we sit down around his working desk. He was very friendly. He then began his speech about the reform of timetable scheduling and some symbolic violence it was generating (the reform has led to large-scale strikes and protests during the past weeks). The minister did not understand why trade unions, associations and political parties were struggling with this issue. The head of Veritas told him that the left was more concerned by the family and no longer considered the horizon of equality. It had to focus on the new familial order in relation to the evolutions of the law and social protection. The minister responded that the reform of timetable scheduling had served as a pro domo argument for its opponents who refused to recognise that pupils were tired. He believed that the risk was that the school system would become a supermarket in which everyone would choose his or her timetable, his or her curriculum and his or her teachers according to his or her preferences. He also observed a big gap between the claims by parent organisations and what was actually happening at the local level.

Then, Mr A, the representative of our working group in the think tank, presented the key elements of the topic the experts were working on. He argued that the issue of governance has hardly been explored in official guidelines and that it was necessary to reflect on a new share of powers and responsibilities in order to achieve better democratisation and better performances for students. I summarised the arguments we had previously discussed to write the report, which focused on a certain number of values that the socialist minister could adhere to: better recognition for the work of teachers; the building of solidarity between schools in the same catchment area; recognition of the merits of each school according to its pedagogical efforts; development of self-evaluation to improve the conditions of further training. The high-ranking civil servant, seated next to the minister, a counsellor specialising in youth issues, took some notes. The minister listened intently and seemed interested.

The retired high-ranking civil servant, influencial in Veritas, took the floor to defend his idea of social mix in schools. The minister did not seem that interested but he continued his speech. He argued that the ministry should not adopt a technocratic policy but consider the true meaning of the reform.

In his opinion, the diagnosis had been established by research and the general inspectorate's reports. The school system is unequal because of social determinisms and it poorly democratises the access to the elite. That is the real problem. Mr A added comments and explained that there is a process of ghettoisation but that some schools in education priority areas are having success. It is important to take into account team work and the psychoc-ognitive dimension of pupils. He spoke about his experience as a principal. Then he went back to the topic of the working group. I intervened to say that reform does not work because local actors are not well informed and supported. It would be useful to reflect on an engineering of reforms as has been done in other countries. The retired high-ranking civil servant spoke again and came back to the idea of social mix as he denounced separatism in local education areas. The minister replied that he believed that social mix is desirable but it raises a question of economic efficiency due to budgetary difficulties. There is also a social obstacle. This reflection has to be made when considering the reform of school catchment areas but this evolution will take time. The head of the think tank shared his idea of creating bigger schools to improve social mix and to achieve some economies of scale. The retired civil servant told us about a survey conducted in Paris in which indicators have been built to measure the progress of each school, in a dynamic way, without stigmatising failing schools but by providing examples of good achievement that can be transferred.

The discussion ended because the minister had a dinner with presidents of universities. The meeting was less than one hour. The contents of expertise from the working group were not really discussed. We agreed that we would keep the minister informed of our progress when writing the report. Outside of the ministry, the Veritas representatives seemed quite disappointed and they shared their doubts regarding the minister's interest. However, this meeting had collateral effects on the working group of experts. I later learnt that Mr B, the chair of the expert group, had been recommended by the retired civil servant who had joined the meeting with the minister. They were friends who for a long time had been in the circles of the same political party. The report was revised during the summer. Mr B was helped by another member of the working group, a high-ranking civil servant close to the cabinet. A table of contents was designed and Mr A, the think tank representative, shared the new document and asked everyone to make comments. He said that he was glad that the report had become more coherent but he had revised the introduction by giving it a strong historical orientation. This rewriting suggested that other members of the think tank who were outside the working group had intervened in the writing of the document. Meanwhile other contributions were made by the other members of the working group.

Afterwards, a meeting of the working group was organised while some experts were pushed aside. Mr B, the chair of the working group, began to question the method and considered that a consensus had been reached for writing the report and it should not to be revised. Consequently, he felt that there was no need for a new table of contents but instead it had now become urgent to finish the writing. In an email sent to all the members of the group, he wrote that he could not continue to work without knowing precisely the objective to be reached, that a method had to be defined, a schedule had to be drawn up, and tasks had to be allocated between experts. He argued about the necessity of working on writing the report and improving its content.

This crisis in the group of experts can be explained in several ways. The head of the working group learnt about the meeting with the minister and he felt that his authority had been undermined: it explained his attempt to take power in the writing of the report. But it was also due to tension with the type of management adopted by Mr A, the think tank representative, who sought to inflect the content of the writing by mobilising external allies. There was therefore a game of subtle negotiations in addition to a latent conflict between Mr A and Mr B. A final meeting was organised to resolve the crisis after which some criticism was addressed regarding the report's form and content. It led to the head of the expert group having more of a withdrawn position. Meanwhile, political circumstances had changed: the issue of governance was no longer a ministerial priority and other topics had arrived on the political agenda, and the minister of education was replaced. Finally, this report was never published.

This expertise characterises a reflexive learning because experts, in developing social interactions, build content and insights while sharing knowledge according to an endogenous process linked to politics. However, while they had autonomy, the expert group was externally framed while members had difficulties in agreeing on common objectives. This work gave birth to a dynamic process of reflectivity and common writing. This case also relativises the idea of a direct link between story telling, think tanks and decision-making. As illustrated by our example, think tanks are subjected to narrative and argumentative constraints so that their arguments can be accepted by policy-makers. They are positioned in a highly competitive market of ideas in which individual visions and affinity relationships can undermine a mid-term strategy. The pressure of the media and political short-term thinking forces them to anticipate decision-making and to react opportunely with regard to current interests and stakes. In terms of influence, think tanks participate in the framing of the political agenda and are subjected to permanent adjustments regarding politics and the media.

## Epistemic communities in evidence-based research and policy

From my position in my research institute I was involved in a European programme coordinated by the Knowledge Centre for Evidence-Based

Technologies (KCEBT) while I became an expert and participated in several meetings in Europe. The objective was to work with the French Ministry of Education and to professionalise some technicians producing literature reviews in our knowledge centre. This training gave me the opportunity to become familiarised with the new tools of evidence-based research, mainly the protocols of systemic reviews of research literature and the use of databanks.

Experts promoting evidence-based research belong to a transnational epistemic community defining new standards for education. In that sense, they have a high level of expertise: some of them are heads of evidence-based knowledge research centres developing technologies of evidence (systematic reviews, controlled randomised trials, etc.), others manage evidence-based research programmes. Medicine is the model of reference for evidence-based education. The argument is as follows: in education, experiments have an intellectual interest but no practical utility while their range is limited. Educational research helps to reflect about the problems of teachers but they are not a response for policy-makers. A more rigorous research demonstrating positive and reproducible effects on students' outcomes will have more chance of being funded.

Technologies of evidence are particularly appreciated by policy-makers as they reduce uncertainty and can give access to knowledge they judge useful for decision-making (Biesta 2007; Lingard 2013).

The European project launched by KCBET fitted this objective. The aim was to develop a knowledge and exchange platform for technologies of evidence. The project brought together various actors: individual experts, policy-makers from ministries, knowledge centres, agencies, universities, specialists of media tools and digital platforms. According to Haas' definition (Haas 1992), KCBET is an epistemic community. The experts involved in the European project were persuaded that technologies of evidence are a means of improving the quality and effectiveness of educational research to serve decision-making better. They were searching to elucidate the multiple links between political actions and the desired results by analysing series of practices and problems related to the contribution of research and teaching to the improvement of student scores.

Haas gives us a clear definition of the learning process in this type of epistemic community. It is an information process for policy-makers' beliefs when confronted with uncertainty. Experts control the production of knowledge thus substantively influencing political arrangements and the states' interests. Two types of epistemic community are generally distinguished (Dunlop 2009): in the first type, experts regulate themselves and they are called upon by policy-makers for advice, the second type corresponds to experts deliberately selected by policy-makers to justify a determined political decision or to depoliticise a disputed issue. We could consider that KCBET belongs to the second type.

The Knowledge Centre for Training in Evidence-based Education project is also related to mode 2 of knowledge production (Gibbons *et al.* 1994). In addition to gathering a vast range of European actors from many countries, it establishes a balance between experts, policy-makers, stakeholders and professionals who are invited to produce new knowledge. It presents itself as a triangulation between the production of evidence, its mediation and use in context. In the formulation of a project, it is considered as an imperative to create incentives encouraging researchers and policy-makers to change their attitudes and behaviour in the production, communication and use of scientific knowledge. The objective is to set up infrastructures able to strengthen the links between research, policy and practice in the field of European education.

Within this context, expertise is not autonomous but subjected to a previous framing through a set of 'work packages' (networking, accessing research, mediation, research products and use, stakeholder engagement, sustainability) with different roles and responsibilities defined and shared between the network's experts. The aim is to develop and extend the transnational European network via the website, to improve evidence-based research both in person and at distance, to encourage the development of innovative projects and experiments, but also to create indicators, to conceive a support service for professionals, to encourage the participation of stakeholders, to ensure the sustainability of the network beyond the European project by the development of other projects and publications.

Progressively, encounters were enriched by a certain number of European policy-makers and experts, invited by the leaders of the network for conferences. Throughout the project, the website is updated by the productions of experts, the findings of conferences, the reports of workshops corresponding to work packages, and the tools and resources specifically produced outside the network by institutions, knowledge centres and agencies pursuing their own development programmes on evidence-based education. During the second phase of the project, the epistemic community became more and more visible in its ramifications and activities while the number of participating policy-makers and stakeholders increased. A final report ended the project and recommendations were addressed to European policy-makers, and a second project has been planned in order to continue the network's activities. It has been agreed that the network of experts will be divided into special interest groups and task groups to develop other issues and to extend collaboration with other European partners.

This apparent unity in the coordination and rhetoric of the project must not hide some extremely heterogeneous realities and implementations in each country. It is in the interest of the manager of European projects to claim relative harmony and coherence with the commission, which funds and regularly evaluates it. This facade can dissimulate strong disagreements with the board in charge of the coordination but it is often unknown by the other experts. Participation in a project varies according to the understanding and interest of policy-makers and stakeholders for evidence-based education. For example, the categories used in the English language do not penetrate easily into the cognitive world of participants from the south of Europe.

On the French side, the project received a mixed reception. While my institute and the Ministry of Education were officially involved, and a working group had been set up, the institutional and political structure was not adjusted to welcome a project of this scope. The members of the small knowledge centre in my institute quickly judged that technologies of evidence could threaten their professional identity while they were not skilled enough to move from documentary reviewing to systematic reviews of research literature. The adoption of protocols was a constraint on their work and they did not want the research community to overview and supervise their work. They were therefore pretty hostile to this evolution. The head of the European network had the opportunity to present the objectives and contents of evidence-based education as a guest speaker at the institute in front of practitioners and researchers. But he was not warmly received and often misunderstood because of the existing gap this epistemology has developed at the international level and which French educational sciences largely introverted within the French-speaking area and were globally hostile to the import of Anglo-Saxon influences.

The ministry itself, albeit interested by a reflection on the conditions for transferring and disseminating research findings, did not have sufficient internal means to build an infrastructure fitting the criteria of evidence-based education. In addition, this operation would have required a significant effort of translation for national policy-makers. The solution was to delegate to the institute the design of a mapping of French research and the building of a databank, while some metrics were developed to monitor general trends and to provide information to policy-makers. Another development was the organisation of consensus-based conferences with a national agency of school evaluation to raise awareness among national policy-makers and stakeholders regarding key evidence-based international research findings. But these initiatives, limited and poorly interconnected, remained loosely coupled with European policy.

## From expertise to benchmarks: instrumental politics at the European level

The objective of the European Commission is to build a European space of research and higher education supported by statistical techniques and performance-based measurements to promote competition between national systems in order to generate innovation and to support higher education systems contributing to growth and economic competitiveness (Ritzen

2010; Aghion *et al.* 2010). In creating a European market and strengthening emulation and competition, European policy-makers' intent is to rationalise training provision and research by avoiding the fragmentation of activities, segmentation between the public and the private, and dispersion of funding. Benchmarking, as rankings, is therefore a statistical tool that enables the adoption of a common language for European policy-makers and creates a platform of coherence for national policies so that a dynamic European territory can be progressively built, and one which is open and attractive in the international rankings landscape (Grek 2012; Hazelkorn 2007, 2008, 2011; Kauppi and Erkkila 2011).

The group of experts we were involved with had the task of building benchmarks for higher education policies in Europe. This work followed an initiative started by three European important policy-makers in education when they launched a common call urging universities to use their potential of innovation and to transform their modes of governance in order to improve their attractiveness and rank in global competition. This manifesto invited universities to be more autonomous under a more performant leadership and management capable of better preparing young people to enter the global labour market. The call also proposed to reflect on guidelines to evaluate better the performance of European member states in the implementation of the new higher education policy.

These policy-makers, high-ranking experts from the European reformist left, characterised a different kind of expertise from that which we have mentioned above: they are political entrepreneurs. They search to promote change in higher education policies in Europe by participating in the definition of public problems. They use opportunity windows to promote their arguments. In this way, they attempt to justify the idea of a crisis or major dysfunctions in European higher education thus making decision-making more urgent. To assert their rhetoric, these experts use their political networks but also expert networks with different knowledge and skills to amplify their message while at the same time benefiting from certified knowledge. The mobilisation or empowerment of experts and policy-makers remain fundamental for the success of the enterprise. These political entrepreneurs also have to prove the realism of political proposals formulated in a conceptual framework or programme that has to produce results and show the example to follow.

They find interlocutors more easily in the high administrative and political spheres, particularly at the European Commission, because they share the same codes and values. They are also aware of the best political timing to advance their cause. The work of European political entrepreneurs is close to that of the advocacy coalitions studied by Paul A. Sabatier (Sabatier 1988; Sabatier and Jenkins-Smith 1993; Weible *et al.* 2011). In the sense that they share values, causal imputations and even the same perception of problems, their size as an expert group and the scope of their mobilisation is less. It is a policy learning in terms of social interaction, to resume Radaelli's classification, with a weak divide between experts and policy-makers but also some possibilities of more important informal encounters.

The task force was quickly active in organising a first meeting in a small European city bringing together a group of experts. The drafting of a review of higher education was scheduled for the European Commission. In order to do so, the task force had designed a set of indicators linking policy, performance and growth, and using methods of regression and European databanks. These indicators were grouped into different topics (policy, performance, economic output) to evaluation the national higher education systems. The discussion between experts was essentially focused on technical problems regarding data collection and their adaptation to national realities, without challenging the global approach. It was supported by official reports or international organisations and recurrent topics such as new mobility, the brain drain, innovation, patents, public costs and expenditure, internationalisation and the recruitment of foreign students. In conclusion, it was affirmed that European universities' autonomy and attractiveness needed strengthening.

During the following months, experts were invited to work at distance before the next meetings to compare the evolution of higher education policies from indicators provided by the task force. Each topic was decomposed into indicators, (autonomy, research, access, fund mix, productivity, attractiveness, competitiveness, innovation) from which countries were ranked in a two-column table. A set of colours (green, orange, red) was used to indicate the positive or negative evolution of each country with regard to the benchmarks formalised by the task force while each indicator was graphically represented. These data were accompanied by comments on each country: each national expert, based on his or her review of the situation of higher education, had to confirm or refute the proposed analysis. A technical document was designed to explain the complexity of statistical calculations and regressions used to frame different benchmarks.

Some members of the networks organised other meetings in Europe while the benchmarks and report were updated after collecting advice from experts. Opportunity was given to reflect on a common programme responding to a European call from the European Commission to lead a project on best practices in the governance of higher education. Meanwhile, the representative of the expert group participated in high level meetings with European policy-makers, from the European Commission, in charge of education, research and innovation, as representatives of the Academic Cooperation Association Conference. Recommendations from the expert group served to justify the development of policies focusing on innovation, autonomy and the quality of higher education, while the idea of a long term strategic plan was put forward. One of these meetings was organised under the auspices of the European Bank of Investment along with the European commissioner for research, science and innovation, and with three ministers of education at the origin of the benchmarking project.

## Institutional expertise in the shadow of European technocracy

We will now describe endogenous expertise at the European Commission characterising policy learning in the shadow of hierarchy, in the sense that a network of experts produces knowledge for the units of the General Directorate of Education and Culture (DGEAC) to help it with its proposals and recommendations in the field of lifelong learning policy. This network, entitled NEXUS, was created by the DGEAC, and was subjected to a narrow frame to deliver its expertise and was supervised by a technocrat, or policy officer, in charge of transmitting the directives of his hierarchy to the head of the expert group. NEXUS's aim is to produce expertise content, supported by international research findings in education, to guide European decision-making and to facilitate DGEAC's negotiations with other general directorates, the cCommission itself, and other European institutions.

The network's first task was to carry out a mapping of research fields in education and training and to identify some issues related to the commission's political agenda. It also had to formulate analyses and proposals to become directly operational in the implementation of policy and to organise meetings at the European level with other experts, policy-makers and stakeholders.

Experts, mostly academics, were extremely reluctant to accept this approach of expertise, which they considered utilitarian and instrumental, and this created problems later. The first meeting held in Brussels with the head of one of the DGEAC units, in charge of the expertise programme, was a shock for most of them. The policy-maker explained that the expertise of his unit was limited but it had a lot of relations with a wide variety of ministries, research and expert communities, practitioners and stakeholders at the European level. He described the functioning of another group of experts as a good example and explained that it was DGEAC's ambition better to link policy, research and evidence while a report was being prepared on the efficiency and effectiveness of education systems. It was also argued that a lot of work had already been carried out and the European Council was ready to promote evidence-based policy and to mobilise stakeholders.

The objective of the meeting was to clarify the work of the NEXUS network; its methods with regard to contractual individual and collective arrangements varied according to national contexts. DGEAC's policy-maker wanted the expert group to prepare the next communication quickly on the topic of evidence-based policy. He then recalled the objectives of the open method of coordination, its indicators and benchmarks, the need to exchange on best practices and to develop peer learning between policy-makers, to find effective methods for the development of education policies in relation to PISA scores. The objective was also to strengthen DGEAC's credibility and to work with the commission alongside member states in producing political documents and effective recommendations. The idea was not to provoke resistance but to have a real impact on the transformation of education systems. This is why the expert network had to be selective in its messages and to work on evidence-based issues to avoid problems with the OECD and European governments.

Quickly, an agenda was fixed to the NEXUS network with precise tasks defining the participation of some experts in seminars and conferences organised by DGEAC in different parts of Europe. Experts had to provide advice regularly on drafts DGEAC wanted to make public, on the initial elements of the mapping assigned to my institute, and the development of the website. Later on, the network of experts received 'ad-hoc questions' sent by DGEAC's services, two to three page documents summarising the European Commission's publications on a topic and formulating three key questions about policy-making or decision-making to which experts had to respond within a limited period of time (15 days to 1 month). These ad-hoc questions, highly precise or on the contrary very broad, corresponded to the concerns of Brussels technocrats, who were incapable of finding a response by exploring internal reports and studies or existing databanks. Sometimes the research in this field did not exist or the question was so broad that it would have required a vast and selective review of international research findings.

The rhythm imposed by DGEAC, based on a quality insurance procedure and control, and the reluctance of some experts to respond to such complex questions, often outside of their disciplinary area, and the highly bureaucratic and inexperienced management of our institute in the design of the mapping and the internet website quickly led to an institutional crisis. DGEAC, through its policy officer, convoked an urgent meeting to specify the European Commission's expectations, to remind the experts of the framework and their duties. They were required to contribute better and more to the formulation of recommendations but also to step outside of their scientific expertise area to provide information to the network and to be more available. As for DGEAC, it had to make an effort to reduce timeframes and the number of ad-hoc questions and to set up a new schedule for achieving tasks. In fact, these tensions were the expression of a larger misunderstanding between DGEAC's representatives and those of the expert group.

Indeed, technocrats are used to manipulating instrumental and positivist scientific knowledge and they do not understand that some issues could lead to tergiversations in the responses of experts who have more mobilised, more reflexive, critical and pluralist knowledge. Furthermore, they wanted to control the production of expertise closely and believed that setting up a quality insurance procedure and tasks schedule would be sufficient to frame the work of experts. As for the experts who were mostly all academics, they were unfamiliar with the requirements of international expertise and were not disposed to abandon their academic freedom to apply norms and conceptions they did not share. They were also busy with other tasks for their research community and they did not always have the time to respond, while other broader questions or those that were too narrowly focused would have required the development of new research projects or an extended review of research literature, which would have taken months or years. A perverse effect of this pressure on expertise was that some academics were resuming the contents of the European Commission's documents or already produced expertise to provide a quick review and to finish tasks within the network. Disagreements grew between the DGEAC and the group of experts regarding the evaluation of quality and the relevance of deliverables as well as the content of expertise.

As has been demonstrated by this case study, the cognitive world of Brussels technocrats is relatively constrained. Urged to find responses to questions and to deliver notes, reports and recommendations within tight deadlines, they do not have time to take into account the problems of interpretation and reflexivity induced by the exploration of international research literature. They also cannot penetrate epistemic and methodological debates. They have to produce a normative discourse embedded in previous programmes and actions while claiming a continuity and coherence of European policy. Taking a step back is impossible because it would challenge the assumptions and foundations of an acquired expertise already accepted and officialised by member states.

To guarantee this continuity and to discipline expertise and experts, the DGEAC forces them to work in a restricted framework and protocol, and uses quality standards and financial penalties to ensure deadlines are respected and the work fits the normative requirements of technocrats. Experts, forced to produce expertise in a very short time, have no real possibility to explore the entire extent of research literature required to respond to complex, technocratic and wide-ranging questions far from scientific questioning. In order to do so, it is necessary to translate and reformulate technocratic statements to make them acceptable with regard to scientific content. Because of lack of time, experts have a tendency to 'cut and paste' elements of expertise close to their work, to select papers, reports and other documents quickly, to privilege existing syntheses produced by the commission itself. These experts maintain a kind of hermeneutic circle through which technocrats learn some expert content that they themselves contributed to develop in other expert networks or other epistemic communities, without gaining any exteriority and reflexivity from an endogenous and self-perpetuating 'technocratic doxa'.

## Conclusion

As we have shown in the previous pages, expertise has led to different policy learning processes, which link experts and policy-makers. Scenes and arenas defining the work and the content of expertise are multiple and entail different types of mobilisation and interaction. The transmission of expertise is not homogenous and linear and it is not always successful. Various interpretations and categorisations, but also heterogeneous and uncertain assemblages, have paved the way for knowledge from the field of expertise to that of decision-making (Gorur 2011; Fenwick and Landri 2014). The worlds of expertise are plural and they have their own logic of action, which, contrary to what the technocrats think, cannot be prescribed in advance through quality frameworks and protocols.

We have explored here the cognitive dimension of the experts' work by emphasising the exploratory and incomplete dimension of expertise in action while demonstrating that experts are also subjected to contingency, doubt, misunderstandings, limited rationality, and that they are not always able to give meaning to their action. As a process of policy learning, expertise is made up of multiple attachments and dependences both at proximity and at distance and which participate in a distributed cognition and learning similar to certain conditions found in academic work.

Albeit that content in the production of knowledge is different, the two activities share similarities: regulating and self-control by peers, a sense of legitimacy and hierarchy, competition, sharing implicit knowledge, networking. Evidently, there are differences in expertise: lack of time dedicated to the production of knowledge, the normativity of content, which puts reflexivity and criticism at a distance (and this is a problem for social sciences), the lack of clear divide between analysis of facts and values generating and maintaining a certain 'doxa' and/or satisficing to 'discursive fashions', a lack of historical perspective regarding several issues, a mono-epistemic dimension recusing interpretative pluralism. Some researchers have not taken into account these differences in reducing the gap between science and expertise and producing sciences of government. For others, the two perspectives cannot really be conciliated but these researchers have been relegated to the periphery of expert networks criss-crossing the traditional boundaries between policy, research and practice.

## References

Aghion, P., Dewatripont, M., Hoxby, C., Mas-Colell, A. and Sapir, A. (2010). The governance and performance of universities: evidence from Europe and the US. *Economic Policy*, 25(61), 7–59.

Bennett, C.J. and Howlett, M. (1992). The lessons of learning: reconciling theories of policy learning and policy change. *Policy Sciences*, 25(3), 275–294.

Biesta, G. (2007). Why "what works" won't work: evidence-based practice and the democratic deficit in educational research. *Educational theory*, 57(1), 1–22.

Bomberg, E. (2007). Policy learning in an enlarged European Union: environmental NGOs and new policy instruments. *Journal of European Public Policy*, 14(2), 248–268.

Dunlop, C.A. (2009). Policy transfer as learning: capturing variation in what decision-makers learn from epistemic communities. *Policy studies*, 30(3), 289–311.

Dunlop, C.A. and Radaelli, C.M. (2013). Systematising policy learning: from mono-lith to dimensions. *Political studies*, 61(3), 599–619.

Fenwick, T.J. and Landri, P. (eds) (2014). *Materialities, textures and pedagogies.* London: Routledge.

Fenwick, T., Mangez, E. and Ozga, J. (eds) (2014). *World Yearbook of Education 2014, Governing Knowledge: comparison, knowledge-based technologies and expertise in the regulation of education.* London: Routledge.

Gibbons, M., Limoges, C., Nowotny, H., Schwartzman, S., Scott, P. and Trow, M. (1994). *The New Production of Knowledge: the dynamics of science and research in contemporary societies.* London: Sage.

Gornitzka, Å. (2013). The interface between research and policy – a note with poten-tial relevance for higher education. *European Journal of Higher Education*, 3(3), 255–264.

Gornitzka, Å. and Sverdrup, U. (2008). Who consults? The configuration of expert groups in the European Union. *West European Politics*, 31(4), 725–750.

Gorur, R. (2011) Policy as assemblage. *European Educational Research Journal*, 10(4), 611–622.

Grek, S. (2012). Learning from meetings and comparison: a critical examination of the policy tools of transnationals. In Steiner-Khamsi, G. and Waldow, F. *Policy Borrowing and Lending in Education.* New York: Routledge World Yearbook of Education, pp. 41–61.

Haas, P. (1992). Introduction: epistemic communities and international policy co-ordination. *International Organization*, 46 (1): 1–35.

Hazelkorn, E. (2007). The impact of league tables and ranking systems on higher edu-cation decision making. *Higher Education Management and Policy*, 19(2), 1–24.

Hazelkorn, E. (2008). Learning to live with league tables and ranking: the experience of institutional leaders. *Higher Education Policy*, 21(2), 193–215.

Hazelkorn, E. (2011). *Rankings and the Reshaping of Higher Education: the battle for world-class excellence.* Basingstoke, UK: Palgrave Macmillan.

Kauppi, N. and Erkkilä, T. (2011). The struggle over global higher education: actors, institutions, and practices. *International Political Sociology*, 5(3), 314–326.

Lawn, M. and Grek, S. (2012). *Europeanizing Education: governing a new policy space.* Oxford: Symposium Books.

Lawn, M. and Normand, R. (2014). *Shaping of European education: interdisciplinary approaches.* London: Routledge.

Lingard, B. (2013). The impact of research on education policy in an era of evidence-based policy. *Critical Studies in Education*, 54(2), 113–131.

Majone, G.D. (1996). *Regulating Europe.* London: Routledge.

May, P.J. (1992). Policy learning and failure. *Journal of Public Policy*, 12(4), 331–354.

Medvetz, T. (2012). *Think tanks in America.* Chicago: University of Chicago Press.

Normand, R. (2010). Expertise, Networks and Indicators: the construction of the European strategy in education. *European Educational Research Journal*, 9(3), 407–421.

Ozga, J. (2011). Researching the powerful: seeking knowledge about policy. *European Educational Research Journal*, 10(2), 218–224.

Radaelli, C.M. (1999a). The public policy of the European Union: whither politics of expertise? *Journal of European Public Policy*, 6(5), 757–774.

Radaelli, C.M. (1999b). *Technocracy in the European Union*. Boston: Addison Wesley Longman.

Radaelli, C.M. (2008). Europeanization, policy learning, and new modes of governance. *Journal of Comparative Policy Analysis*, 10(3), 239–254.

Rich, A. (2005). *Think Tanks, Public Policy, and the Politics of Expertise*. Cambridge: Cambridge University Press.

Ritzen, J.M.M. (2010). *A Chance for European Universities: or, avoiding the looming university crisis in Europe*. Amsterdam: Amsterdam University Press.

Robert, C. (2010). Who are the European experts? Profiles, trajectories and expert 'careers' of the European Commission. *French Politics*, 8(3), 248–274.

Sabatier, P.A. (1988). An advocacy coalition framework of policy change and the role of policy-oriented learning therein. *Policy sciences*, 21(2–3), 129–168.

Sabatier, P.A. and Jenkins-Smith, H.C. (1993). *Policy Change and Learning: an advocacy coalition approach*. Boulder, CO: Westview Press.

Sherrington, P. (2000). Shaping the policy agenda: think tank activity in the European Union. *Global Society*, 14(2), 173–189.

Stone, D. and Denham, A. (eds) (2004). *Think tank traditions: policy research and the politics of ideas*. Manchester: Manchester University Press.

Ullrich, H. (2004). *EU Think Tanks: generating ideas, analysis and debate*. Manchester: Manchester University Press.

Weible, C.M. (2008). Expert-based information and policy subsystems: a review and synthesis. *Policy Studies Journal*, 36(4), 615–635.

Weible, C.M., Sabatier, P.A., Jenkins-Smith, H.C., Nohrstedt, D., Henry, A.D. and Deleon, P. (2011). A quarter century of the advocacy coalition framework: an introduction to the special issue. *Policy Studies Journal*, 39(3), 349–360.

Chapter 6

# Ranking and structuration of a transnational field of higher education

*Niilo Kauppi*

> Without data, you are just another person with an opinion.
> (Andreas Schleicher, head of the OECD's
> directorate for education and skills)

This chapter explores the transnational governance of higher education (HE) by focusing on the production and uses of ranking lists of universities and more broadly HE institutions. Since the creation of the so-called Shanghai list of world universities in 2003, an intensification of competition in HE has occurred. Today competition does not take place only between scholars, departments, universities, or even countries, but has moved to a meta level, to a global competition between the providers of knowledge and data that frame HE (past and future) developments. Specialised research institutions like the German Center for Higher Education and international organisations like the OECD as producers of data have become central in HE governance as institutions of HE have become global governable objects.

While everyone agrees on their shortcomings, there is clear evidence that for the stakeholders and public opinion ranking lists are part of the reality of HE. They are widely used and legitimised for setting strategic goals, and thus creating forms of ontological dependence that bind the actors involved in HE to certain conceptions of what is desirable and valued. In ways that need to be empirically documented they help create through (variable) positive feedback the reality they describe, framing the globe as a unified playing field for HE institutions.

## Introduction

There are constant, structural challenges to freedom of thought. These include who can determine what is being taught and studied in HE institutions. In his study *Der Streit der Fakultäten* (Kant 1789) Immanuel Kant divided the university into major and minor faculties. The role of government and the Prussian state was central in the major faculties of medicine, law and theology. These faculties were involved in activities that had to do with practical interests whereas the minor faculty of philosophy was involved in theoretical interest, the pursuit of truth (for a defence see Flexner 1939). Another key dimension of HE has to do with the financing of teaching and research. It can be private, public or a mixture of the two. These two dimensions, the aim of the activity and the economic basis of this activity do not have permanent solutions but vary depending on time and space. These distinctions give us clues of what kind of model of governance is applied to HE. Two ideal typical models can be distinguished: epistemic governance that follows the Haldane principle according to which scientists themselves set the goals and principles of scientific activity, and non-epistemic governance, in which government or business sets research priorities on the basis of mostly non-epistemic interests and goals (profit, political utility...). In reality, these ideal types of theoretical and practical interest are mixed and create contradictions of various kinds, but nevertheless as ideals they influence the way those involved in science governance (and beyond) see their roles and the rules that govern scientific activity and HE.

In this chapter, I will analyse some of the recent transformations of HE in the European context. Higher education has been under major transformations for some time, especially in Europe, where the public university has been reformed since the beginning of the 2000s following the principles of new public management (see for instance Kauppi 2015). HE has been transformed from a public good into a measurable, exploitable private good. This structural shift has been accompanied by a series of transformations. Because these transformations are very similar in different national settings analysing them requires a transnational point of view that enables scrutinising the mechanisms that enable the circulation of models and concepts between different national contexts. The topic is large. Global university rankings provide an empirically pertinent entry point to the analysis of the mechanisms of the transformations of global HE. Rankings and more broadly the practice of producing numerical data on the performance of HE institutions are symbolic technologies that describe and prescribe transnational convergence/divergence processes. They are knowledge driven and knowledge producing. I will focus on the links between these tools and governance practices and the formation of discursive hierarchies and more broadly dominant values in HE.

The development of new symbolic technologies of governance such as ranking lists of HE institutions has a broader significance. Economic development is dependent on the diffusion and sharing of knowledge (Piketty 2013: 50). Consequently, economic development is to a highly significant degree dependent on policies in the area of education, as these have to do with access to formation, the definitions of job qualifications, of valued skills and so on. In other words, epistemic governance is crucial not just for HE and research but more broadly in order to understand current political and economic development. The knowledge tools used shape reality in certain form and direction. They favour certain types of developments at the expense of others, contracting reality in certain ways (eliminating certain options that might have before seemed reasonable, such as developing a democratic university) and focusing on certain chosen aspects of HE reality (such as publication outputs in English language journals). The issue of focus (Kahneman 2013) is crucial. If in the literature focus has been approached from the point of view of psychology, it is also a significant social psychological mechanism that enables collective action. It gives indications on what aspects of political reality actors concentrate, or which aspects of reality are valued and legitimised and which are delegitimised, which parts stand out and which fade into the background. Those parts that stand out will be the focus of further attention, etc. In other words the link between education and economy, which has since the 2000s taken the shape of knowledge-based economy, goes deeper as economic development has always been crucially dependent on the availability of knowledge and technologies, and on their transnational diffusion.

The practice of ranking is part of a broader development of global governance that relies heavily on numerical measures such as indicators of corruption, gender equality, the school performance of students, the economic performance of countries, etc. as evaluations and justifications of public action. These enable creating a reality that is considered objective and legitimate, because the tools used to describe this reality are presented as being divorced from human judgement and thus error (Porter 1996). Since Pythagoras, numbers have been seen as providing a direct access to that part of reality that is considered as being fundamental. Often, numbers have been attributed magical properties. They have been key tools in the mastery of nature and society. With information technologies a real data revolution has taken place. Big data is the latest innovation in this respect. As it supposedly collects all data on a specific phenomenon, big data seems to dispense us with the use of statistical techniques in analysing numerical information. Of course, somebody always produces numbers with a certain interest in mind and with certain tools at her disposal, and numbers need to be interpreted and used by someone to have meaning. But the dramatic development of big data and of numerical data in connection with informational technologies means that they have taken the place of knowledge and information as valued categories, relegating expert opinion and related concepts that rely on human judgement to history books. While the value of knowledge will always depend on who produces and uses it, in general if knowledge or information cannot be converted into numerical form it will be less useful, convincing and thus legitimate. In other words individuals and social groups who have access to numerical information or are able to produce it hold considerable power compared to those who are not able to have access to or produce numerical information. This is especially clear in the development of HE.

The practice of ranking HE institutions is an example of the transnational convergence/divergence tendencies that are knowledge-driven and knowledge-producing processes. While there are clear convergence tendencies that support the theory of global culture theory (Meyer 2010), clear divergence tendencies can also be observed. These will depend on the strategies and interests of dominant groups in national settings as well as political culture and need to be studied more in detail.

Monopolies have traditionally provided a valued model in terms of reproducing and contesting discursive hierarchies and dominant values. In global HE the current dominant model includes an organisational form (the American private research university, epitomised by Harvard) as well as discursive strategies (the scientific language of efficiency and evidence-based knowledge and data). Today, these values emphasise global competition as a means to achieve excellence. This paradigm contrasts with the more classic educational ideal of *Bildung*, which centres on personal development and competition with oneself, on the idea of improving the individual as a moral person, or with the idea of educating citizens and forming the nation.

Until now, academics have played a minor role in reforms of the European public university. Or rather, a very small minority has played a key role as policy advisers and experts to public officials at national and EU levels. But overall, given that they are the first ones affected by these policies, they have not taken part in the reforms, except as their passive objects. A framework has to be devised that would enable bringing academics back into the picture of HE. I will provide such a theoretical framework that includes them, their role and activities in current transformations.

Additional difficulties in studying HE stem from the entanglement of scholarly and non-scholarly discourses. As in other European policy areas, scholars often merely reproduce the terms and categories used by public officials at European and national levels. This is understandable as the source of information is often the object of study. The national and the European levels are also increasingly fused, as national HE and research programmes copy policy blueprints and organisational models from the European level, which itself has been formed in the interaction of dominant interests at European and global levels. In HE the latter is represented by international organisations like the OECD and the World Bank. Access to information is thus a crucial issue in knowledge-driven global developments as the EU, the OECD and the World Bank are its primary providers. These institutions have the resources necessary to produce up-to-date numerical data that can then be transmitted to and used by other organisations like universities or national ministries of education and research. This undoubtedly partly explains some of the current convergence developments. I will concentrate on two aspects of this development: the transnational field of HE, and the mechanism of ranking as a symbolic tool used to structure this field.

## The transnational field of HE

The transnational refers to over the border activities that are not part of official politics or ritualised international cooperation. Compared to the international it mobilises a distinct ontology that focuses on the actors involved in various policy areas. Actors operate at various scalar levels and institutions. A more precise way of approaching the transnational is to conceptualise it in terms of fields of activity (Kauppi and Madsen 2014). Hence we could talk about a transnational field of HE and research, which involves a variety of actors at various scalar levels, united in an interest in HE and research. Actors operate in the context of institutions that are variably powerful. Dominant institutions seek to keep up the status quo and protect their positions whereas dominated institutions seek to propose alternative values. In HE, dominant institutions can systematically be found in the USA and some other countries like the UK. They are then English language institutions, often private with important financial resources at their disposal. They accumulate most of the signs of scientific excellence such as Nobel prizes. According to the standard theory as developed by Pierre Bourdieu (see for instance Bourdieu 1975), fields exist when field effects can be detected. However, as the standard theory does not focus on change and transformations, the disadvantage of this formulation is that it sets the game into one mould, a hermetic, interactive space where the value of the actors and their resources are internally set. From this perspective the idea of weak field developed by some is an oxymoron, as a field does not exist if there are no field effects and if external causes or exogenous resources explain the activities of the actors. These methodological biases can be avoided by approaching the issue of HE and research from a historical or developmental point of view as an evolving uneven space, necessarily more structured and socially regulated in some parts than in others (for a similar approach on EU integration see Kauppi 2005). As a form of self-governance of the HE and research community, it strives to set its rules of functioning, but is internally divided between a pole that represents epistemic governance and an opposite pole that revolves around various types of non-epistemic governance. Reality is somewhere between the two, but both types of legitimation are used by different actors to transform or criticise the changes that are under way.

Until recently there seemed to be a consensus concerning the principles that should govern HE and research. But since the introduction in the 2000s of a new paradigm of HE governance that revolves around principles of new public management this consensus has been shattered. Since then, with the economic crisis hitting much of the western world, non-academics, mostly politicians and administrators have dominated science governance and set the tone of reforms. These have been governed by a formal approach that seeks to measure the value of science by using so-called objective measures.

Following Kant, the main structuring principle of the transnational field of HE is between epistemic governance and non-epistemic governance of HE, that is governance that follows the interest of science (epistemic value) or governance that follows the interest of society (non-epistemic value). Habermas used the Kantian terms of theoretical and practical interest to describe these positions (Habermas 1972). I will combine these various theoretical tools in my analysis. In the European context, the autonomous pole is represented by institutions governed by academics and representing in the name of something that comes close to the interest of science. Institutions like the European Science Foundation (ESF) and the European University Association represent at the European level this position, whereas key financers, Germany and the UK, more closely monitor the activities of Science Europe, a relatively new organisation that is poised to replace the ESF, and which aims at promoting more practical interests such as the links with business and economic development. In general, development in European science funding has involved a tighter government control of resources. But this has not meant that epistemic values have been totally pushed to the background. European Research Council (ERC) funding promotes excellence, while at the national level the model for scientist-led organisations comes from the USA and the Institute for Advanced Study in Princeton. These types of organisations have proliferated in Europe since the 2000s. In France, the Network of French Institutes for Advanced Study was established in March 2007 and regroups four institutes in Nantes, Lyon, Marseille and Paris. It provides a significant outlet for top-level research in all disciplines.

Since the 1950s the goal of European integration in all policy areas has been to get rid of the culprit of two devastating world wars, the nation state. Economically, and following the USA as a model, the goal was to create a unified European market. This has more or less worked with the euro. Politically, by favouring intra-European mobility, citizens were believed gradually to distance themselves from their nation state and embrace Europe and a European identity. This has not worked as well, as the low turnout level to European parliament elections and the low level of intra-European mobility testify. In science, a stateless science seemed to be the goal, the model being the American National Science Foundation. Ideally, the same scientific skills could be obtained if one studied in Warsaw or Paris. Globally, this has not worked so well either. However, in some areas like nuclear research and molecular biology, integration has gone further than in other disciplines. EURATOM and CERN have succeeded in pooling European research in physics. EMBO has done the same in molecular biology. Both are very internationalised and Europeanised research areas and require state of the art equipment that is very expensive. In contrast, the social sciences and the humanities are still very tied to national structures. The ESF and more recently the ERC have been key institutions in the Europeanisation and internationalisation of European science. While the

ESF has since 1974 provided European and global-level peer review services and has coordinated the activities of national funding agencies such as the French *Agence nationale de la recherche* (ANR) and the Finnish Academy of Finland, the ERC provides individual funding for scholars. Created in 2007 by the European Commission, it is the first organisation that provides funding for individual scholars on the basis of the epistemic value of scientific excellence. The grants, typically ranging from 2 to 3 million euros, are portable, and are given for 3–5 years. This funding can be contrasted with nation-level funding, which is typically for 3 years and is in the range of 200–300,000 euros. The ERC grants are clearly in today's European science the grand prize in research. At the same time as ERC grants have become the most prestigious science funding instruments, research funding has shifted from block funding to project funding that takes place mostly in universities and not research centres like the Max Planck system in Germany or the CNRS in France, and it is increasingly internationally evaluated using foreign scholars and numerical data.

In Europe, the pressures to create similar funding structures are strong, as can be seen in the cases of the ANR in France, the French Evaluation Agency for Research and Higher Education, the *Fonds national de la recherche du Luxembourg*, and the Academy of Finland, for instance. The forms and criteria of funding application are the same and follow the blueprint provided by the ERC. Structural isomorphism is supposed to create more efficiency between these institutions. Similar processes have taken place in universities. There are strong pressures to create larger units. The three universities in Strasbourg fused into one University of Strasbourg in 2009. Aalto University in Finland regroups three separate institutions. Examples could be multiplied. One reason for this tendency is that university rankings like the Shanghai ranking are based on the number of Nobel prizes or articles in journals like *Nature* and *Science*. The larger the unit the more likely there will be more of these. International visibility has become a key component in the competition between universities. Even in France, where most academics are openly critical of the reforms of HE and research, successive governments have been following similar policies in HE that mirror transnational developments. In 2006, a new law, loi relative aux libertéset responsabilités des universities, was passed that aims at making HE institutions responsible. The *Pôle de Recherche et d'Enseignement Supérieur* was launched in 2006, aiming at regrouping institutions to gain more international visibility, to reach a critical mass, and more broadly to develop a coherent research and educational policy through economies of scale. New funding initiatives include Operation Campus, Investissements d'avenir, various Idex projects, all seeking to create a globally competitive Ivy League of French universities, five to seven world-class universities. This process of stratification of HE institutions can also be observed in other EU member states, Germany, Poland, Finland, etc.

While the European Commission has, in theory, a limited role in HE and member states have primary responsibility in organising their education systems, reality is more complicated. With increased cooperation between member states through an open method of coordination with intergovernmental 'soft law' and public policy instruments such as guidelines, benchmarks and sharing best practice, the European Commission in fact plays a key role in the development of European HE. Without it current institutions such as the European research area and funding instruments such as ERC would not exist. The Bologna Process that started in 1999 aims at creating a unified European HE area with similar curricula and diplomas in all EU member states. The European Commission has served as the engine of the process, coordinating the unification process.

Rankings and numerical governance technologies more generally can be viewed as key tools in this struggle between various positions to determine the direction of scientific development in Europe and globally. Dominant institutions such as the OECD, the European Commission and national science administrators have successfully used these to reinforce their position in science governance, setting the game and its rules. Since the 2000s collecting data on HE has become the main means through which HE institutions are governed. Defining alternative strategies that would challenge the monopoly of dominant values would require significant organisational and financial resources that are missing today.

## Rankings

> Some number better than no number.
> (Popular saying)

The influx of numerical data into HE governance has meant decision-makers increasingly rely on these data to make decisions. Or rather, through the production and use of data decision-making itself has changed. It does no longer involves to the same extent evaluation in terms of the comparison of different expert opinions for instance. Rather, it involves relying on data and through comparison of data a more and more usual numerical comparison of scholars if filling a position or universities if deciding on which place to choose for one's studies. The logical end result of this development is the increasing use of automation and algorithms. These are step-by-step automatic operations that determine the value of a candidate, a journal, a department or a university. For instance with Research Gate, academia.edu, Google scholar and other web tools the 'value' of individual scholars is constantly monitored in real time through the number of citations in English language publications. Likewise, universities compare themselves to their competitors using ranking lists like the Shanghai list, or data provided by private companies like Quacquarelli Symonds through their service packages, or by relying on publications like Times Higher Education. These have become the GPS of global HE that enable the positioning of a HE institution, a faculty member, a student or a parent in real time vis-à-vis developments in HE.

Measurement or quantification or commensuration has become the normal state of affairs, and through a process of institutionalisation of rankings this practice is integrated into the normal functioning of HE institutions, into their DNA. In this knowledge and evidence-based activity, knowledge is valuable only to the extent that it can be converted into numerical form. Cases can then be compared on a similar metric. The quality of a scientific journal and of its producers is equated with the impact factor, how many citations per article published in a journal during the two years following its publication. The silent revolution we have been witnessing since the 2000s consists in quality becoming an emergent property of quantity (Kauppi 2015). The structural biases favour generalist journals, journals with other publications than articles and research notes (editorial, letters to the editor, science news, like in *Nature*), large language groups such as English and certain disciplines like the natural sciences where citation cultures cite a lot, preferably several authors instead of just one like in the humanities and the social sciences.

According to a survey among administrators of HE institutions in 41 countries reported by Thomson Reuters, 68 per cent used rankings as a management tool to bring about strategic, organisational, managerial and/or academic change (Adams and Baker 2010). Since 2003 and the introduction of the so-called Shanghai ranking, numerical evaluation has become a specified field of activity with its professionals and institutions, which are public and private. Twelve years later there is an increasing number of rankings that measure the performance of universities and HE institutions. These include the two major ones, the Shanghai ranking and the Times Higher Education ranking, as well as a slew of competitors that include a Russian ranking REITOR and a European one (for details see Erkkilä and Kauppi 2010). The generic, or first generation rankings that measure the performance of whole universities have been replaced by measures of disciplines, or for instance regions such as Latin America. The European Commission launched the U-Multirank in 2013. Intended as a transparent tool of information on HE and also of science and research management, it aims at providing users with a number of performance indicators instead of just the usual research output. The U-Multirank also stresses the similarity of universities, comparing 'like with like'. The user interface allows the grouping of universities based on certain criteria, such as the investments in research. This undoubtedly better takes into account the massive differences that prevail in the funding of HE institutions globally. Altogether, the U-Multirank has been promoted with the argument that it makes a fairer assessment of universities than other global rankings. Without a doubt, the U-Multirank mapping sponsored by the European Commission seeks to promote continental European universities.

It was born out of the frustration of French and German politicians toward the Shanghai ranking, which each year reminded them that continental European universities are not the best in the world.

Today, the methodologies developed are more varied than before, and some measures are very specialised. For instance the European mapping lets the user choose the variable used in the search. The second development is the diversification of different kinds of rankings. They have become more complicated knowledge products (single league table, ranking according to discipline, interactive interfaces that enable multiple ranking...). A third feature has been the involvement of more economically and politically powerful actors in the ranking industry (private actors include Thomson Reuters, Bertelsmann Foundation, Elsevier, Quacquarelli Symonds, and public institutions the OECD, the World Bank and the European Commission). These have considerable economic and organisational resources at their disposal. They contrast with the artisanal activity of the first Shanghai ranking, basically a product of the mind of a Chinese chemistry professor. Ranking, and producing data on the performance of HE institutions, has become a lucrative business for many, which also raises issues concerning the reliability of the data collected and used by companies such as Thomson Reuters. Private companies are of course mainly interested in selling data and various kinds of service packages, for instance on close competitors. All of this has taken on the background of a major shift in HE. Instead of knowledge and education as public goods, dominant before the 2000s, key organising principles are now autonomy, accountability, competition, all linked to the knowledge economy.

Who produces the knowledge that enables this knowledge-driven process? What is the quality of this knowledge? How reliable is it? One pathological effect of this data collection and the production of quantitative information is increasing fraud. Knowledge production through measurement leads to attempts to manipulate these. According to a survey by Thomson Reuters (Adams and Baker 2010), 74 per cent of respondents who were HE professionals strongly agreed or somewhat agreed with the statement that institutions manipulated their data to move up in the rankings. Strategies have consisted of inviting a Nobel laureate to give a talk, and then including the name of the person on the list of faculty members. Or inviting visiting scholars for 1–2 weeks a year with a high salary, something King Abdullah University in Saudi Arabia is remembered for. Another one has been the manipulation of the ratio of teacher/student by not calculating graduate students, who in reality teach more and more in all HE institutions, as teachers. A third very common one has been to exaggerate the amount of external funding, something that is difficult to check. The problem is that data production is complicated. It can be either endogenous as when the European Commission collects the data or exogenous as when the universities involved provide the data. The first one is very costly, and requires significant resources that large organisations like the European Commission and its Joint Research Center have at their disposal. With a staff of more than 3000 persons the Joint Research Centre is the European Commission's in-house science service. It is independent of any national, private or industry interest and provides sound and relevant scientific input to European policy-making (Joint Research Center 2015). But even they are dependent on universities to provide some of the information. However, depending solely on universities is risky. Checking the quality of the data is expensive, often even impossible as it is dependent on the goodwill of university administrators. The lack of transparency and reliability of the data collected is the problem, as the universities and the firms involved in producing the data might not have an interest in providing all their data, or revealing the data that are at the basis of the indicators produced. This seriously prevents the development of better indicators.

It is in this context of escalating competition that the European Commission has financed the development of something it has called a game changer that aims at mapping HE institutions instead of ranking them. However, this U-Multirank (2007) takes part in the game of fighting numbers with alternative numbers, testifying to the existence of an ontological trap: it is not possible to talk legitimately about HE today without the use of data. For this reason some research centres like the Center for Higher Education in Germany, funded by the Bertelsmann Foundation, play a key role in the development of HE policies; as does the University of Twente in the Netherlands whose scholars are integrated in powerful transnational policy networks that include the OECD, the European Commission and the World Bank. They cater to European and global political and administrative decision-makers.

## Conclusion

We need more studies on the historical development of HE in transnational contexts as the vertical circulation of models and ideas between global and national levels shape national HE policies and give us indications on the power mechanisms involved in the setting of HE agendas. This is key to understanding many aspects today, such as the success of new public management, the dominant role of international organisations like the OECD, the increased use of numerical technologies of power, the fusions of universities, the stratification of national university systems into first – and second-class institutions, and many other developments that have directly affected academic work.

The abstract goal of ranking, defining excellence or quality, or that which is considered valuable, is turning in the name of pursuing excellence into something else. It is as if concentration on quality through emphasis on technique and measurable value were counter-productive to the pursuit of quality itself. The quantification of quality (impact factors for reviews, points in HE institution ranking) does not seem to produce more quality but rather, by moving the goal posts, a new set of measures of quality that seeks to dispense of human agency and evaluation. While it creates a sense of control through collective self-governance, it is dependent on everyone accepting the rules and principles of social domination that is involved in the new public management of HE and research.

## References

Adams, J. and Baker, K. (2010). *Global Opinion Survey: new outlooks on institutional profiles.* February. Available at: www.thomsonreuters.com [Accessed 1 March 2016].

Bourdieu, P. (1975). The specificity of the scientific field and the social conditions of the progress of reason. *Social Science Information,* December, 14, 19–57.

Erkkilä, T. and Kauppi N. (2010). Alternatives to existing international rankings. *World Social Science Report 2009–2010.* Paris: UNESCO, pp. 239–241.

Flexner, A. (1939). The usefulness of useless thinking. *Harper's Magazine,* October, 544–552.

Habermas, J. (1972). *Knowledge and Human Interests.* Boston: Beacon Press.

Joint Research Center (2015). *Presentation.* Available at: https://ec.europa.eu/jrc [Accessed 16 September 2015].

Kahneman, D. (2013). *Thinking, Fast and Slow.* London: Penguin.

Kant, I. (1789). *Le conflit des facultés en trois sections.* Paris: Vrin.

Kauppi, N. (2005). *Democracy, Social Resources and Political Power in the European Union,* Manchester: Manchester University Press.

Kauppi, N. (2015). The academic condition: unstable structures, ambivalent narratives, dislocated identities, in Evans L. and Nixon J. (eds). *Academic Identities and the European Academic Landscape,* London: Bloomsbury.

Kauppi, N. and Madsen, M.R. (2014). Fields of global governance. *International Political Sociology,* 8(3), 324–30.

Meyer, J. (2010). World society, institutional theories, and the actor. *Annual Review of Sociology,* 36, 1–20.

Piketty, T. (2013). *Le capital au XXI siècle.* Paris: Le Seuil.

Porter, T.M. (1996). *Trust in Numbers.* Princeton: Princeton University Press.

Chapter 7

# Higher education

From 'unclear technologies' to human resources management techniques

*Jean-Émile Charlier and Sarah Croché*[1]

Even though a consensus has not emerged on the proper concept of a university, many sociologists have for a long time based their research on the work published in the 1970s, in which universities were regarded as organisations that operate in a particular way. They were approximated to 'organised anarchies' (Cohen *et al.* 1972) or to 'loosely coupled systems' (Weick 1976; Orton and Weick 1990), which were considered host to 'unclear technologies' (Cohen and March 1974). This article called into question these concepts and confronted them with the evolution of the piloting way of contemporary establishments of higher education.

This chapter is divided into five parts. The first briefly recalls in broad terms the impulses shaping the interventions of international organisations in the higher education systems in Europe. The second and the third parts concern the different instruments (such as the European credit transfer system (ECTS) and diploma supplement) developed by international organisations and their integration in an apparatus (in Foucault's sense) of standardisation of higher education. The fourth analyses the effects of these instruments and of the apparatus on the academic profession and inscribes the article in the whole of the works (see for example Derouet and Normand 2012; Evans and Nixon 2015; Lucas 2014; Normand 2015) examining the nature and extent of the changes experienced by the academics in their teaching profession in recent years. The fifth studies how these instruments (and notably the learning outcomes approach) transforms each segment of the university and generates a deep interdependence between all of them.

## From the promotion of mobility to the normative intervention of international organisations in establishments of higher education

Since the 1950s, different initiatives have been taken by various international organisations, in particular the Council of Europe and UNESCO, each one at its own degree, to facilitate the movement of higher education students and staff.[2] These initiatives did not give rise to the request for mobility. Instead, they were intended to provide a first framework to allow for the mobility of university staff and students and to foster further the development of an academic exchange network. These initiatives, thus, supported and accompanied a structural movement towards greater mobility, exchange and collaboration between higher education establishments, researchers and students. In 1987, the European Commission started the Erasmus project, which benefited only a very small proportion of students. Some commentators take the view that the Erasmus programme has not really democratised student mobility (Ballatore 2010). However, Papatsiba (2006) provides us with another interpretation. Based on the analysis of official texts, emanating, in particular, from the European Commission, she shows that support for student mobility was a means used by the European Commission to stimulate the convergence of European systems of higher education:

> Without disregarding the tension between popularity and limited impact of EU mobility programmes, I argue that promoting student mobility was not an act of a limited ambition, but on the contrary, an initiative aiming at the foundation of a system of higher education institutions at a European level.
>
> (Papatsiba 2006: 93)

The Erasmus programme, thus, reinforced a structural movement that already existed. It strongly contributed to promoting the idea of mobility and to its integration into the strategies of distinction[3] of higher education students in European countries. In doing that, it changed the perception of Europeans towards higher education. Furthermore, it prepared the cultural ground for the reforms adopted by all the systems of higher education following the launch of the Bologna Process in 1999. The Bologna Process started at the Sorbonne in 1998. Not surprisingly, the arguments made in the Joint Sorbonne Declaration remained focused on the promotion of mobility:

> Universities were born in Europe, some three-quarters of a millennium ago. [...] In those times, students and academics would freely circulate and rapidly disseminate knowledge throughout the continent. Nowadays, too many of our students still graduate without having had the benefit of a study period outside of national boundaries.

The main objective of the Sorbonne Declaration was, thus, the promotion of mobility. In order to realise this goal, it was necessary to take technical measures, such as the use of credits and semesters, or improvements in the transparency and comparability of programmes. These technical measures were not put forward for their intrinsic value; they were justified only by their possible contribution to achieving the goal of supporting the mobility that they served. We see that the reasoning of the authors of the Sorbonne Declaration is in line with the programmes of the European Commission to support mobility. The European Commission had no mandate to intervene in the functioning of higher education establishments; its only authorised act was to support mobility. The *Memorandum on Higher Education in the European Union* (European Commission 1991), which announced the intervention of the European Commission in higher education, reflects this understanding. The competence of the European Union as regards education was first recognised by the Treaty of Maastricht of 1992. In this text, the European Union's competence was, however, restricted by the principle of subsidiarity, which necessarily limited the capacity of the European authorities to intervene in higher education.

Nevertheless, after the false start at the Sorbonne in 1998, the project to create a European higher education area took shape in Bologna in 1999. With regard to its objectives, the promotion of mobility was relegated in importance and the primary focus shifted to the imposition of technical measures. The promotion of mobility was, of course, recalled in the Bologna Declaration, but it was subordinated to the adoption of technical measures, which were to 'adopt a system of easily readable and comparable degrees', to 'enhance transparency' and to reinforce the 'cooperation in quality assurance'. In other words, starting from 1999, the realisation of these technical measures became the ultimate goal. The Bologna Process was then integrated into the Lisbon Strategy – which envisaged construction of a European knowledge-based society[4] – and became an essential axis in this strategy (Croché and Charlier 2009).

The subsuming of the Bologna Process into the Lisbon Strategy reinvigorated the commitment to the attainment of the technical measures. Indeed, the project to ensure the comparability of academic degrees ceased to be used solely for improving mobility between establishments of higher education; it also became essential to stimulating the economy. From that point on, the sole challenge was the development of technical means to measure students' learning accurately. On the one hand, it was of paramount importance that increased mobility would enable students to expand their educational profile and contribute to a European professional elite. This required that they would move only between establishments having comparable academic levels. On the other hand, it was imperative to measure accurately the professional skills of candidates dispersed across the vast territories comprising the countries participating in the Bologna Process. This process was integral to providing high calibre candidates to companies, which, benefiting from the contributions of such candidates, would achieve profit maximisation. In 2010, the proclamation of the European higher education area was accompanied, inter alia, by a review of the Bologna Process' objectives. In contrast with the 1999 declaration, it was emphasised that the main aim of the

Bologna Process was to make the European higher education systems more comparable, more compatible and more coherent.

> As the main objective of the Bologna Process since its inception in 1999, the EHEA was meant to ensure more comparable, compatible and coherent systems of higher education in Europe. Between 1999–2010, all the efforts of the Bologna Process members were targeted to creating the European Higher Education Area, that became reality with the Budapest–Vienna Declaration of March, 2010.[5]

This trajectory of the discourse on the objectives of the Bologna Process mirrored the evolution of the policies implemented by the Bologna Process piloting group, particularly by the European Commission. Starting with the Berlin summit in 2005, normative instruments of the organisation of higher education were proposed and adopted. This initiative was taken with the full agreement of state representatives. A fresh instrument was adopted during each summit of the ministers of higher education from the European higher education area. Thus, having regard to the democratic process of their adoption, the instruments are cloaked with an undeniable legitimacy.

## Multiple and interconnected instruments in European higher education

By their very nature, some of these instruments appear not to be very constraining and, further, seem to bind only the establishments that adopt them. This is, for example, the case with respect to the labels 'diploma supplement' (DS)[6] and 'ECTS',[7] which have existed since 2003 and 2004, respectively, and are 'honorary distinctions'[8] granted by the European Commission 'to higher education institutions which show that they are implementing ECTS and/or the DS correctly' (European Commission, 2014: 3).

Although they appear not to be very constraining, these instruments – in particular the ECTS label – contribute both to the reinforcement of constraints that weigh on the establishments and to the control that can be exerted on their functioning. The quantitative data suggest that the impact of the ECTS label is very weak, almost negligible. Indeed, only 91 establishments were granted it between 2009 and 2013,[9] a mere 11.4 per cent of the 850 universities from the 47 countries that are affiliated to European University Association[10] or – and this comparison is more relevant – 1.5 per cent of the 6400[11] recognised establishments of higher education in the European higher education area (Table 7.1).

The analysis of the list of countries whose universities received the ECTS label since its creation has some surprises. The number of universities that received the ECTS label in Turkey (31 out of 139) and in the Czech Republic

Table 7.1 Number of universities having received the label ECTS from 2009 to 2013, by country

| | | | |
|---|---|---|---|
| Turkey | 31 | Slovak Republic | 3 |
| Czech Republic | 12 | Lithuania | 2 |
| Belgium | 6 | Norway | 2 |
| Portugal | 6 | The Netherlands | 2 |
| Austria | 5 | Sweden | 2 |
| Italy | 5 | Germany | 1 |
| Finland | 4 | Bulgaria | 1 |
| Poland | 4 | Denmark | 1 |
| Cyprus | 3 | Latvia | 1 |

Source: Authors' computation, based on the Erasmus+ 2015 tables, pp. 40–55.

(12 out of 73) contrasts with the ratio identified in the majority of the other countries. The four signatory countries to the Sorbonne Declaration (Germany, France, Italy, the United Kingdom) – which preceded the Bologna Process – showed little interest in being granted this label, whereas, in 1998, these four countries counted for more than 50 per cent of European higher education students. No university in the United Kingdom and France was granted this label, whereas only five Italian establishments (out of 219) and only one German establishment (out of 355) received it. This observation highlights the highly differentiated relationships that the countries of the European higher education area maintain with the regulations or recommendations emanating from the Bologna Process. In the large countries, with a strong university tradition, conformism is rare. This is not the case for the countries located at the periphery of the European higher education area, or for those of small size, which intend to weigh on the orientations of the European higher education system. In these countries, conformism constitutes a rational strategy.[12] The empirical observations supporting this contribution should be interpreted in light of the fact that the evolutions recorded in various 'small countries' were stimulated by factors from which no country of the European higher education area has escaped. That being said, the reaction of these small countries may be interpreted as being marked by a concern for overconformity, which had not been observed in any of the large countries.

It should be added that not all the establishments that obtained the label ECTS seemed overly eager to preserve it. Prestigious universities, some of which hosted summits of the ministers of higher education in connection with the creation of the European higher education area, did not file an application to renew their ECTS label. This occurred, for example, in the case of the universities of Aarhus (Denmark), Bologna (Italy), Leuven (Belgium), and the technical universities of Karadeniz (Turkey) and Lisbon (Portugal).

That being said, even if, objectively, there has been no massive movement of the universities towards the ECTS label and, even if, in the large countries with a strong university tradition, the interest in this label seems very weak, the creation of the ECTS label was not without value for the European authorities. In the application request that universities submit for the label, they offer information that the European Commission would have difficulty in obtaining by other means. This information relates of course to the purposes for which the establishments intend to use the ECTS label, but it has, in fact, a much broader application. The European authorities do not attempt to conceal this fact. In fact, they have publicly announced that the requests introduced by the universities are not examined only from the angle of ECTS label use:

> DS label applications have [...] also shown that the concept of 'learning outcomes' is applied in various ways, and that the question of student workload is tackled in different ways when designing programmes and curricula. These important issues will be part of the new ECTS User's Guide [...]. The ECTS User's Guide should help all institutions and academics to meet the challenge of applying ECTS, and particularly of ensuring a learning outcomes based approach at every stage of the design, delivery and assessment of an education programme.
>
> (European Commission 2014: 5)

Whether or not it was conceived with this intention, it appears that the ECTS label constitutes a very effective means both of obtaining information on the universities' internal policies and practices and of testing the effectiveness of the tools promoted by the European authorities to pilot higher education. It is undeniable that the implementation of this label necessarily implies the standardisation of study structures, which is made explicit by the European Commission as well in the quotation above and in the definition it gives. The ECTS label is accorded only to establishments that 'correctly' apply the ECTS system. The goal of standardisation was, in fact, the impulse for the creation of the label. Starting in 2003, the report on *Les avancées de l'espace européen de l'enseignement supérieur* suggested that 'The introduction of the label ECTS will lead to a clear qualitative improvement in the uses of ECTS' (Reichert and Tauch, 2003: 12).

## Increasingly precise instruments integrated into an apparatus of standardisation of higher education

In order to update and specify the contents of the ECTS Users' Guide, the group in charge, set up by the European Commission, held various consultations. The guide was then adopted by ministers for higher education of the European higher education area during the ministerial conference at

Erevan, on 14 and 15 May 2015. 'It is therefore the official Guide for the use of ECTS' (European Commission 2015: 7). This adoption does not automatically give it binding force but, nonetheless, it enjoys total legitimacy in all the countries of the European higher education area. A short section of this guide is entitled 'ECTS and quality assurance'. It opens with a sentence that takes for granted that the ECTS contributes to improving the quality of higher education and that the implementation of the ECTS must be the object of an evaluation. 'This section outlines how the ECTS contributes to quality enhancement in HEIs ([Higher Education Institutions] and gives examples for the evaluation of ECTS implementation.' (European Commission 2015: 50). No demonstration, however, comes to back up these two assertions. However, once again, the European authorities will point out that the ECTS must be used appropriately so that it improves the quality of higher education: 'Good practice in using ECTS will help institutions improve the quality of their programmes and their learning mobility offer' (European Commission 2015: 51). The guide specifies how to evaluate the use of the ECTS.

> ECTS use should be quality assured through appropriate evaluation processes (e.g. monitoring, internal and external quality reviews and students' feedback) and continuous quality enhancement. In evaluating the effectiveness of a programme (including the learning outcomes, workload and assessment methods) a number of measures will be used. These may include high dropout or failure rates or longer completion times. A programme can be considered effective when its goals are attained in due time, that is to say when students achieve the defined learning outcomes, accumulate the required credits and obtain the qualification as planned in the programme.
>
> (European Commission 2015: 51)

It is no longer a question of awarding honours to the establishments which use the ECTS in an adequate way. It is now a question of integrating the evaluation of the ECTS use into the establishments' quality control procedures. The consequences are very different. An establishment can do perfectly well without the ECTS label; the low number of those that have acquired it attests to its expendability. Nevertheless, an establishment runs undeniable risks of isolation if the quality assessment of the educational programmes that it offers is poor.

The implementation of quality control instruments in higher education establishments has been progressive (Croché 2009; Saarinen 2005).[13] All these instruments appear interconnected today; they mutually reinforce each other to form a European higher education apparatus (Charlier and Croche 2013). Two of the essential parts of this apparatus are the standards and guidelines for quality assurance in the European higher education area[14]

(ESG) and the European quality assurance register for higher education (EQAR). The ESG establishes the standard, whereas the EQAR sanctions the institutions that do not follow the standard. The ESG were published for the first time in 2005 by the European Association for Quality Insurance in Higher Education, created pursuant to a proposal of the European Commission in 1998. They define the various aspects of their functioning and delineate the criteria higher education establishments must comply with if they seek to adhere to a quality enhancement perspective. They also regulate the quality assurance agencies for higher education. These agencies are included in the EQAR only if they scrupulously conform to the regulations set forth in the ESG. 'In order to appear on the register, the applications should be evaluated on the basis of substantial compliance with the ESG, evidenced through an independent review process endorsed by national authorities.'[15]

Thus, the European higher education apparatus appears perfectly integrated. In each country of the European higher education area, all the establishments that seek to profit from the Erasmus programme are required to be evaluated by a quality assurance agency, recognised by the EQAR. In the knowledge that all the prestigious establishments tend to validate their image of excellence by the quality of the international exchanges that they establish, one can easily deduce that, for an average establishment, the cost of being excluded from the exchange system is extremely high.

The power of the apparatus is due to the fact that prescriptive messages are sent to all the facets of the organisation and of management of the higher education establishments. Even if they appear independent from one another, and even if they possibly emanate from different sources, they tend to converge on their reformulated definition of the role of higher education. In this new definition, the emancipation of the individual and the group holds a less important place than their contribution to economic prosperity and social cohesion. For example, Parker (2011) considers that contemporary accounting and accountability techniques in use in different countries aim to modify the identity and the role of the academic community. According to Scott (2003), accounting systems are among the most important conventions that connect institutionally defined belief systems to technical activities. None of the implemented instruments is, thus, neutral, even those that appear strictly technical. Each instrument contributes to produce an image of the role that higher education should play in contemporary society.

Based on a lexicometric analysis of the European Commission's official texts related to higher education, Cusso (2006) concluded, as early as 2006, that the Bologna Process and the European Commission were working to implement a standardised quality assurance system and to promote a managerial functioning in higher education. The evolutionary process that has taken place since that date largely confirms this analysis.

## The apparatus reaches the heart of the teaching profession and acquires a new legitimacy

Listing the entire range of instruments set up to standardise higher educa-tion in all facets of its functioning would probably be a somewhat taxing task and would serve little useful purpose. We are interested here only in those instruments related to the organisation and the practice of higher education, and do not, therefore, intend to treat those related to the management[16] of the actual educational establishments. One of the common characteristics of such instruments is that they were presented as trivial, a fact that contributed to hide their potential for change. The majority of them did indeed involve reforms that could be regarded as strictly cosmetic. Let us take two examples. The passage on the architecture of studies according to the '3-5-8' model frequently failed to produce any change as regards the exercise of the aca-demic work.[17] This new configuration of studies would, however, require that the first cycle ('3') provides graduates with marketable skills. Moreover, its framework defines the doctoral thesis as an applied exercise that can be accomplished in three years; this vision reformed the manner in which the doctoral thesis was perceived – as a product of one's long line of thought. These two requirements are frequently neglected; but this does not mean that the potential for change of the '3-5-8' architecture is definitively neutral-ised. Likewise, in many establishments, the conversion to the ECTS system did not have any effect on academic practices and it was mainly mechanical. A certain number of lecture courses was transformed into an ECTS equiva-lent. However, conceiving and organising teaching in the manner envisaged by ECTS would necessitate a major transformation of practices. For example, it would imply a strong reduction in the activities dedicated to the transfer of knowledge. In this case, as in the case of the '3-5-8' framework, observing that the requirements related to the ECTS are often by passed leads us to the conclusion that the instruments' potential for change is negated.

The potential for change of these various instruments can appear only if favourable circumstances allow it, and if actors, therefore, choose to activate them. Illustrations are provided by A. Gorga and M. Souto Lopez. Gorga (2011) highlights in her research the structural factors that encouraged the Swiss and the Romanian authorities to create quality assurance and quality control procedures in higher education. Souto Lopez (2015) shows how the challenges addressed to universities regarding the rate of failure of their stu-dents contributed to legitimating multiple teaching experiments. The con-text studied was French-speaking Belgium where the level of public funding for each establishment is directly determined by its market share, and where the scientific field is structured by its own logic. The commitment of the French-speaking universities in Belgium to over-conform to applications of the learning outcomes model can be read only as a consequence of the conjunc-tion of two distinct elements. On the one hand, an incentive was provided to establishments by the European authorities to organise their teaching according to defined learning outcomes. On the other hand, a particular restructuring of power in the university led decision-makers to give the necessary authority and means to technicians to impose this logic on the establishments.

Among all the standardisation instruments of higher education, learning outcomes undoubtedly have the highest potential for transformation of the university teaching profession. The definition of learning outcomes is given for the first time in the European prescriptive texts, in particular, in the ECTS Users' Guide 2004. The learning outcomes are, thus, defined as: 'statements of what a learner is expected to know, understand and/or be able to demonstrate after a completion of a process of learning' (European Commission 2004: 44).[18] This explicit presentation of the results that the learner can expect at the end of his or her personal learning pathway is common in countries where the financing of studies is either totally or partially provided by the students. However, defining learning outcomes goes against all traditions in countries where this financing is provided by the community. Today, in countries where the volume of public funding of education depends directly on the market share of each establishment, the learning outcomes model is applied on a voluntary basis.

Souto Lopez (2015) presents a history on the introduction of learning outcomes to the piloting system of the European higher education area's establishments. He shows that the learning outcomes' potential of control as regards the effectiveness of the professors' work was suggested starting with the European texts of 2005 and the report 'A Framework for Qualifications of the European Higher Education Area' published by the Bologna Working Group on Qualifications Framework (BWGQF). In order to produce this report, the BWGQF based itself, inter alia, on the report of the conference 'Using Learning Outcomes', that took place in Edinburgh between 1 and 2 July 2004 (Adam 2004). Three expected effects of the learning outcomes were highlighted at the conference: at the international level, they could support the recognition of qualifications; at the national level, they were useful within the framework of the quality assurance mechanisms; at the local level, they made it possible to identify the best adapted teaching practices and methods. It goes without saying that this identification of the 'good practices' goes hand in hand with measures intended to both support such practices and to discourage less effective practices.

The potential for the influence of learning outcomes on professors' practices will be achieved only if standardised measurements are carried out on a scale sufficient to facilitate reliable comparisons. The project assessing higher education learning outcomes (AHELO) of the OECD was launched to this end in 2010. This project was an answer to a request addressed by the ministers of education from the OECD countries at a meeting in Athens in 2006. In January 2008, assembled at an informal meeting in Tokyo, the ministers specified their request and encouraged the OECD to set up one 'PISA for the superior' (OECD 2008). A feasibility study, focused on the studies of economics and civil engineering, was completed in 2012 in 17 countries. The next objective is to carry out tests in other sectors in all the OECD countries in 2016 (OECD 2014).

The modus operandi here is very similar here to that used in the PISA investigation or to the open method of coordination. Data are made public and accessible by national decision-makers. They allow for a swift comparison of the performance of various systems, which encourages the persons in charge of the least efficient systems to adopt measures to improve their output. If it is still too early to affirm that the AHELO project will achieve a dynamic of this kind, based on the observation of the effects produced by PISA, one may assume this will occur.

While providing means for controlling and conducting the educational activity of professors, the Bologna Process was subject to reinterpretation. In September 2014, the Bologna Process' follow-up group (BFUG) gathered in Rome and adopted 'The Bologna Process Revisited: The Future of the European Higher Education Area'. This document preceded the ministerial conference, which took place in May 2015 in Yerevan (Armenia). In this new document, one can read:

> the construction of the EHEA [European Higher Education Area] is a supranational endeavor resulting from a jointly developed common vision [...] the governing bodies of the process must ensure that it maintains its supranational nature and at the same times generates sufficient added value for each country to be willing to continue to be committed to it.
>
> (BFUG 2015: 4)

Since its inception, it was the first time that the Bologna Process was described as a supranational enterprise. One may recall that one of the objectives of the Sorbonne summit in 1998 was to prevent any supranational influence on higher education. The Bologna summit had not, however, disavowed international inputs. The calibre of the members of the BFUG, among which was the European Commission, dispels the assumption of an act of thoughtlessness. Mayrgündter (2015) highlights the current trend to develop an 'intergovernmental supranationalism' in Europe. However, the document adopted by the BFUG does not evoke the intergovernmental character of the process. It underlines instead its 'supranational nature', a pronouncement that does not appear to have caused any adverse reaction in countries that are members of the European higher education area.[19]

## The willingness to put an end to the organised anarchy by means of the instruments

After this brief examination of some standardisation instruments of higher education, let us return to the theories presented in the introduction.

According to these theories, universities are seen as 'organised anarchies' or 'loosely coupled systems', in which one can find 'unclear technologies'. The efforts both of the European Commission and the OECD seem to aim at correcting the characteristics of the university that these concepts underline. For Friedberg and Musselin (1989), an organised anarchy is the product of rational strategies used by professors to avoid any quantitative evaluation of the research and teaching activities at the university. Thus, anarchy is only presumed and it does not concern all aspects of university work. The question of the coexistence of both supposed organisational anarchy and the rationality of scientific work can be answered by Thompson (1967). He shows that organisations search at the same time for rationality and indetermination: the technical core constitutes a closed system, where uncertainty is excluded, whereas the institutional level maintains openness, thus giving the appearance of anarchy. The concept of 'loosely coupled system' makes it possible to explain this double nature. Both rationality and indetermination are necessary for the effective performance of the organisation – here the university. The only possible manner in which to preserve rationality and indetermination at the same time is by locating them at different places and by preventing cross-contamination.

The research carried out, which is summed up in the underlined statements above, mentioned that the organisation is not homogeneous and the actors involved seek to preserve the heterogeneity of the segments that constitute it. The decoupling dimension is also addressed by Meyer and Rowan (1977: 58). They consider that educational establishments must try to reconcile incompatibilities between institutional and technical pressures. They do this by decoupling the formal structures from activities in order to maintain the 'ceremonial conformity'. Decoupling is 'a logout deliberated between the organisational structures which reinforce legitimacy and the organisational practices which are regarded by the organisation as being most efficient'.

In the universities, the rationality core is easy to identify and is designed around research and administration methods of scientific proof. Meanwhile, the sources of uncertainty are diverse and each one of them is likely to cause or maintain the strategies of segmentation or decoupling. They relate to the political and societal expectations as regards the university, the labour market's reaction to graduates' skills, the effectiveness of the teaching methods used, the relevance of the research protocols, etc.

The outcomes-based model in higher education highlights both the learning outcomes and the incentives provided to researchers to focus their work on concrete applications; it seeks to generate each one of these uncertainties by an explicit procedure. The project assumes the distinction between teaching and research activities and also the clarification by control indicators of the effectiveness of both types of activities. With regard to teaching activities, piloting by learning outcomes seeks to provide to decision-makers and operators the means for measuring teaching efficiency.

Measures of learning outcomes also hold important promises for higher education faculties and leaders in providing evidence-based diagnosis tools on the strengths and weaknesses of their courses and programmes to be used as part of their quality improvement efforts.

(Tremblay *et al.* 2012: 56)

It is not sure that the project's promises carried through the learning outcomes could be held. The learning outcomes aim to create a consistency between the objectives of teaching, the evaluations and the teaching methods. In short, it is an instrument that seeks to make the teaching result more predictable and even more programmable (see Legendre 2012; Brancaleone and O'Brien 2011). It does this by proposing a specific managing system of uncertainty that defines the manner in which the learner will react to the stimuli that are presented to him. On the one hand, the instrument – here the learning outcomes – is underlined by the recognition of what is obvious. The obvious, in this case, is the fact that it is up to each student to develop his competences. On the other hand, it provides means for measuring the effectiveness of the various methods used to lead the student to the intended learning outcomes (Biggs and Tang 2007). The unpredictable character of the learner's reactions ceases, thus to be a factor of uncertainty. It becomes simply one of the variables that the learning outcomes have the authority to manage.

The learning outcomes can also contribute to disarm the argument of the irreducibility of the teacher's work, put forward, in particular, by authors denouncing 'academic capitalism'. 'Learning, and research require reflection, engagement, collaboration, trial-and-error, processing, practice; all of which take time' (Walker 2009: 68). Higher education ceases to be one of those 'professions with prudential practice', defined by Champy (2009) as professions where it is impossible to envisage precisely the result of the actions initiated. In this case, the choice of whom does not imply the application of an unquestionable scientific framework. The choice results then from the professional's conviction, and from his approval of the risk, which is a risk in respect of which he may be held to account.

All the instruments presented above were created in order to divest the universities of the characteristics that led some analysts to approximate such establishments to organised anarchies, with weak interdependence, using unclear technologies. Such instruments lead to extreme specialisation of tasks, which, thereby, triggers changes in collegial management. Management is entrusted to managers who may be strangers to the university world. The organisation of education is delegated to technicians of applied pedagogy, who may come from private offices of engineering[20] (see Kalpazidou-Schmidt and Langberg, 2007). Research is entrusted to specialised researchers, assisted by professionals in the drafting of file requests for funding. Teaching becomes the responsibility of professors specialised in pedagogic animation, surrounded by technicians who guide them.[21] In this way, each segment of the organisation utilises those technologies considered to be the most efficient by the professionals of that particular segment. Each one is, thus, controlled in the most rational way. The question of interdependence then arises in renewed terms: the specialisation of tasks and techniques reduces the interferences between the segments, but generates a deep interdependence between all the segments and activities conducted within the same segment.

To conclude, given the increasing competitiveness and greater geopolitical significance of higher education and research, under the pressure of international organisations (such as the European Commission and the OECD) and the instruments they adopted, the apparatus of standardisation of European higher education attains from now on both the universities management and the professions, including the work of academics who benefited from a great autonomy in teaching.

## Notes

1 The authors would like to thank Oana Panait and Miguel Souto Lopez for their comments and discussions that helped to improve this chapter.
2 See the description of these initiatives in Croché 2010.
3 We use here the concept in the sense of Bourdieu (1979). For Bourdieu, the different choices people make are all distinctions, that is, choices made in opposition.
4 Cf. http://ue.eu.int/ueDocs/cms_Data/docs/pressData/fr/ec/00100-rl.f0.htm.
5 See the European higher education area website http://www.ehea.info/#.
6 The diploma supplement (DS) is a document accompanying a higher education diploma, providing a standardised description of the nature, level, context, content (for example mobility of the student) and status of the studies completed by her/his holder. This document is produced by the higher education institutions according to standards agreed by the European Commission.
7 The ECTS (European credit transfer and accumulation system) is a system designed to make it easier for students to move between different countries members of the Bologna Process. As they are based on the learning achievements and workload of a course, a student can transfer their ECTS credits from one university to another so they are added up to contribute to an individual's degree programme or training. One academic year corresponds to 60 ECTS credits that are equivalent to 1500–1800 hours of study in all countries.
8 Cf. http://ec.europa.eu/education/ects/ects_en.htm.
9 The number given at page 3 in Erasmus+ (2015: 3) is 97. The number given at page 39 is 91 (Erasmus+ 2015: 39). The last number corresponds to the tables of pages 40–55.
10 Cf. http://www.eua.be/eua-membership-and-services/Home.aspx.
11 These are the authors' computations, based on the national data provided in Eurydice (2010). France's data were corrected and were established to 527 using the data of Campus France (http://www.canada.campusfrance.org/fr/faq/quels-sont-les-etablissements-d%E2%80%99enseignement-superieur-en-france). The number of establishments retained in the Eurydice source, namely 4.343 establishments, integrates various initiatives, which do not have the same equivalent in other countries.

12  Another illustration of this phenomenon could be observed after the summit of the Sorbonne of 25 May 1998. All the European countries were invited to sign the declaration, which was signed in the Sorbonne only by the ministers of higher education of Germany, France, Italy and the United Kingdom. Only Bulgaria, Romania, the German-speaking community of Belgium, the Dutch-speaking community of Belgium, Switzerland, Denmark and the Czech Republic agreed to sign during the following months, from July 1998 to May 1999.
13  For a history of the way in which the European Commission set up the instruments of higher education quality control, see Croché 2009 and Saarinen 2005.
14  Cf. http://www.enqa.eu/wp-content/uploads/2013/06/ESG_3edition-2.pdf.
15  London communiqué, 18 May 2007, *Towards the European Higher Education Area: responding to challenges in a globalised world*, p. 4.
16  The changes in this matter were also considerable. See, for example, Degn and Sorensen 2015.
17  Cf. beyond, part four of this paper. It will be necessary to expect the installation of instruments such as the mechanisms of quality assurance and the learning outcomes so that changes of the academic work appear gradually in some countries (see Souto Lopez 2015).
18  The definition hardly varied through time, the ECTS Users' Guide of 2015 defines them as 'statements of what the individual knows, understands and is able to do on completion of a learning process' (European Commission, 2015: 72).
19  Since the beginnings of the Bologna Process, the European Commission continued the work that it had started a few decades before while trying, by soft methods, to orient the policies of higher education of the countries of the European Union, then of large Europe (Croché 2010) and beyond (Charlier and Panait 2015). It firstly integrated the Bologna Process in 2001, obtained after the right to vote in the follow-up group of the Bologna Process, as well as the states. The reference to 'supranational nature' attests that a step moreover is taken and that the states do not seem reticent any more with the intervention of the European Commission in the orientation of their national policies.
20  In certain countries (as in the Scandinavian countries), the private is engaged in the organisation of higher education teaching. This commitment concerns today until the production of the knowledge to transmit and the manners of transmitting the knowledge (see Kalapazidou-Schmidt and Langberg 2007).
21  As far as we know, few countries are engaged in the specialisation of the four spheres presented above. However, examples of commitments to carry out radical reforms in one or the other spheres are easy to find. The country undergoing these reforms is then presented by the pilots of the Bologna Process as examples of good practices that must inspire all the others.

# References

Adam, S. (2004). Using Learning Outcomes. A consideration of the nature, role, application and implications for European education of employing 'learning outcomes' at the local, national and international levels. *United Kingdom Bologna seminar 1–2 July 2004*, Heriot-Watt University, Edinburgh, Scotland.
Ballatore, M. (2010). *Erasmus et la mobilité des jeunes européens*. Paris: PUF.
BFUG (2015). The Bologna process revisited: the future of the European higher education area. *EHEA Ministerial Conference*. Yerevan: BFUG.

Biggs, J. and Tang, C. (2007). *Teaching for Quality learning at University.* Maidenhead: McGraw-Hill and Open University Press.

Bourdieu, P. (1979). *La distinction: critique sociale du jugement.* Paris: Les éditions de Minuit.

Brancaleone, D. and O'Brien, S. (2011). Educational commodification and the (economic) sign value of learning outcomes. *British Journal of Sociology of Education,* 32(4), 501–519.

Champy, F. (2009). *La sociologie des professions.* Paris: PUF.

Charlier, J.É. and Croche, S. (2013). Comment le processus de Bologne a modifié la signification et les enjeux de l'évaluation des enseignements. *Éducation comparée,* 8, 43–62.

Charlier, J.-É. and Panait, O. (2015). The Bologna Policy Forum: the temptation to act on non-European higher education systems, in Olson, J.R., Biseth, H. and Ruiz, G. (eds) *Educational Internationalisation: academic voices and public policy.* Rotterdam: Sense Publishers.

Cohen, M.D. and March, J.G. (1974). *Leadership and Ambiguity: the American college president.* New York: McGraw Hill Book Company.

Cohen, M.D., March, J.G. and Olsen, J.P. (1972). A garbage can model of organizational choice. *Administrative Science Quarterly,* 17(1), 1–25.

Croché, S. (2009). L'université circonscrite par Bologne. Quand l'Europe impose sa définition de la bonne institution, du bon enseignement et de la bonne science en réseau, *Émulations,* 6. Available at: http://www.revue-emulations.net/articles/croche.pdf.

Croché, S. (2010). *Le pilotage du processus de Bologne.* Louvain-la-Neuve: Academia-Bruylant.

Croché, S. and Charlier, J.É. (dir.) (2009). Le processus de Bologne et ses effets. *Éducation et sociétés,* 33.

Cusso, R. (2006). La Commission européenne et l'enseignement supérieur: une réforme au-delà de Bologne. *Cahiers de la recherche sur l'éducation et les savoirs,* 5, 193–214.

Degn, L. and Sørensen, M.P. (2015). From collegial governance to conduct of conducts: Danish universities set free in the service of the state. *Higher Education,* 69, 931–946.

Derouet, J.-L. and Normand, R. (2012). Les nouvelles épreuves d'Homo Academicus. Revisiter la condition universitaire dans une société de la connaissance, in Charlier, J.-E., Croche, S. and Leclercq, B. (dir.). *Contrôler la qualité dans l'enseignement supérieur.* Louvain-La-Neuve: Academia.

Erasmus+ (2015). *Celebrating ECTS and Diploma Supplement Label Holders 2019 & 2013. Internationalisation in Europe's universities.* Luxembourg: Publications Office of the European Union.

European Commission (1991). *Memorandum on Higher Education in the European Union.* Brussels: CE.

European Commission (2004). *ECTS Users' Guide. European Credit Transfer and Accumulation System and the Diploma Supplement.* 17 August. Brussels: European Commission.

European Commission (2014). *ECTS and Diploma Supplement Label Holders 2011 & 2012. Internationalisation in Europe's universities.* Luxembourg: Publications Office of the European Union.

European Commission (2015). *ECTS Users' Guide*. Luxembourg: Publications Office of the European Union.

Eurydice. (2010). *Focus on Higher Education in Europe 2010. The Impact of the Bologna Process*. Brussel: Eurydice.

Evans, L. and Nixon, J. (dir.) (2015). *Academic Identities in Higher Education. Changing European Landscape*. London: Bloomsbury Academic.

Friedberg, E. and Musselin, C. (1989). *En quête d'universités*. Paris: L'Harmattan.

Gorga, A. (2011). *Les jeux de la qualité: impacts sur les politiques éducatives et la vie académique en Suisse et en Roumanie*. Louvain-la-Neuve: Academia.

Kalpazidou-Schmidt, K.E. and Langberg, K. (2007). Academic autonomy in a rapidly changing higher education framework: academia on the Procrustean bed? *European Education*, 39(4), 80–94.

Legendre, F. (2012). Processus de Bologne dans l'enseignement supérieur hongrois: représentations et pratiques enseignantes. *Carrefours de l'éducation*, 34, 211–226.

Lucas, L. (2014). Academic resistance to quality assurance processes in higher education in the UK. *Policy and Society*, 33, 215–224.

Mayrgündter, T. (2015). The 'Enlargement Paradox': intergovernmental supranationalism survives despite the winds of change, *Les études du CERI*, 211. Available at: http://www.sciencespo.fr/ceri/sites/sciencespo.fr.ceri/files/Etude_211.pdf.

Meyer, J.W. and Rowan, B. (1977). Institutionalized organizations: formal structure as myth and ceremony. *American Journal of Sociology*, 80, 340–363.

Normand, R. (2015). The challenges of the French 'homo academicus': modernization, identities and the sense of justice, in Evans, L. and Nixon, J. (dir.) *Academic Identities in Higher Education: the changing European landscape*, part III (chapter 9). New York: Bloomsbury Academic.

OECD (2008). Réunion informelle des ministres de l'éducation des pays de l'OCDE sur l'évaluation des résultats de l'enseignement supérieur, Tokyo, 11–12 janvier. Available at: http://www.oecd.org/document/20/0,3343,en_2649_33723_39926612_1_1_1_1,00.html.

OECD (2014). Testing student and university performance globally: OECD's AHELO. Available at: http://www.oecd.org/edu/skills.

Orton, J.D. and Weick, K.E. (1990). Loosely coupled systems: a reconceptualization. *Academy of Management Review*, 15(2), 203–223.

Papatsiba, V. (2006). Making higher education more European through student mobility? Revisiting EU initiatives in the context of the Bologna Process. *Comparative Education*, 42(1), 93–111.

Parker, L. (2011). University corporatization: driving redefinition. *Critical Perspectives on Accounting*, 22(4), 434–450.

Reichert, S. and Tauch, C. (2003). *Trends 2003. Progress towards the European Higher Education Area*. Bruxelles: EUA.

Saarinen, T. (2005). Quality in the Bologna Process: from 'competitive edge' to quality assurance techniques. *European Journal of Education*, 40(2), 189–204.

Scott, W.R. (2003). *Organizations: rational, natural and open systems*. Englewood Cliffs, NJ: Prentice-Hall.

Souto Lopez, M. (2015). *Resserrer le dispositif européen de l'enseignement supérieur par les acquis d'apprentissage*. Thèse de doctorat en sociologie, Université Catholique de Louvain, École normale supérieure de Lyon, Mons, Lyon.

Thompson, J.D. (1967). *Organizations in Action: social sciences bases of administrative theory.* New York: Mc Graw-Hill.

Tremblay, K., Lalancette, D. and Rosevaere, D. (2012). *AHELO. Feasibility Study Report. Volume 1 Design and Implementation.* Paris: OECD.

Walker, J. (2009). Time as the fourth dimension in the globalization of higher education. *The Journal of Higher Education*, 50(5), 483–509.

Weick, K.E. (1976). Educational organizations as loosely coupled systems. *Administrative Science Quarterly*, 21, 1–19.

Chapter 8

# Universities, the risk industry and capitalism

## A political economy critique

*Susan L. Robertson and Chris Muellerleile*

## Introduction

This chapter explores the growth of what we are calling 'the risk industry' and its rapidly expanding role in both servicing and governing the university as a social institution (Huber 2011) during a period of significant transformation in the reorganisation of contemporary capitalism.

Risk was at the centre of Ulrich Beck's claim that societies were moving into a new phase of modernity. For Beck, we not only face the collapse of modernity's certainties around progress, but a darker, more uncertain, reality; a risk society shaped by fragmentation, individualisation, globalisation and environmental disaster (cf. Beck 1996, 1999).

Risk has also emerged as a newer strategy for governing the university and those within it. Originating in the finance sector, 'risk' has become the lingua franca of business management, and is rapidly colonising public policy domains, including higher education. As of 2000 in the UK, universities are required to accompany all of their decisions with risk management calculations as well as produce and maintain risk strategies. Entangled with new public management (NPM) (Hood 1991), risk technologies have transformed NPM governance into what Hood and colleagues (1999) now describe as a 'risk regulation regime'.

Risk has also become big business, and selling risk solutions to universities a new market to be serviced. Risk templates, tools, frameworks and training are developed by consultancy firms and sold to universities. Newer products and approaches replace those that no longer meet the ISO 31000 standard for quality risk management. Universities are even told their 'reputations' are at risk if their position on any of the 'world university' rankings or 'good university guides' plummets. This, despite the fact that these guides and rankings are largely commercially driven activities, with a commercial interest in generating sufficient turbulence and a sense of vertigo for universities (Robertson 2014). After all, this is what sells newspapers, on the one hand, and the possibility of new services, on the other.

Yet there is a problem with much of the literature on risk and the university in that it fails to locate universities in the context of contemporary capitalism, and the relationship between growing social and economic inequalities. Furthermore, risk management has not been considered in light of greater education inequalities and the unfolding commercialisation and commodification of universities. This is despite the burgeoning risk industry, which services the university, or the ways in which products, like world rankings, are parasitic upon, and turn the wheels of, the risk industry. Similarly, Beck's risk society thesis has very little to say about the changing nature of capitalism and what this means for social institutions, such as universities, who play an important role in the production of political elites, in social reproduction, and increasingly as a producer of wealth for the economy (Matthewman 2015). Much like Fraser's cunning of history argument (Fraser 2009); that the feminist movement unwittingly supplied a key ingredient of the 'new spirit' of neoliberal capitalism through the way in which the cultural turn in second wave feminism 'swallowed up' political economy, our argument is that the failure to link risk and the university to the dynamics of contemporary capitalism in turn occludes important social and political processes and outcomes (Piketty 2014; Streeck 2014). Ours is thus a political economic critique of the risk industry and universities in contemporary capitalism.

Our chapter will proceed in the following way. We begin with Beck's risk society thesis, and then discuss risk governance and the risk university thesis. In the final section we argue that when 'risk' theories become anchored in either a limited engagement with capitalism, on the one hand, or a depoliticised view of risk tools, on the other, that it deflects attention away from broader understanding of the wider political, economic and social class dynamics shaping universities and their futures.

## Beck's risk society

Ulrich Beck (1996) outlines a powerful analysis of the ways the rise of the risk society is transforming social reproduction, nature and ecology, intimate relationships, politics and democracy. From his highly influential 1992 volume *Risk Society* through to *World Risk Society* (1999), Beck insisted that the notion of risk was becoming central to global society. Beck's core thesis is that modernity introduces global risk parameters that previous generations have not had to face, in a large part because modern institutions are not able to control the risks that they create.

At the same time, societies attempt to intervene in and control the future and as a result what were once incalculable hazards (natural disasters and so on) become political issues to be managed. The rise of this more instrumental form of rational control permeates all forms of modern society – from the individual to the institutional to the nation. Risk calculations in turn come to dominate all spheres of activity – from calculations around medical treatments to returns on investments in higher education, including the potential rate of return (private wages/public good) into the future as a result of one's 'financial investment'.

Beck's second pillar centres on the idea of reflexive modernisation – which he argues emerges from the 'self-confrontation' of the dark side-effects of progress. These side-effects come to dominate thinking and behaviour, and the short-circuiting of this through organised irresponsibility (Beck 1996: 28). In other words, a contradiction emerges between public awareness of the risks produced by and within the social institutional system on the one hand, and the lack of attribution of systemic risks to this system on the other. And as Elliott (2002: 298) observes: 'This self-created dead end, in which culpability is passed off on to individuals and thus collectively denied, is maintained through political ideologies of industrial fatalism: faith in progress, dependence in rationality and the rule of expert opinion.'

A third pillar is individualisation – which is not so much about risk, but 'choice' (Beck 1996). For if risks are an attempt to make the incalculable calculable, then risk monitoring presupposes agency, choice, calculation and responsibility. And as more and more areas of social life are disembedded from tradition, or opened up to free market logics, as we see in education sectors in many parts of the world, then existing social forms and categories, such as 'student', 'lecturer', 'university', are forced into making decisions about lives, courses of action and futures, guided by ideas such as choice, risk and uncertainty. Yet this, as Beck points out, is not without problems, as choice and experimentation can be both progressive and regressive. For instance, choice policies can be regressive because the wherewith all to choose is not evenly distributed across the social field. Indeed there is much evidence in the education choice literature that the middle and upper social classes are able to exercise choice in a way that the working classes are not (Ball 2003). This is because of the 'positional good' nature of education, meaning there is intense competition for acquiring a particular kind of education that can be valorised in the labour market, and/or as a means of social mobility (Brown 2000). Furthermore, this competition is increasingly global, and thus feeds back on the globalising of the university.

Beck's thesis received a great deal of airplay in the 1990s and continues to be influential, particularly among contemporary risk and regulation theorists, including Michael Power (see Power *et al.* 2009). And it is true; the language of 'risk' has penetrated the lexicon that is put to work reorganising the management of all sorts of firms and institutions, including the university.

However, we want to suggest, following Alexander (1996: 135) and Matthewman (2015), that Beck's risk thesis offers us a rather unproblematic understanding of risk – as utilitarian and objectivist – and that his model is deeply entangled with neoclassical economics, rational choice theory and methodological individualism. As a result, it shares the conceptual and political limitations of this work. For instance, political conflicts for Beck (see Beck 1992: 35), along with power and domination, are recast as a risk that is equally shared, and thus has an equalising effect. Yet there is a considerable body of evidence that our worlds are even more unequal than they were in the 1980s and 1990s, and that these inequalities are directly linked to neoliberalism as a political project (cf. Streeck 2014; Dorling 2015; Sayer 2015). Beck's underlying thesis – that 'we are all in it together' – underplays the unequal distribution of power, resources and opportunities in neoliberal market societies, and furthermore distracts us from addressing these dynamics and their outcomes.

## Risk governance

There is now a huge literature on risk and its management, leading Rothstein *et al.* (2006: 92) to suggest not only has risk become the lingua franca of business management, but that it has also begun to colonise public policy domains. In short, risk is seen to be all pervasive; it is expanding and demands attention, and in turn requires more and better tools to ensure its management.

Yet this was not always the case. In the business management literature in the 1990s, ideas like 'risk and regulation' were broadly understood to refer to '...the organised control of environmental and human health and safety hazards through a range of legal instruments and management systems' (Rothstein *et al.* 2006: 92). This could include what to do with hazardous chemicals, workplaces and issues of safety, the consequences of pandemics for health services, or the likelihood of traffic accidents. To deal with such risks there are increasingly complex insurance policies – ranging from health to life-expectancy and vehicles, with the risks being calculated by actuarial science experts working mostly for insurance companies.

Over the past two decades, however, risk has emerged as a key organising concept for governments and their regulatory regimes, enabling an extension in the reach of governance deep inside organisations, on the one hand, and as a means to shape the behaviours of individuals, on the other. In the UK, a risk-based approach to regulation was adopted by the New Labour government in 2000, and progressively rolled out to policy domains that included education, housing, the environment, and financial services (UK Cabinet Office 2002). There is now a proliferation of different kinds of risks to be managed with their own approaches to management. For instance, Verbano and Venturini (2011) identity seven different types – including financial risk management, strategic risk management, clinical risk management, engineering risk management and project risk management.

Rothstein *et al.* (2006: 92–93) argue that risk has been embedded in regulation in two ways; one societal and the other institutional. First, regarding societal risks, they argue that there has been a quantitative expansion of risk across policy domains to include more areas of social life – from the management of risk around criminals to stress and risk in the workplace.

In short, there are fewer areas of social life that then are not subject to risk scrutiny mechanisms. Second, regarding institutional risks, these are the risks to organisations who are regulating and managing societal risks. This then results in both the regulated and the regulator now engaging in a dance around the risk of risk management, ranging from cost overruns, the failure to deliver, potential loss of reputation, and so on.

Much of this risk governance research describes the ongoing development of risk management tools and toolkits (cf. Jordan *et al.* 2013) including risk maps (Jordan *et al.* 2013), the development of risk management guidance and standards (such as the 2004 Committee of Sponsoring Organizations of the Treadway Commission – COSO) (cf. Power 2009; Huber and Scheytt 2013), the development of more comprehensive, all-encompassing approaches to risk, such as enterprise risk management (ERM) (Arena *et al.* 2010), and its conceptual innovations – including risk maturity, risk appetite and risk transfer. More serious, however, is that ERM assumes that all risks for organisational strategies can be rendered commensurate in financial terms – a legacy of its origins as a tool in the finance sector, and a conception of risk management that is positive, entrepreneurial, and explicitly at the service of wealth creation (Power, 2009: 850).

This radical expansion has been accompanied by the emergence of voluntary risk standards, such as ISO 31000, which open new opportunities for specialist firms to offer training for key personnel in their organisation while further legitimating risk as a technology for governing. At the same time these firms make profit by selling various risk management products. Bywater Excel (2015) is one such specialist company located in the Midlands in England, close to many agencies and regulatory bodies. It offers one day training courses on ISO 31000 risk management aimed at managers, design teams and auditors. Amongst others, it promises that its delegates will be able to interpret the principles of risk management within ISO 31000 and the generic risk management framework, evaluate how business risks impact on each other, and how to identify appropriate treatments and controls and choose those best suited (Bywater Excel 2015).

Yet despite the promise of certainty, risk governance is full of tensions, contradictions and ambivalences, leading commentator on audit and risk, Michael Power, to argue that an impoverished concept of 'risk appetite' is part of the intellectual failure at the heart of the 2008 financial crisis (Power 2009). More importantly, he points to the ways in which risk models like ERM tend to act rather like a thermostat which '…adjusts to changes in the environment, subject to a pre-given target temperature' (Power 2009: 849). The problem here is that in adopting this 'canopy-like view' of the organisation, risk management approaches like ERM assume it can represent an organisation as an integrated whole; a view that comes from financial accounting. Yet all organisations, including universities, are embedded in wider social networks and flows (such as finance, people, ideas), whose dynamics create a high level of contingency in the system. This is also increasingly the case for universities the more they are pulled into the circuits of capitalism – for while the future cannot be known, risk management tools promise to be able to know, and direct that future. This has led Power to ask:

> How has the ERM conception of risk management gained such a strong institutional toe-hold? The answer is complex but would point to the cultural and epistemological processes of financialization which have shaped the increasingly reductive manner in which organizations are conceptualised, known, managed and regulated.
>
> (Power 2009: 851)

We share some of Power's questions. Where do risk technologies come from? Whose interests do they strategically advance? And what are their consequences for the institutions and societies where they play a growing role? One answer is that

> the knowledge base of ERM connects to the wider political economy of professional advisory firms – the very firms who will be enlisted and will offer themselves for reforming risk management practice. ERM systems cannot represent embeddedness in the sense of interconnectedness; its proponents seem only able to demand an intensification of embedding at the level of the individual entity.
>
> (Power 2009: 853)

The expansion of risk as a socio-economic imaginary, and risk technologies as the solution, arise in part because they are promoted particularly by large global consultancy firms like PricewaterhouseCoopers (2015) with whole divisions devoted to risk consulting services that in part train 'risk leaders' as specialists in particular kinds of markets. There is considerable money to be made in promoting risk frameworks and tools aimed at ensuring 'mission effectiveness' and 'profits'. Risk in PricewaterhouseCoopers' terms is not just a threat or a hazard, but an opportunity.

An organisation's ability effectively to mitigate and capitalise on risk is a growing differentiator in the marketplace with direct impact on business profits and mission effectiveness. In a world of greater complexity, uncertainty and accelerating change, PricewaterhouseCoopers' advisory risk consulting practice positions resilience as a strategic imperative. Teams work cross-functionally within client organisations and with other PricewaterhouseCoopers specialists to factor risk into strategy, finance, operations and compliance, while distinctively integrating the traditional disciplines of risk management. PricewaterhouseCoopers supports clients in defining their strategy, formulating business objectives and managing performance while achieving a balance between risk and opportunity/return (PricewaterhouseCoopers 2015).

Despite the ubiquity of risk as an imaginary and set of technologies, Schiller and Prpich (2014) point out it is not a well-researched field as it is dominated by the same consultants who produce confidential reports for clients and selected surveys for wider audiences. As a result: 'The former does not permit wider dissemination of findings and subsequent advancement of explanations, and the latter is largely based on subjective perceptions, e.g. of risk officers reporting their perception of the field' (Schiller and Prpich 2014: 1000).

There is a further problem with the development of a more critical approach to risk; most of the research is conducted in business schools. And as Foucade *et al.* (2014) argue not only are these researchers from disciplines like economics, or the less well respected accounting and management fields, but their material circumstances in the academy that are buoyed by consulting fees, their world views, and their social and political connections to corporations, have resulted in a very high degree of insularity from the wider social sciences. There is little incentive here to develop a more critical account of risk, particularly in an environment where academics in business schools have '…provided the scientific justification for the management practices favoured by a new generation of corporate raiders, such as leveraged buy-outs, mergers and acquisitions…' (Foucade *et al.* 2014: 17).

## 'The risk university'

The university has been a producer of ideas and expertise around risk and regulation, as we have outlined above, but it has also become subject to regulation via risk governance. In 2000, England's Higher Education Funding Council (HEFCE) required all universities to introduce risk management as a governance tool (Hood *et al.* 2001; Rothstein *et al.* 2006; Huber 2011) as a means for 'improving decisions'. Its approach drew explicitly from the world of finance, when it stated: '…there are genuine business benefits to be gained… quite apart from improvements in accountability and shareholder confidence' (HEFCE 2001: 1). But who was the shareholder here, unless of course they meant the public as stakeholder?

In 2002 HEFCE launched a risk tree, where eight main areas of risk were identified and a set of sub-risks attributed to each area (Huber 2011: 128). Gradations of risk were proposed – from 'early warnings' to 'mitigating actions' – and with 'damage values' were assigned.

HEFCE has also published a 'risk prompt list' containing examples of potentially significant risk elements – from reputational risks to financial risks – many of which have been taken up as a template in many UK universities. Cambridge University, for example, visibly promotes its risk structures and policies on its website; this includes membership of its risk steering committee, the content of its risk management policy and the detail of its risk management strategy. Many UK universities also now spend considerable time filling out risk assessment columns, gathering risk data, and making risk-implicated decisions, calculations, and predictions (for example on numbers of students expected to be successfully recruited.) Risk is a practice in anticipating and attempting to know the future in order to plan accordingly, plan accordingly when in effect this future is neither knowable and nor is it certain.

Risk calculations are also now found in a widening range of activity within the higher education sector: they include, for instance, ensuring particular levels of international student success in university courses, or the possibility being struck off the register of 'trusted' providers kept by UK immigration officials to approve the movement of international students into university places. Similarly, the number of grant applications submitted to funding councils that fall below the fundable category can result in the university being excluded from bidding for research funds into the future. The performance of the university according to its prior risk-infused research 'management' process, and its final scores, are then read as either meeting or falling short of performance targets. This process opens the university, or parts of it, to formal scrutiny not only for the results of decisions, but also for the (in)capacity to anticipate the correct decision in the first place.

Since 2010, and the implementation of austerity policies in the higher education sector in the UK, regulators have tended to formalise this approach in a whole set of spheres to do with university life. A key argument used by the UK government (2010) to justify introducing risk-based regulation as a means of mechanism of external quality assurance of universities and colleges in England is that a more selective focus or prioritisation by the regulator on those institutions that create most risk to the regulator's objectives would lift the regulatory burden on most other providers. This is imagined to enable them (read high status universities) to be more enterprising, innovative and globally competitive. Regulation, it was assumed, would also be 'better' because agency decision-making would be more open to scrutiny as well as being more focused and evidence based.

Yet the UK higher education system is highly differentiated, and increasingly so, following the introduction of market mechanisms into the sector. This means that universities are differently placed regarding their student intakes, levels of retention of students, capacity to perform on league tables, recruitment of international students, and so on. There are a number of axes of differentiation in terms of the increasing uncertainty as universities find themselves implicated in flows of international students, the outcomes of investment decisions, fluctuating credit ratings, and so on. For instance, the social class composition of the student population in any university will shape levels of retention and the nature of their students' future employment opportunities (Reay 2011). As Reay (2011: 117) argues:

> massification of the higher education sector has resulted in the reproduction of the UK's school system's highly polarized and segregated

hierarchy, with those new universities with sizeable cohorts of working class students languishing at the bottom of the university league tables, while the Russell [sic. elite] group universities, with equally sizeable privately educated students, are at the pinnacle.

(Reay 2011: 117)

Almost all universities in the UK have a high level of dependence on international students. Of the full-time graduate students enrolled at the University of Bristol, a Russell Group university, almost 50 per cent of the total are full fee-paying international students (HESA 2015). Changes in the wider political economy, immigration laws, tightened international security, or greater competition from other higher ecucation providers, will all have an impact on the final numbers of international students who will be enrolled. With universities depending more and more on this market, fluctuations will create major financial and programming issues for the provider. We'll return to these wider issues in the following section.

There is now a growing body of work on risk and the university (cf. Huber 2009; Power *et al.* 2009), including the idea of *The Risk University* (Huber 2011). Calling the university 'a special organisation', Huber (2011: 2) sketches out what we regard as rather functional, and uncritical account as to why universities have found themselves subject to the new managerialism and risk. For Huber this includes more efficient use of taxpayers' money, greater accountability to stakeholders, and the demand for greater value for money. Little is said in this literature around the deepening role of the university in creating competitive service sectors, and what this might mean for the university and its governance.

For in truth, universities in many countries have been placed under closer political scrutiny and tightening regulatory pressures, to align their missions and purposes to deliver on global competitiveness agendas for the nation (Marginson and Considine 2000; Barnett 2005). Universities were also being reigned in, from being self-governing institutions to being more closely regulated through research assessment frameworks, quality assurance systems, teaching excellence frameworks and rankings exercises. Risk tools are another demanding regulatory device that sets in train a further burden of 'accounting' for more aspects of organisational life by trying to anticipate the future; from decision-making to financial losses, overseas operations or the research assessment exercises.

These growing external constraints on institutions – aimed at improving accountability – have the potential also to make universities highly risk averse. This is a paradox in that they are also accused of being more reluctant to undertake the entrepreneurialism and innovation that governments want them to adopt. To counteract this negative consequence, managed risk-taking, rather than mere risk avoidance, has become the governmental policy objective in England – and this is captured in the notion of risk-based, external quality assurance. The key question for university leaders and external quality assurers is which risks can be tolerated. King (2016) argues that risk-based frameworks require first, identification of the risks that must be managed, which in turn requires evidence. However, this neglects the fact that robust evidence-based judgements of risk (intended to result in a more selective approach) require large amounts of data. In other words, risks must be translated into calculable events with calculable impacts. But risk calculation is clearly also a 'risky business', as risk is constituted by a future unknown, not a more easily evidenced present or past. Being able to relocate blame – to the 'autonomous institution' or 'choosing agent' thus becomes important – although any major collapse (such as with the financial regulators in 2008) will in turn have wider social and political ramifications.

However, it is reputational risk that is regarded in the risk literature on universities as particular to universities, and is the other side of financial risks. The idea of 'reputational' risk (Power *et al.* 2009), particularly in relation to ranking systems and their management, has therefore come to be an important tool through which universities and those inside them become objects for governing.

> The idea of reputation in science acts as a signalling system in that it simplified the monitoring of the scientific debate for all scholars by pre-selecting promising contributions on the basis of previous accomplishments. ...This reduction of complexity only works if reputation is attributed by the invisible hand.
>
> (Huber 2011: 14)

Yet as we have already pointed out, this invisible hand is nonetheless a hand largely guided by economic wealth and political power; and is a 'class hand'. Reputation and status have historically been features of universities, and are central to the production of political elites. What is increasingly important here is the ways in which 'reputation' is being valorized in new ways (as a risk to reputation), from which new value and value chains are being created.

That the 'Russell Group' universities, with their class-based capital in the UK, do significantly better than any other kind of institution in securing students, funds, publications in highly reputable outlets, and wealthy benefactors and alumni, in turn produce and reproduce the capitals that benefit social class reproduction. Universities also calculate the risks of their decisions, such as the recent research excellence framework, and whether reputation or financial returns need to be secured, and how. Losses in height in relation to global rankings can send the calculators into a downward spiral. These all matter for they are also the 'material' on which ratings agencies, like Standards and Poor's, build their calculations around the financial stability of a university and therefore determine how much interest the university will be required to pay for borrowing.

This temporal shift – bringing the future into the present – promises in turn to manage the future while sheeting home any shortfall in this capability to the individuals making the decisions in the first place. The 'cunning' here of course, if we can paraphrase Fraser (2009) is that by promising to know the future and bring it into the present, risk imaginaries and technologies create a level of certainty on one hand, and dependency on the other. This quickly becomes a seduction for university managers who long for more simplistic solutions in an increasingly complex environment. At the same time, it has been a license for risk consultants to print money. There is now a huge 'risk management' industry that both services and is serviced by the university; experts in risk management sell risk management frameworks to university administrations; risk research centres (including the influential Centre for Analysis of Risk and Regulation established in 1999 located at the London School of Economics, funded by the Economic and Social Research Council) focus attention on risk by pumping out papers and making academic careers; a proliferating number of dedicated risk research journals make it clear risk is an important social topic; while risk-oriented research in management, accountancy and organisation studies journals locates and legitimates risk research as an important governing and management tool.

## The 'risk' of ignoring the relationship between class, the university, and global capitalism

Imaginaries like 'risk society' and its flanking technologies, 'risk governance' and 'risk university', all emerged at a time when: (i) neoliberalism was being advanced as a political project with risk a key tool for self- governing (Rose 1999); (ii) the state was disinvesting in social programmes while mandating risk as a self-governance tool (Streeck 2014); (iii) finance capital was able to benefit from the creation of porous boundaries around the nation state and tax havens while trading in risk (Davies, 2015); (iv) a tiny super wealthy elite have emerged who have benefitted hugely from the notion that entrepreneurs deserve wealth because of the 'risks' they take (Piketty, 2014); and (v) when neoclassical economists have dominated important policy-making domains at all scales of governing where risk is viewed as manageable by rational actors and market relations (Beckert 2014; Fourcade et al. 2014).

Risk is only one of a range of technologies that neoliberal states have 'bought' from economists and the world of finance, and imposed on their public sectors as well as their societies. Represented as a project concerned with competition to ensure more efficient public sectors, together with freedom through choice in the market, risk is simply one more tool for individualising decisions and responsibility, as if power and politics did not matter – all the while waging a class war (Harvey 2005). This is a war that has seen disinvestment in public sector institutions, like universities, while giving tax breaks to the wealthy (Streeck 2014). More to the point, all of this matters more for those universities who do not have alternative sources of wealth, such as endowments, investments, or the capacity to raise money through bonds or third mission activities (McGettigan 2013). And if we are left with any doubt that this is a class war, it is instructive to take Warren Buffett – the fourth richest person in the world, with estimated wealth of $44 billion, at his word. In an interview with the New York Times stated: 'There's class warfare alright, but it is my class, the rich class, that's making war. And we're winning'. And it is this wealthy class (e.g. Gates, Meritosis), especially in the United States, who have also weighed in on what policies ought to be in place to run sectors like higher education (Scott 2009) (with the adage that we are all in it together), or that the future can be controlled. Yet the cunning of 'risk talk' is that with the adage of 'we are all in it together', promises to wipe away social inequalities.

It is clear that 'risk imaginaries' privilege some groups over others. Some benefit directly because it is the source of new forms of value creation. By diagnosing the problem to which you have the answer, and by constantly changing the range of products used to respond to this or that new risk, we see capitalism at its inventive best. Others benefit because academic careers can be made, and made profitably. Still others benefit as it normalises a view that risk is an individual responsibility and any opportunities and profits that might flow are fairly and squarely the result of anticipating well, and that the wealth they acquire is deserved. Because it feeds off a view that risks are shared, and that those taking the most risks have the right to the super salaries that have in turn produced a small elite of very very wealthy, it reinforces the kinds of world views that have also come to shape state policies. The political elites create the conditions for the new economic elites, and vice versa.

Thomas Piketty's (2014) book *Capital in the Twenty-First Century* demolishes the widely held view that free market capitalism, in releasing the entrepreneurial spirit and invoking risk, spreads wealth around as well as shares the risks. Piketty documents in detail how social inequality of both wealth and income has evolved over the past century, with particular emphasis on the role of wealth. More importantly for our argument, he points to the ways the dangerous combination of the free market with finance capital that we saw emerge over the period, if left without major redistributive interventions on the part of neoliberal states, produces anti-democratic oligarchies.

Here 'risk' works not just as a regulatory and disciplining' tool for neoliberalism but its constant focus on individuals and individual institutions (e.g. improvement through competitive comparison on global and national league tables), also acts as a new development ideology – much as modernisation theory did in the post-World War II period (Ferguson 2006). But the ontology that drives neoliberalism's theory of development – of liberty and freedom through (free) market relations – overstates the security one might gain from gaming the future (alone) and underplays the insecurity and anxiety that inevitably follows from perpetual competition and the possibly of loss (of reputation, wealth, job security) (Sennett 2006). What is also excluded from view are the ways in which the game rules for capitalism are controlled, and how these drive deeper social inequalities and social justice outcomes arising from economisation, privatisation and commodification of higher education in many countries. The outcomes are evident: the stalling of social mobility (particularly noticeable in the USA), the rise in graduate unemployment in both the west and the east, along with a growing democratic deficit in the governing of education as the economic and power elites use their think tanks, foundations and memberships of boards, to advance their own agendas.

Crouch (2015: 13) points out that the relationship to risk and uncertainty is a 'classic class relationship because it is very closely related to the relationship to property ownership. Far from class in this sense declining in post-industrial societies, it has become increasingly important'. And as he argues, this results from the central role of the financial sector, the area of the economy where pure wealth counts more than anywhere else. The fact that, compared with the first half of the twentieth century, far more people own property does not reduce this. 'There are severe limits to the risks one might take with one's own residential property, and therefore in the interest rates one can expect to earn, compared with liquid assets that one is using just for investments' (Crouch 2015: 13). Attempts to transcend this by mortgaging a property – such as to generate a living wage, finance a holiday or a student at university – and the resultant debt then being traded as a liquid asset, was one of the causes of the 2008 financial crisis.

Similarly, Streeck (2014: 35) argues that more than any time since the Second World War, capitalism is in a critical condition, and that its crisis symptoms are simply one register of a deeper set of disorders. Rather than the uncertainties being derived from the collapse of modernity as the dominant narrative, as we have with Beck, Streeck's focus is on contemporary capitalism and the new vulnerabilities it sets in train for groups of workers whose lives are organised around flexibility and insecurity (Crouch 2015: 18). Measures to protect workers from insecurities are regarded as market impediments. If public policy has a role it is in facilitating this ideal so as to ensure labour market participation but with levels of flexibility that benefit the owners of capital and managers of corporations (The 1%) and not those having to 'sell' their labour.

The contemporary university has not been exempt from this practice. Shorter term and flexible contracts have become the norm in US universities (20 per cent are tenured faculty; in the UK it is around 35 per cent) – with pressure also on existing tenured staff to take cuts in salaries as the university tries to steer a difficult road between increased student fees and student protest, or lower academic salaries and the loss of 'star' professors. Risk is used as a key tool here to try and navigate a future and its risks with sufficient flexibility and agility.

Streeck outlines three long trends in the trajectories in rich (de)industrialised capitalist countries: (i) a persistent decline in the rate of economic growth, aggravated by the events of 2008; (ii) a rise in overall indebtedness of leading capitalist states as governments, private households and non-financial, as well as financial, firms have piled up financial obligations; and (iii) growing economic inequality in both income and wealth. The net effect of these policies has been to depress wages, drive up debt, and increase social inequalities, and this has an ongoing cumulative effect. The rich in turn get richer, the state in turn becomes poorer and more indebted, and the middle class and poor become disenfranchised and exploited further. All of these dynamics have direct consequences for higher education as its capacity to be a public institution is dependent on the redistribution of public funds.

Sayer advances a similar argument in his recent book *Why We Can't Afford the Rich* (Sayer 2015). His account is located in a wider reading of the history of capitalism, and historic tendencies towards financialisation in any epoch as the rentiers seek out new ways of extracting wealth through the economic system through rent seeking (Sayer 2015: 179). Of course finance is necessary to oil the wheels of capitalism. But when its role reverses – from being a servant to a master – then we begin to see the concentration of wealth in a very small percentage of the population. And as Sayer observes, one of the hallmarks of financialisation is the spread of the practice of selling everything off that it is believed to be able to produce a predictable income stream in order to get the cash now (Sayer 2015: 199). The university has been badly damaged as a result of its deeper and deeper insertion into the world of global capital – as engine as well as a sector generating tradeable education services in the global economy.

So what does the deepening enmeshment of higher education institutions in capitalism and its flows mean for how to think about the university and how it understands and manages uncertainty. Here the work of Jens Beckert (1996) is particularly helpful. He refutes the underlying assumptions of the neoclassical economists; that markets are self-organising, that markets generate trickle-down wealth, and '...the action theoretic model of an individualised homo-economicus who strives restlessly for the maximization of utility' (Beckert 1996: 804), which we have argued is at the heart of most of the risk theories, including Beck's (1999).

As Beckert argues, '...this is not much of a starting point for a *sociological* contribution to the understanding of economic phenomena' [emphasis added], and most certainly does not help us understand how capitalist markets work. As Beckert points out, we cannot know the future, and therefore agents must reach decisions when they do not know what is best to do. The task of the sociologist is thus to develop theoretical concepts and engage in empirical investigations into how actors attempt to make this future is made more certain.

Beckert challenges the idea that agents manage uncertainty by increasing their calculative capabilities – as risk technologies propose. Rather, he argues that as intentionally-rational actors, we live in, and structure, our social worlds using social devices, such as rules, social norms, conventions, institutions, social structures and power relations. These in turn limit our choices as actors, but also make actions more predictable (Beckert 1996: 820). Much of Beckert's work goes on to look at what he describes as the micro-foundations of economic action; that is, the mental representations of future states he calls 'fictional expectations' that guide and structure action. As he says:

> Recognition of the human capability of imagining future states of the world provides a basis for anchoring a theory of capitalist economy in a theory of action; it is also crucial for understanding the value of goods, and of how cooperation dilemmas are overcome.
>
> (Beckert 2014: 220)

In our view, this kind of approach is more helpful for understanding the dynamics shaping universities and their futures that it moves us towards a social critique that places political economy and class strategies more firmly in the visible centre.

## Conclusion

These developments within capitalism more generally have in turn created a crisis within universities – where paradoxically 'risk' is also mobilised as a tool to manage the crisis. At every turn, finance and risk are ever present; as a technology for governing in the interests of finance capital. And the contradictions are growing, which may – at some point – end in a crisis of the tool for crisis management that the state has deployed: the crisis in risk management as a crisis of the state and capital accumulation (Streeck 2014). To begin, in a low wage economy (for a growing proportion of the population) and a low or no taxation environment for the wealthy, there is a shortfall in tax receipts, the state has to increase its expenditures to make up a living wage. And with household debt increasing at the same time that the state is asking families to take on more and more of the cost of higher education, it is clear that this formula is in trouble – not least because of the health and social inequalities it produces but even in its own terms, it is failing to create healthy and fit labour for a vibrant, creative economy.

We have been arguing that 'risk' as a tool for governing the university has strategically and selectively concealed rather more than it has revealed around class strategies, interests and outcomes. Those universities that win in the reputation stakes are those universities who produce the political elites and provide important legitimation for the economic elites. This is not a game of risk, but one of class and privilege that is the outcome of wealth, social networks, and the strategic use of cultural and economic resources.

It seems to us that a number of things need to happen. First, that we show the ways in which the production of knowledge in the academy can act to shore up these projects of the powerful; in this case finance capital and its legitimators in the academy. Fraser (2009) makes a similar point in her paper on feminism and capitalism and 'the cunning of history'. That is, second wave feminism and post-structural theory is to be lauded for the ways it revealed binary thinking and focused on culture and identity. But at the same time it produced its own blindside – the lack of analysis of political economy more generally and capital and class in particular.

Second, we need to make visible the ontological and epistemological basis of risk tools as means of governing the future, and rather see that futures can rarely be known. In the struggle to imagine and stabilise those futures to ensure the ongoing reproduction of capitalism and class interests, certain possible futures are strategically selected over others (Beckert 2014). These micro-foundations for political economy – in turn create motifs for engaging in potentially profitable and incalculable outcomes – and shift attention to the management of expectations. The more the world of higher education enters the world of capital accumulation, the more these micro-foundations depend upon, and refashion, the system of expectations within the academy. This profoundly changes the purpose of the university as well as its temporal rhythms and social and spatial relations.

Finally, we need a different conceptual grammar to talk about the transformation of the university in the twenty-first century; one that has the potential to recover the revolutionary potential of the academy in creating knowledge without reverting to a script that romances the pre-1970s academy. This means also putting risk in its place socially, politically and economically. It means resisting the temptation to talk of the calculating university, as if this was an ontological state of being. Instead we need to see risk imaginaries, technologies and tools, as either wittingly or unwittingly being promoted or legitimated by those who benefit from the growth of the risk industry.

## References

Alexander, J.C. (1996). Critical reflections on reflexive modernization. *Theory, Culture and Society*, 13(4), 133–138.

Arena, M., Arnaboldi, M. and Azzone, G. (2010). The organizational dynamics of enterprise risk management. *Accounting, Organization and Society*, 35, 659–675.

Ball, S. (2003). *Class Strategies and the Education Market*. New York: Routledge Falmer.

Barnett, R. (ed.). (2005). *Reshaping the University: new relationships between research, scholarship and teaching.* Berkshire, UK: Open University Press.

Beck, U. (1992). *Risk Society: Toward a New Modernity.* London and New York: Sage.

Beck, U. (1996). World risk society as cosmopolitan society: ecological questions in a framework of manufactured uncertainties. *Theory, Culture and Society* 13(4), 1–32.

Beck, U. (1999). *World Risk Society.* Cambridge: Polity.

Beckert, J. (1996). What is sociological about economic sociology? Uncertainty and the embeddedness of economic action. *Theory and Society,* 25, 803–840.

Beckert, J. (2014). *Capitalism as a system of fictional expectations: toward a sociological micro-foundations of political economy.* Working Paper, Max Planck Institute for the Study of Societies, Koln, Germany.

Brown, P. (2000). The globalisation of positional competition? *Sociology,* 34(4), 633–653.

Bywater Excel (2015). ISO 31000 risk management training. Available at: https://www.bywater.co.uk/course/iso-310002009-fundamentals-risk [Accessed 24 November 2014].

Crouch, C. (2015). *Governing Social Risks in Post-Crisis Europe.* Cheltenham: Edward Elgar.

Davies, H. (2015). *Can Financial Markets be Controlled.* Cambridge: Polity.

Dorling, D. (2015). *Inequality and the 1%.* London and New York: Verso.

Elliott, A. (2002). Beck's sociology of risk: a critical assessment. *Sociology,* 36(2), 293–315.

Ferguson, J. (2006). *Global Shadows: Africa in the Neoliberal World.* Durham and London: Duke University Press.

Fourcade, M., Ollion, E. and Algan, Y. (2014). *The Superiority of Economists.* Maxpo Discussion Paper No. 14/3. Paris: Max Planck Sciences Po Centre.

Fraser, N. (2009). Feminism, capitalism and the cunning of history. *New Left Review,* 56, 97–117.

Harvey, D. (2005). *Spaces of Global Development.* London and New York: Verso.

HEFCE (2001). *Risk Management: a guide to good practice for higher education institutions.* Bristol: HEFCE.

HESA (2015). Table 3 – HE student enrolments by HE provider, level of study, mode of study and domicile 2013/14. Available at: https://www.hesa.ac.uk/stats [Accessed 25 November 2015].

Hood, C. (1991). A public management for all seasons? *Public Administration,* 65, 3–19.

Hood, C., Rothstein, H., Baldwin, R., Rees, J. and Spackman, M. (1999). Where risk meets the regulatory state: exploring variations in risk management. *Risk Management,* 1(1), 212–234.

Huber, C. (2009). Risks and risk regulation in higher education institutions. *Tertiary Education and Management,* 15(2), 83–95.

Huber, C. (2011). *The Risk University: risk identification at higher education institutions in England. Discussion Paper No. 69.* CARR. London: London School of Economics.

Huber, C. and Scheytt, T. (2013). The dispositif of risk management: reconstructing risk management after the financial crisis. *Management Accounting Research,* 24, 88–99.

Jordan, S., Jorgensen, L. and Mitterhofer, H. (2013). Performing risk and the project: risk maps as mediating instruments. *Management Accounting Research*, 24, 156–174.

King, R. (2016). Regulating risk in the higher education state: implications for policy and research, in John P. and Fanganal J. (eds). *Dimensions of Marketisation in Higher Education*. London and New York: Routledge.

McGettigan, A. (2013). *The Great University Gamble*. London: Pluto Press.

Marginson, S. and Considine, M. (2000). *The Enterprise University*. Cambridge: Cambridge University Press.

Matthewman, S. (2015). Risk society revisited, again. *Thesis Eleven*, 128(1), 141–152.

Piketty, T. (2014). *Capital in the 21st Century*. Boston: Harvard University Press.

Power, M. (2009). The risk management of nothing. *Accounting, Organizations and Society*, 34, 849–855.

Power, M., Scheytt, T., Soin, K. and Sahlin, K. (2009). Reputational risk as a logic of organizing late modernity. *Organization Studies*, 30(2 & 3), 301–324.

PricewaterhouseCoopers (2015). Risk Consulting Services, PWC. Available at: http://www.pwc.com/us/en/risk [Accessed 24 November 2015].

Reay, D. (2011). Universities and the reproduction of inequalities, in Holmwood J. (ed.). *A Manifesto for the Public University*. London: Bloomsbury.

Robertson, S.L. (2014). *World Class Higher Education: thoughts toward an alternative mobilities paradigm*. A paper presented to the Academic Mobilities Conference, Johannes Gutenberg Universitat, Mainz, 26–28 June, 2014.

Rose, T. (1999). *Powers of Freedom*. Cambridge: Cambridge University Press.

Rothstein, H., Huber, M. and Gaskell, G. (2006). A theory of risk colonization: the spiralling regulatory logics of societal and institutional risk. *Economy and Society*, 35(91), 91–112.

Sayer, A. (2015). *Why We Can't Afford the Rich*. Bristol: Policy Press.

Schiller, F. and Prpich, G. (2014). Learning to organize risk management in organizations: what future for enterprise risk management? *Journal of Risk Research*, 17(8), 999–1017.

Scott, J. (2009). The politics of venture philanthropy in Charter School policy and advocacy. *Education Policy*, 23(1), 106–136.

Sennett, R. (2006). *The Culture of the New Capitalism*. New Haven and London: Yale University Press.

Streeck, W. (2014). *Buying Time*. London: Verso.

UK Cabinet Office (2002). *Risk: improving government's capacity to handle risk and uncertainty*. London: Strategy Unit, Cabinet Office.

Verbano, C. and Venturini, K. (2011). Development paths of risk management: approaches, methods and fields of application. *Journal of Risk Research*, 14(5), 519–550.

# Chapter 9

# 'Silencing the disbelievers'

## Games of truth and power struggles around fact-based management

*Isabelle Bruno*

> 'Fact, fact, fact!' said the gentleman.
> And 'Fact, fact, fact!' repeated Thomas Gradgrind.
> 'You are to be in all things regulated and governed', said the gentleman,
> 'by fact. We hope to have, before long, a board of fact, composed of
> commissioners of fact, who will force the people to be a people of fact,
> and of nothing but fact. You must discard the word Fancy altogether.'
> (Charles Dickens, *Hard Times*, 1854)

## Introduction

The same applies to Mr Thomas Gradgrind's utilitarian school as it does within the state apparatus, international organisations, think tanks and other networks of experts tasked with developing teaching policies: the only thing that counts is 'facts' built as targets, points of reference and spurs of education practices in the same vein as public action. This attachment to facts as assessment and decision-making criteria is fully incarnated by the Dickensian character, depicted as 'a square man', 'a man of realities. A man of facts and calculation. A man who proceeds upon the principle that two and two are four' (Dickens 1994: 2). Via this school principal who counsels his students to 'be in all things regulated and governed by fact', to 'ban the word imagination forever', Victorian literature of the nineteenth century was taking into account a bureaucratic method of government which was in its early stages, but which today has been materialised into mechanisms which are as diverse as the battery of tests which measure the skills of students; the reporting system and performance-based pay to which teachers are subjected; the development of so-called 'evidence-based' educational policies; the use of benchmarking to compare national performances, etc.

We have entered into the 'total performance' era (Jany-Catrice 2012). At every echelon – at the national level of the 'education system' or at the local level of the school, or even at the individual level, that of the teacher or the student – with each one adding up to legitimise its raison d'être by proving its effectiveness.

In other words, in education as in other fields, we could paraphrase the poet by saying that 'there's no such thing as performance, only proofs of performance'. Whether it is from a comparative, experimental or statistical point of view, you must show that positive results are registered or expected. You must show them backed up by figures, backed up by evidence, hence an intensive documentary activity – the document being (etymologically) what is used as evidence. Yet, the documentary activity is the true principle of the managerial bureaucratisation which has proliferated all forms of organisation (Bruno 2013b). In this regard, educational organisations are no exception.

Those who wish to understand the meaning of this managerial bureaucratisation are attacking an old problem: that of the art of governing by facts, an art which is concerned above all of with effectiveness and objectivity. And anyone asking the governmental question, the question of power, cannot escape the question of resistances. In other words, governing by facts implicitly raises the problem of possibles: which 'real possibilities' opposed to a reality supposedly irrefutable of facts. We therefore need to revisit the question – a classic one – of governing by 'facts' in the light of the current proliferation of evaluative technologies aiming to produce 'convincing data', whether they are statistics, experimental results, comparative data such as benchmarks or 'best practices'.

The systems producing such facts for governmental use are part of a plurality of objectivities inextricably linked to certain conceptions of social order and political policy. In the spirit of the works of Lorraine Daston and Peter Galison (Daston and Galison 2007), who gave a historical overview of objectivity as an epistemic virtue, we should first of all recall and outline how it has also become a political virtue, which redefines the relationships between rulers and the ruled and transforms the exercise of governmental power, both its instrumentation and its finalities. We shall then take into account the political force of facts by examining three check systems that translate them into recognised evidence. This input via systems aims to highlight the plurality of objectivity schemes claimed by the entrepreneurs of 'proving data', instead of revering their scientificity indiscriminately. The challenge is not to separate the more or less true from the more or less false, reality and chimeras, but to understand how the normativities which operate within these schemes work in practice. We will focus more specifically on the example of benchmarking (Bruno and Didier 2013). This comparative assessment technique is indeed interesting with regard to our aim, in that it effectively equips an art of governing by 'facts', which tends to neutralise policies – both at the corporate level and the state level – by tying up organisational practices to 'evidence', which is considered to be indisputable.

Finally, we will open up the perilous issue of possibles, more specifically their objectification and the role of social sciences in this objectification of possibles. To what extent can social sciences – or must they – help actors 'to see reality from the point of view of its possibilities'? Where is the border situated – inevitably political – between scientific and extra-scientific statements taking possibles as their object? And how to reflect about possibles objectively? Admittedly, the critical approach, inherent in social sciences, always strives to re-establish its contingence to reality. Constructivist approaches are notably characterised by paying particular attention to the production of facts to undermine authority better. But more often than not, the possible is reduced to notions of contingence, the space of possibles or the room for manoeuvre; the possible therefore remains very abstract and underdetermined. And yet there exists works that are precisely attempting to define, measure, document, in one word to objectify the possible(s) according to diverse paths, which an excellent article in the *Tracés* journal recently showcased (Jeanpierre *et al.* 2013).[1] Among these paths, we shall develop two of them: on the one hand, that of 'statactivism', which consists of statistically objectifying possibles of thought in order to transfer them into possibles of struggle… and inversely; on the other hand, those of 'real utopias' (Wright 2010), which consists of feeding a culture of micropolitical precedents.

## The art of governing by facts: 'silencing the disbelievers'

Since the 1980s, the increasing recourse to statistical ratios, econometric data or even performance indicators in the decision-making process, to justify a measure, to be used as the basis for a strategic programme, has become a routine practice both in states and the corporate environment. In both cases, we are talking about management by performance, the culture of results, the 'policy of setting targets'.

There is nothing new, nor enigmatic a priori in rulers basing their policies on 'facts', which are as hard and indisputable as possible, in order to exercise power. This was already proposed in the liberal politics of the eighteenth century, with the aim of 'ending the violence, domination, oppositions of interests and the shock of passions'. As written by Arnault Skornicki in a thesis on French political economics in the eighteenth century, the liberals wished

> to finish, in a way, with politics itself, by rationalising and naturalising this field of objectivity which is society under the sign of a physically based natural order. Consequently, we must less govern men and women than administrate things in their naturality, in other words, to manage the population by manipulating things, by directing the desire of men and women against which we can do nothing, and this what Foucault called without any apparent irony 'governmentality'.
>
> (Skornicki 2008: 19)

In the nineteenth century, literature talked about these methods of governing by facts. Charles Dickens' well-known extract, which was quoted in the epigraph (Dickens 1994: 6) dramatises the school principal, Thomas Gradgrind, and a civil servant inspecting the school who explains to the students what the government is hoping for: 'We hope to have, before long, a board of fact, composed of commissioners of fact, who will force the people to be a people of fact, and of nothing but fact.'

Obviously, it was not just literature which precociously took as its subject this art of governing by facts. Philosophy was another major critical body. If we take for example, the School of Frankfurt, in particular Max Horkheimer, who targeted the authority invested in facts. As explains Katia Genel, the analysis of the transformations of authority led this author to diagnose 'the end of traditional authorities', such as the family, the chief, mass culture, and the 'the growing advent of an authority of "facts" or even the real' (Genel 2013: 110). There is disillusionment in these findings: the criticism of authority by Horkheimer and his subordinates did not lead to the discounted emancipation of the critical topic, and seems even to have armed a new form of authority which is based on 'a method of presenting reality' designed as data, and which can be found to be 'reinforced by the sciences themselves' (Genel 2013: 108). According to Horkheimer, the 'authority no longer assumes a personal form, but becomes the authority of the social-economic order which is given as a necessity'; and this 'passionate attachment to the given' will close the revolutionary possibles (Genel 2013: 110). As stated by Genel, this closure of the possibles extends to 'the double meaning of a loss of traditional vectors ensuring the possibilities of emancipation and a closure of facts assumed by the positivist transformation of the theory' (Genel 2013: 108).

From a completely different point of view, Michel Foucault also attacked this issue of governing by facts by showing that political economics has made reality both the target and the instrument of liberal governmentality. In his lessons in 1978, he proposed a genealogy of this liberal governmentality by going back to the physiocrats and their conception that both the economy and politics were physical. By 'physical', by 'nature', the physiocrats effectively saw this reality as the only datum upon which politics must act and with which it should interact. In this regard, he quoted Dupont de Nemours who wrote in the preface of his *Journal de l'agriculture, du commerce et des finances* [Journal of Agriculture, trade and finance] (1765): '[The political economy] is not a science of opinion, in which we contest between verisimilitudes and probabilities. The study of physical laws, which are all reduced to calculations, decide the least results' (quoted in Foucault 2004: 55). He also quoted Le Trosne, another great figure of physiocratie, who wrote in 1766: 'As economic science is nothing but the application of the natural order of the government of societies, it is as constant in its principles and as likely to be the demonstration of the most certain physical sciences' (Foucault 2004).

And Foucault commented:

> Only positioning oneself in this game of reality with itself, this is what I believe, the physiocrats, the economists, the political thought of the 18th century intended when it said that, in anyway, we remain in the order of the physical and that acting in the order of politics, is still acting in the order of nature. And you can see at the same time as this postulate, I mean to say this fundamental principle that the political technique should never detach itself from the game of reality with itself, that this is profoundly linked to the general principle which we call liberalism.
>
> (Foucault 2004: 49)

Foucault insisted on the leading role that economists play in the constitution of a field of reality, which appears as the correlative of governmental power. By doing so, they open the door to statistics, the technology of government par excellence. Until the seventeenth century, the art of governing constituted a manipulation of laws. We expected the prince to act wisely and prudently. 'Being wise, is knowing the laws' (positive, natural, divine, moral). Being prudent, was 'knowing to what extent, at what moment and in which circumstances to effectively apply this wisdom' (Foucault 2004: 279).

Foucault suggested that

> from the 17th century onwards, that something else entirely appeared as a characteristic of the knowledge necessary for those who govern. The sovereign or the one who governs [...] must know not just the laws, and not even first hand or fundamentally the laws (even though we always refer to them, of course, and that it is important to know them), but what is at the same time new, capital and decisive, is that the sovereign must know these elements which constitute the State [...] the person who governs must know the elements which are going to enable the State to be maintained [...]. In other words, the knowledge which the sovereign must have shall be a knowledge of things rather than a knowledge of the laws, and that these things that the sovereign must know, these things which are the actual reality of the State, are specifically what we called at the time, 'statistics'.
>
> (Foucault 2004: 279–280)

Liberal governmentality thus took as a target and instrument a reality economically and statistically objectified in data held to be indisputable facts.

And yet, it is not just a case of indenturing statistics to the liberal political economy. As a 'science of the state', statistics have always served as a 'tool of evidence' and a 'tool of government' (Desrosières 1998, 2014). But the operations collecting and registering, quantificating and modelling data are not immutable. They participate in a game of co-construction with the conceptualisations of society and the economy, as well as with public action modes. This is what Alain Desrosières demonstrated via a periodisation extricating five types of state (the engineer, liberal, welfare, Keynesian and neoliberal states), characterised by the specificities of organisations of knowledge and instruments (demographic, accounting, econometric, etc.), which equip their interventions and, by doing so, retroact on governmental forms (Desrosières 2003).

It is not just statistical quantification that objectifies reality as a target and instrument of government. With experimental 'facts', we have a type of evidence which is summoned in support of the political action, especially in the field of education. In this case, the work of objectification does not just aim to have a discriminating knowledge of the populations and territories to govern. It puts into place processes to develop policies and organisational management in order to give them a so-called scientific rigour. By adopting the methodology of clinical trials, evidence-based policy proceeds by empiric corroboration, in the manner of 'evidence-based medicine' (Marks 1997, 2010). Issued from the agronomics work by the statistician Ronald Fisher (Labrousse 2010), this experimental approach found great success in the medical field during the 1980s, in the education field during the following decade (Normand 2011), and then in the economics of development under the impetus notably of Esther Duflo and her colleagues in the Jameel Poverty Action Lab (Banerjee and Duflo 2009; Labrousse 2010). In France, for instance, the public policy impact experimentations were put on the back burner following lively controversies in favour of so-called pluralist assessments (Monnier 1987; Spenlehauer 1998), but experienced renewed interest during the 2000s, in particular in the field of social policies, with the income support benefit known as the *revenu de solidarité active* (RSA), being an emblematic case study in this regard (Gomel and Serverin 2009; L'Horty and Petit 2010; Chauffaut 2012).

With statistical facts on the one hand and experimental facts on the other hand, we have two examples of facts built for governmental purposes which draw their power to convince from the scientificity of knowledge and the tools mobilised to build them. We shall now develop a third example of facts steering the practices of government: benchmarks that designate models, 'best practices', assessable targets and performance indicators. Benchmarks are an offshoot of the practice of benchmarking, which is nothing more than a managerial technique of evidence-based government.

What is benchmarking? Benchmarking was rationalised in the industrial sector during the 1980s, in particular by engineers in the multinational firm Xerox, before being invested with a certain scientificity by the managerial discipline. It would be interesting for us to look at the political rationality which led to the creation of this technology of power. Benchmarking consists of a process objectifying 'best practices', by assessing the results and comparing them. It is designed as a process which measures and compares performances in order to 'support the decision-making process' or, more specifically, in order for middle management to accept senior management's decisions.

How to they get them on-board? By the administration of hard evidence regarding the existence of 'best practices' observable elsewhere, by recording results higher than theirs and thus creating performance gaps which are competitiveness differentials that bring into play the survival of the organisation. Thus, benchmarking is a way of governing by the real: it is in the real, by an empirical method in the search for 'best practices', and not by forecasting, and even less so by negotiation, that we search for benchmarks which can be translated into targets to be achieved. Thus, benchmarking opens up a space of possibles, which limits itself to the feasible, in that it proceeds by an empirical search for 'best practices'; a search that is deployed within a competitive space which significantly overflows from the competitive market, as the best performances can be potentially found anywhere, in any sector and throughout the world (Bruno 2009).

Governing by the means of benchmarking thus makes it possible to assign assessable objectives to an undisputable realism as they are drawn from the real. This art of governing by using probing data is what is commonly called in the corporate world evidence-based management; at Xerox, they tended to speak management by fact. Facts drawn from the corporate environment thus function as incentive standards – not legal in this case – but it should be noted that these facts do not pre-exist their translation into accounting and statistical data, comparable to internal results. Between the market and the worker, there is an entire sociotechnical chain which documents 'best practices' and assesses their performance. Via this chain, the company builds standards which draw their force from their supposed naturality and serve as a point of support for management to mobilise the irrefutable register of necessity, the imperious reality, instead of asserting their decisional authority.

The challenge is not just to obtain the obedience of subordinates, but to collect a consensus regarding 'objectively' determined targets, and thus to motivate a freely consented action, carried out under exogenous and not hierarchal pressure, objective and not interpersonal.[2] Benchmarking is in fact a method of governing based on initiative, self-assessment, empowerment, voluntary will, personal or even intimate engagement. Instead of submitting ourselves to orders and rules, it is supposed to orientate our engagement towards action, govern what we tend to think is the most personal: our initiatives. Everything happens as if it was neither the supervisor, nor the boss, nor financers who exercise authority. It is facts that are supposed to order, and not arbitrary subjectivities. Political negotiations yield before the authority of facts. This apparent de-personalisation of the power relationships, supposedly cushioned by the administration of facts and figures, bases the exercise of governing on evidence taken to be indisputable. It replaces negotiable standards by the 'harsh reality' of competing performances, and by doing so attempts to paralyse within both the corporate world and the state, the collective apparatus of social and political democracy, which functions via debate, dissensus and compromise.

In periods of crisis, such an approach has enabled the industrial leaders of united states to offer tangible and incontestable evidence that the highest levels of performance are observable elsewhere, therefore accessible here. Any argument justifying a practical impossibility is de facto invalidated by the existence of a precedent, translated into an assessable target to be achieved: the benchmark. By using benchmarking, Xerox's senior management wanted to arm themselves against the conservatism and scepticism of middle management – two symptoms which compose a well-known syndrome in management: the 'invented here syndrome' (NIH).[3] According to Robert C. Camp, the engineer responsible for implementing benchmarking at Xerox, NIH is a 'protector mechanism', a natural defence mechanism that benchmarking can heal because it does not content itself with pointing out differentials of performance, the identification of problems, it instead equips managers to solve problems by bringing them solutions in the form of best practices.[4] In his opinion, if benchmarking was systematised at Xerox, it was above all to defeat those who were resisting change, to overcome the mistrust of the processes adopted by other organisations, in other words to 'silence the disbelievers'.[5]

By bringing tangible proof that a performance is accessible by the demonstration that elsewhere others achieved it, benchmarking gave management arguments of authority that enabled them to discredit any contrary justification. This is what the chief executive officer (CEO) at the time, David T. Kearns, expressed directly in an interview: 'That's one of the things that benchmarking does: it takes away the excuses.'[6] It is interesting to note that in 1990, Kearns left his job as CEO to become the deputy secretary of education in the Bush Senior administration. He was an active promoter of the benchmarking of schools in the United States (Bruno 2013a).

## 'Real utopias': arming political imagination by objectification

After having given an overview on how the objectification of facts acts as a governing technique, we must now envisage how it is a resource of resistance. We outlined above how statistical, economic, managerial knowledge, among others, could be enrolled by the exercise of governmental power, which consumes it as much as it produces it. It remains for us to envisage how this knowledge and other types, notably history and sociology, can advance realistic possibles which are not mistaken for the correlative reality of neoliberal governmentality.

The article in the *Tracés* journal on 'the realities of the possible in SHS' invites us to 'reflect on an epistemological, empirical and critical level, the treatment of the possible in our disciplines' (Jeanpierre *et al.* 2013). In opposition to what Karl Marx called 'abstract possibilities' or general ones, the authors defined 'realistic possibilities' as

> the possibilities of which the description is sufficiently constraining to have a cognitive and possibly critical interest. Not all the possible worlds are also describable or pertinent. Obtaining, in research, a better determination of possibles occurs via the possession of a conceptually accurate apparatus and by a close articulation between the description of alternative possibilities and empirical observation.
>
> (Jeanpierre *et al.* 2013: 8)

But the exploration of realistic possibles by social sciences is not limited to intellectual initiatives aiming better to design the possibles or to capture them via increasingly sophisticated mathematical tools. They can have the ambition of rendering possible certain realities: in other words, better knowing the possibles in order to envisage change, or in other terms, to rearticulate 'the possible of the theory and the possible of the practice (Jeanpierre *et al.* 2013: 16). 'Statactivism' is a modality of this re-articulation (Bruno *et al.* 2014, 2014). 'Real utopias' are another (Wright 2010).

'Statactivism' is a neologism forged to design a type of militancy by statistics, which is already practised by certain militants, artists and researches. As a descriptive concept, it qualifies diverse experiences aiming to re-appropriate the emancipating power of statistics. This concept was created not just as intellectual flirting but because it seemed useful to us to reassemble struggles, which are quite diverse by their purpose but which share a common process, to rally them under a single flag so that they gain in visibility and strength. This is the subject of a collective work entitled *Statactivisme* (Bruno *et al.* 2014), which brings together a series of contributions focusing on the forms of militant action which use statistics, either to make visible categories of populations that have been victims of bureaucratic indifference and to enable them to be heard, such as casual workers, the precarious, people of colour, or more specifically the high rate of workers from the French telecommunication company Orange committing suicide, etc.; or to build other indicators with the aim or re-orientating public policy or corporate strategies (this is the vocation for example of the forum for other wealth indicators – FAIR); to bypass rules, or even to cheat in a competition which is judged to be illegitimate (in France, this is called 'chanstique' in the police).

Certainly, in a certain manner, this is nothing new. The period between the 1950s and the 1970s were in fact rich in terms of historical precedents in the field: the information supplied by the public statistical departments were seen at the time as the pillars of democratic society; it armed social critique which often based itself on statistical arguments to express and showcase the requirements of equality and justice. Statistics have also shown, in the past, that another reality is possible or have rendered other possibilities real. This looked into in the first part of the book with texts by Alain Desrosières, Luc Boltanski, Howard Becker and the artist Hans Haacke. But Desrosières highlights that recently it is precisely the trust accorded to this type of tool that has been eroded by the increasing power of the neoliberal-inspired quantification policies. This is what is called 'new public quantification', in echo of New Public Management (Bruno and Didier 2013).

During the collective research that we carried out on benchmarking and its uses in state administration and the organisations of public services between 2009 and 2012, it appears that statistics were less and less seen as resources of resistance and political imagination and more and more considered as power techniques of power. In this respect, Alain Desrosières writes of an anecdote he was told in the spring of 2009 by a young militant statistician and a member of the Committee for the Defence of Public Statistics, which had just been created. She was participating in a union demonstration against one of President Nicolas Sarkozy's multiple reforms. And in the cortege, she went up to demonstrators and asked them to sign a petition supporting the public statistics service, and was surprised to hear that 'Your statistics are only used to control us, to spy on us, to worsen our working conditions!' By this anecdote, a sad one in his opinion, Desrosières illustrates the reversal of perception operated by the neoliberal use of statistic indicators as assessment and control tools.

This observation was our starting point – an observation in which the actors of social movements are increasingly reproaching the connivance of statistics with power and sanction, even though the history of their links with social reform and emancipation is as long and rich. By documenting the diverse practices of statactivism – artistic, militant but also scientific – we wanted to show how statistics can produce collectives and categories and, in doing so, change reality. 'Statactivism' thus participates in a realistic approach of possibles in that it does not reduce objectivity – in this case, statistics – to an instrument of pure domination. It pleads for an understanding of the work of objectification as a conflictual process caught up in a tension between power and resistance.

Yet, one must make sure that this tension between power and resistance is not confused with another polarisation, that which opposes facts with imagination. Imagination is not by essence emancipating, whereas facts by nature are alienating (see Figure 1). The 'art of governing by facts' thus coexists with forms of 'mythocracy', in the terms of Yves Citton's concept (Citton 2010). In other words, the elites in power's arsenal are composed both of 'probing data', which we talked about in the first part of this chapter and narrations produced by storytelling techniques. Whether they produce facts like benchmarking or fictions like storytelling, these techniques of power are well documented today. However, we know a lot less about alternative resources of objectification and the creativity mobilised for the purposes of resistance.

# POWER

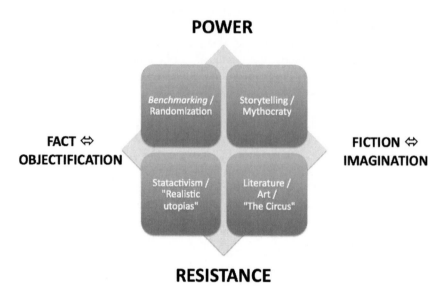

FACT ⇔
OBJECTIFICATION

FICTION ⇔
IMAGINATION

# RESISTANCE

*Figure 9.1* The facts between power and resistance.

Work exists – for example those of the anthropologist and political scientist James C. Scott who wrote about the arts of resistance or the art of not being governed (Scott 1990, 2009), but this needs to be completed in order to produce a genealogy of knowledge and political practices, which are more attentive to local experimentations, to minority practices, to micropolitical actors. In other terms, it is incumbent upon social sciences to feed a 'culture of precedents' (Vercauteren 2011). Feeding a culture of precedents by documenting over the long term a self-government experiment as carried out by the historian Jérôme Baschet:

> We are bogged down in reality. It sticks to our skin, like a piece of clothing which is impossible to remove. In a world which prides itself on flexibility and fluidity, reality is paradoxically constituted as an increasingly dense and heavy matter [...]. It multiplies the traps of constraint, of urgency and the inevitable adaptation of globalised processes in which none has control. [...] Even a good dose of scepticism, or even a solid critical capacity cannot attack, in most cases, this adherence to a system which has maybe renounced to convince us of its virtues in order to simply content itself to appear as the only possible reality, outside of absolute chaos, as François Furet's emblematic sentence summarises: 'We are condemned to live in the world in which we live in.' There is no alternative [Thatcher's famous TINA]: such is the conviction that the forms of the current domination have managed to disseminate in the social fabric.

Beyond each person's opinions, such is the norm of fact, by virtue of which acting complies with an implacable logic of matching the socially constituted reality.

(Baschet 2014: 7–8)

In order to become unstuck from this imperious reality, Baschet proposes fine-tuning the critique of the existing and above all to give consistency to alternative universes in order to shake and weaken the dominant production mode of reality. In other words, working to detach oneself from the surrounding reality. According to him, 'other possibles have already started to take shape and it is in the soil of these concrete experiences and their creativity that reflection should take root' (Baschet 2014: 10–11). It is in this perspective, that he documented the organisation and knowledge practices developed by the Zapatista community of the Chiapas. These communities experimented with a non-state-based political form based on de-specialisation and the collective re-appropriation of the capacity to participate in the decision-making process. This is a not an anecdotic experiment as it has been in place for more than a decade and is deployed in a territory as large as Belgium. In order to understand this self-government experience, Baschet conceptualises it in terms of a 'real utopia' in reference to Erik Olin Wright, an American sociologist who, over two decades, has been looking into new, potential articulations between scientific approaches of social sciences and political practices constituted of forms of alternative experiences to capitalism.

If he has forged the concept of 'real utopias' it is in opposition to two dominant ways of linking the present to the future: the 'real realism' according to which 'the possibility of changing the world has lost all meaning' and 'imaginary utopism', which is a simple critique of what exists. In contrast with these two approaches, sterile according to Wright, the approach in terms of 'real utopias' is a search for realistic utopias in that they have already been implemented at a small scale, or that their 'social feasibility' has been deeply thought out but has yet to be tested. This approach is an 'evidence-based social science', which works to 'collect data on real utopic projects, to analyse the variations in the results and to try and understand the conditions for success and failure' (Wright 2010). But he specifies how such an 'evidence-based social science' cannot be confused with the Duflo style randomised control trials, because randomised sampling is not applicable to real utopia projects, which engage a process of institutional construction deployed at a scale and a temporality that is imperceptible by this technique.

## Conclusion

In the era of management by objectives and the obligation of results as in the utilitarian era of Dickens, these are difficult times for the promoters of an emancipatory vision of education, concerned by social justice rather than management performance. How can social sciences help? By endeavouring to re-establish a historical contingence and a sociological density to voluntarily imperious 'facts', but also to minority utopias, which are too often excluded from the field of possibles even though they have occurred or still exist. In other words, it is by sharpening the critique of a social reality which positions itself as necessary, that social sciences must differentiate themselves from government knowledge and their dominant political imagination. As Bourdieu wrote, it is up to them to create 'the social conditions of a collective production of realistic utopias' (Bourdieu 2001). To banish Mr Gradgrind's demons, which are facts and figures, there is the option offered by Dickens, for whom the alternative universe to bureaucratic hell is the circus. Critical social sciences offer another option, no doubt less poetic – but we hope – as creative: in opposition to necessity and fatalism, to produce 'a knowledge of the probable in order to make the possible come true'.[7]

## Notes

1  Online. Available at https://traces.revues.org/5606 [Accessed 10 April 2016].
2  'It removes the subjectivity from decision making' (Camp 1989: 15).
3  According to a recent manual published by AFNOR (French Standards Association), benchmarking opposes NRIH 'not re-invented here' to NIH. The first is displayed 'with arrogance', the second 'with pride' (Achard and Hermel 2010: 119–122).
4  Interview by the author in 2009 in Ithaca (New York, USA).
5  Taken from *Best Practice Benchmarking: the path to excellence*, communication by R. Camp as the director of the Best Practice Institute, 2010 (private archive).
6  From *Payment in Kind*, *Quality Progress*, April 1989, pp. 16–20, p. 19.
7  This is the objective pursued by a collective of researchers, which launched in October 2014 a 'call for a forum on critical social sciences', which was held on 17 January 2015 in Paris https://lectures.revues.org/9396 [Accessed 10 April 2016].

## References

Achard, P. and Hermel, L. (2010). *Le Benchmarking*, Paris: AFNOR.
Banerjee, A. and Duflo, E. (2009). L'approche expérimentale en économie du développement. *Revue d'économie politique*, 5: 691–726.
Baschet, J. (2014). *Adieux au capitalisme: autonomie, société du bien vivre et multiplicité des mondes*. Paris: La Découverte.
Bourdieu, P. (2001). *Contre-Feux 2*. Paris: Raisons d'agir.
Bruno, I. (2009). The "Indefinite Discipline" of Competitiveness: benchmarking as a neoliberal technology of government. *Minerva*, 47(3), 261–280.
Bruno, I. (2013a). Le Malcolm Baldrige National Quality Award: des "gourous" aux "missionnaires" de la qualité. *Sociétés contemporaines*, 89: 47–71.

Bruno, I. (2013b). "Faire taire les incrédules". Essai sur les figures du pouvoir bureaucratique à l'ère du benchmarking, in Hibou B. (ed.). *La bureaucratisation néolibérale*. Paris: La Découverte.

Bruno, I. and Didier, E. (2013). Benchmarking. L'État sous pression statistique. Paris: La Découverte. Available at: http://www.editions-zones.fr/spip.php?page=lyberplayer&id_article=171 [Accessed 20 November 2014].

Bruno, I., Didier, E. and Prévieux, J. (2014). Statactivisme. Comment lutter avec des nombres. Paris: La Découverte. Available at: http://www.editions-zones.fr/spip.php?page=lyberplayer&id_article=184 [Accessed 20 November 2014].

Bruno, I., Didier, E. and Vitale, T. (eds). (2014). Statactivism: state restructuring, financial capitalism and statistical mobilizations. *Partecipazione e Conflitto. The Open Journal of Sociopolitical Studies*, 7(2). Available at: http://siba-ese.unisalento.it/index.php/paco/issue/view/1248 [Accessed 20 November 2014].

Camp, R. (1989). *Benchmarking: the search for industry best practices that lead to superior performance*. Milwaukee: Quality Press.

Chauffaut, D. (ed.). (2012). Innovations et expérimentations sociales. *Informations sociales*, 174.

Citton, Y. (2010). *Mythocratie: storytelling et imaginaire de gauche*. Paris, Editions Amsterdam.

Daston, L. and Galison, P. (2007). *Objectivity*. New York: Zone Books.

Desrosières, A. (1998). *The politics of large numbers: a history of statistical reasoning*. Cambridge, MA: Harvard University Press.

Desrosières, A. (2003). Managing the economy, the state, the market and statistics, in Porter T. and Ross D. (eds). *The Cambridge History of Science volume 7. Modern Social and Behavioral Sciences*. Cambridge: Cambridge University Press.

Desrosières, A. (2014). *Prouver et gouverner: une analyse politique des statistiques publiques*. Paris: La Découverte.

Dickens, C. (1994). *Hard Times*, London: Penguin Books.

Foucault, M. (2004). *Sécurité, territoire, population. Cours au Collège de France. 1977–1978*. Paris: EHESS/Gallimard/Seuil [(2007). *Security, Territory, Population: Lectures at the College De France, 1977–1978*. New York: Palgrave Macmillan.

Genel, K. (2013). L'autorité des faits: Horkheimer face à la fermeture des possibles. *Tracés*, 24: 107–119. Available at: http://traces.revues.org/5658 [Accessed 20 November 2014].

Gomel, B. and Severin, E. (2009). Expérimenter pour décider? Le RSA en débat, *Document de travail du CEE*, 119. Available at: http://www.cee-recherche.fr/publications/document-de-travail/experimenter-pour-decider-le-rsa-en-debat [Accessed 20 November 2014].

Jany-Catrice, F. (2012). *La performance totale: nouvel esprit du capitalisme?*, Villeneuve d'Ascq: Presses universitaires du Septentrion.

Jeanpierre, L., Nicodème, F. and Saint-Germier, P. (eds) (2013). Réalité(s) du possible en sciences humaines et sociales. *Tracés*, 24. Available at: http://traces.revues.org/5606 [Accessed 20 November 2014].

Labrousse, A. (2010). Nouvelle économie du développement et essais cliniques randomisés: une mise en perspective d'un outil de preuve et de gouvernement. *Revue de la régulation*, 7. Available at: http://regulation.revues.org/7818 [Accessed 20 November 2014].

L'Horty, Y. and Petit, P. (2010). Évaluation aléatoire et expérimentations sociales, document de travail du CEE, 135. Available at: http://www.cee-recherche.fr/publications/document-de-travail/evaluation-aleatoire-et-experimentations-sociales [Accessed 20 November 2014].

Marks, H.M. (1997). *The Progress of Experiment: science and therapeutic reform in the United States. 1900–1990.* Cambridge: Cambridge University Press.

Marks, H.M. (2010). What does evidence do? Histories of therapeutic research, in Bonah C. *et al.* (eds). *Harmonizing Drugs: standards in 20th century pharmaceutical history.* Paris: Éditions Glyph.

Monnier, E. (1987). *Évaluations de l'action des pouvoirs publics. Du projet au bilan.* Economica: Paris.

Normand, R. (2011). *Gouverner la réussite scolaire: une arithmétique politique des inégalités.* Berne: Peter Lang, Presses de l'Ecole Normale Supérieure.

Scott, J.C. (1990). *Domination and the Arts of Resistance: hidden transcripts.* New Haven: Yale University Press.

Scott, J.C. (2009). *The Art of Not Being Governed: An Anarchist History of Upland Southeast Asia.* New Haven: Yale University Press.

Skornicki, A. (2008). Fin de la violence ou fin de l'utopie? La gouvernementalité entre libéralisme et socialisme. *Labyrinthe*, 29: 17–27. Available at: http://labyrinthe.revues.org/3413 [Accessed 20 November 2014].

Spenlehauer, V. (1998). L'évaluation des politiques publiques, avatar de la planification, PhD Dissertation, University Pierre Mendès-France of Grenoble. Available at: https://tel.archives-ouvertes.fr/tel-00342592 [Accessed 20 November 2014].

Vercauteren, D. (2011). *Micropolitique des groupes: pour une écologie des pratiques collectives.* Paris: Les Prairies ordinaires.

Wright, E.O. (2010). *Envisioning Real Utopias.* New York: Verso.

# Chapter 10

# Compliance and contestation in the neoliberal university

## Reflecting on the identities of UK social scientists

*Alan Cribb, Sharon Gewirtz and Aniko Horvath*[1]

The UK higher education (HE) system, driven by the neoliberal project of successive governments, has seen significant reforms to its financing and structure in recent years. Designed to subject the sector more directly to the rigours of market competition, these reforms have prompted concerns about rising levels of student debt, a deterioration in the working conditions of academics, the replacement of traditional public sector values with a preoccupation with profitability and league table positioning and the increased prevalence of corrupt practices. Although student and university staff protests against these reforms have been stronger and longer lasting than anticipated, and many social movements have formed around academia to challenge current transformations,[2] these have not been very successful in impeding or reversing them. Furthermore, despite having produced a substantial critical literature on HE reform, UK social scientists do not seem to have been very effective in resisting HE neoliberalisation, and in many cases could be said to be relatively compliant – even complicit – with the very measures critiqued in the literature.

This chapter discusses this seemingly puzzling contradiction. Searching for answers, we reflect on the changing working conditions and experiences of UK social scientists and consider their implications for the possibility of critical social science scholarship and action. In doing so, we hope to stimulate discussion about the potential relevance of the analysis in other European settings.[3] The working assumption is that understanding the potential contribution of critical social science depends upon understanding how the working conditions of social scientists shape both their capacity to act and the kinds of academic and civic virtues that are encouraged and valued. The chapter is based on a narrative analysis of 22 academic life histories conducted during 2014 and early 2015. However, before turning to that analysis, some contextual detail on the changing landscape of British HE is required.

## The changing landscape of UK higher education

At the end of 2010 the UK Conservative–Liberal Democrat coalition government decided to radically restructure funding for English universities.[4] It was announced that by the 2014/2015 academic year, government funding for teaching would be discontinued for the disciplines of business, law, social sciences, arts and humanities. For science, technology, engineering and mathematics – 'teaching that cannot be covered by tuition fees alone' (Higher Education Funding Council for England 2015) – funding was reduced, but not terminated. To make up for the shortfall, the cap on student tuition fees was raised from £3,375 to £9,000 per year. The government predicted that most academic programmes would not charge the £9,000 cap, but a figure within the £6,000–7,000 range. Despite this, by 2011 most universities announced that they would raise their fees to the £9,000 maximum. In response, protests and university sit-ins were organised across the country, requesting that fee increases be reversed and government funding restored. For months thereafter, university fees, student debt, academic freedom and autonomy, and the role of universities in society took centre stage in public and academic debates. Nevertheless, the coalition government – under its budget-rebalancing and deficit reduction plans – moved forward with structural changes.[5]

Other changes, no less important, were concomitantly implemented. In 2012 the government opened the sector to privatisation: on the one hand, by removing the cap on student numbers and allowing tuition fees to triple, they stimulated the 'internal privatisation' of the sector (McGettigan 2013). On the other hand, by allowing the formation of new corporate institutional structures that made it much easier for 'external' money to enter the sector and extract profits, the government opened the sector to 'external privatisation' and marketisation.

By early 2014, tuition fees and student debt were not the sector's only concern. Several universities had already discontinued academic programmes deemed to be 'non-profitable'; made hundreds of academics redundant in the name of 'efficiency savings'; introduced zero-hour contracts for many of their teaching staff, thereby casualising academic work even further; renegotiated and reduced academic pensions; increased top management salaries and bonuses; brought in consultancy firms to help restructure universities to be more 'productive'; partially replaced university management with people from large corporations and/or US/Australian for-profit universities; began changing their governance and legal/corporate structures to enable more investment and borrowing;[6] and embarked on large scale real-estate developments, to 'improve the student experience' and 'provide value for money'.[7]

Suddenly, corporate practices that had previously been rare in the sector were being implemented at a dizzying pace. Universities were 'disposing' of whole programmes and departments by 'selling' (transferring) them to 'competitors'.[8] Management at various universities searched for 'buy-ups' that would enhance their academic prestige and research and, according to some, prime location 'real-estate portfolios'.[9] At the other end, the new private providers that entered the 'market' were allowed to enrol students receiving state financed tuition fees and maintenance loans. As a result, these newly created institutions expanded on a breathtaking scale, increasing initial student populations from a total of six to ten to as many as several thousands in a matter of one or two years, sometimes by employing fraudulent practices.[10] Government officials – not having proper regulatory and supervisory frameworks in place – ended up in the position of barely being able to influence how taxpayer money was used. Based on this, analysts argue that 'as universities and colleges are forced to operate in commercial terrain, it is basic business imperatives that come to the fore. Our habits of thought about higher education are no longer appropriate for this new terrain' (McGettigan 2013: ix).

However, given the diversity of institutional structures and conceptions of what universities are for, focusing only on the business and financial aspects would miss some of the other important processes that structure British HE. As Ken Jones argues, to focus solely on policy or finances as the object of study 'seems to overly privilege the actions and projects of government and of organizations that contribute supportively to its programmes – and, thus, *a priori* to decentre other social actors' (Jones 2011: 210). Jones suggests focusing on 'educational contestation' and the range of social actors that participate in it, exploring 'the intellectual and political resources with which they work'. In his view, such a focus might lead to a stronger understanding of the politics of educational policy-making, and 'the ways in which key decisions, strategies, projects, and achievements bear the marks of contestation, and express an orientation – perhaps accommodating, perhaps uncompromising – towards other actors and projects' (Jones 2011: 211). Such a lens has the potential to illuminate the many 'unintended' consequences that have emerged in response to educational contestation following the 2010 policy changes, creating a complex web of networks of interests, new forms of institutional structures that reach well beyond mainstream academia, and new forms of cooperative/fragmenting labour practices and (global) social organising that disrupt and alter initiatives of those in office. Yet, parallel to these developments, there is also a discourse of disillusionment and fatigue and a feeling of powerlessness within academia, reflecting what Jones describes as the 'pattern of continuing but low-level and only sporadically organized discontent' in England, which is 'increasingly at odds with the response to educational reform in other countries' (Jones 2011: 193). The research reported here represents an attempt to contribute to Jones' project of 're-centring' other social actors, with a specific focus on academics working in social science disciplines.

## Analytic approach

As noted earlier, this chapter is based on a narrative analysis of 22 academic life histories.[11] Our analytical approach is influenced by Vieda Skultans (1997, 1998), who argues that similarities found in life histories revolving around similar events derive from both shared histories and 'membership of a symbolic and textual community' (Skultans 1997: 761). For Skultans, '[n]arratives of lives bring together the past, present and future' and, in her participants' narratives,

> coherence was constructed not only internally by the relationship of different elements of the narrative to each other, but also by relating the personal narrative to other shared narrative... In trying to make sense of their lives and communicate them to others, narrators sought shelter for their life histories within widely shared literary traditions.
>
> (Skultans 1997: 762, 765)

In our research, narratives of individual academic lives were constructed primarily as dialogues not grounded in broader literary traditions (although 'campus novels' and television series have had a long and popular history in depicting academic life in Britain),[12] but rather in the shared narratives found in social science literature. To understand how social scientists' strong criticism of HE reforms might co-exist with practices that comply with, and often support, the very same policies they criticise, we use our data to interrogate disjunctures between these broader shared narratives and everyday academic practices, and the way such practices are recollected in the life history narratives.

Our approach is also informed by conceptual lenses drawn from work that, like Jones's, takes a 'bottom up' approach to policy analysis by focusing on the experiences and perspectives of social actors whose voices tend to be marginalised in top-down accounts of political and social change, in particular the work of Wacquant (2012, 2013) on 'actually existing neoliberalism', Stef Jansen (2014) on statecraft, and Harms (2011) on the strategic mobilisation of binary discourse in everyday political acts. We begin by relating a widespread 'simple story' about shifting academic identities and virtues that circulates within broader social science narratives about HE policy change, showing how it is also evident within the narratives of our participants. We then go on to use our data to highlight some of the inadequacies of this 'simple story'. In the final section of the chapter, we explicitly problematise, and use our data to try to explain the relatively diffuse and fragmented nature of organised opposition to the neoliberalisation of HE among UK academics.

## The 'simple story'

A 'simple story' found in widespread critiques of managerialism and market-isation in HE, including our own previous accounts,[13] is one of the erosion of traditional and the emergence of new academic identities and virtues. In a nut-shell, the story is one of dispositions of collegiality and the disinterested pursuit of truth being replaced by dispositions of entrepreneurialism and an orientation towards social impact/public relations. These accounts are frequently couched in a neo-Foucauldian language of governmentality, academic self-regulation and subjectification. In what follows we do not suggest the story is wrong, only that it is simple. There is no doubt that there have been major changes to the HE sector – with implications for what counts as valued identities and dispositions – including: the erosion of the very idea of the public sector and service, the corporatisation of universities, the fostering of institutional com-petition, the increased salience of the branding of institutions and of units and individuals, and sustained pressures towards cost effectiveness and auditability, leading to increased bureaucracy and use of technologies, the intensification of labour and the reduced salience of face to face or local relationships.

The 'simple story' also points to an important change in the relationship between universities and governments – 30 years ago students and staff, including vice chancellors, joined together to protest against government cuts to HE funding. There is very little evidence of this in recent years, and fur-ther, there has been a very conspicuous strengthening of the alliance between senior university managers and official government policies and discourses. Thirty years ago the academic as critically subversive of the government was a legitimised academic identity within the university. Now such an identity is increasingly incompatible with being a good employee. However, this simple story needs qualification and elaboration, and we will turn to this in the next part of this chapter. But before doing so, in what follows, we will use some extracts from our interviews to illustrate how elements of this simple story were evident – and frequently mobilised – in our life history narratives.

Quite often these narrative 'recollections' of the past revolve around and are coupled with 'narratives of loss'. Most of our interviewees reflected in one form or another on how managerial technologies – for example, performance development reviews, strategic investment initiatives – harness people's sense of self-worth to institutional goals and produce diverse forms of compliance:

> We all have to have these performance and development review meet-ings every year where you're supposed [to] discuss your work load and what you're gonna do next year.... And I think it's very clever the way they do it, because academics in lots of ways are quite pre-programmed to be good and to want to show how good we are. So you put down everything you've done last year and everything you want to do next

year... and you want your head of whatever it is to say how clever you are 'cause you've got [this] grant and you got this paper published and you developed this new module and da...da...da...da... But of course that's the wrong way to approach it if you don't want them to ask you to do twice as much next year.

(...)

So everybody's focused on trying to get this [strategic investment] money and the only way to get it is to come up with some brand new wonderful idea that they might want to support. Then they might give us the money, but you then create a whole new set of work that you have to do and you still don't have what you needed to underpin the work that you were doing in the first place.

(Ruth)

What these quotes capture very powerfully is the insidious way such measures seem to colonise the souls of academics, producing compliance and implicating them in their own oppression. The data also show how corporatisation works at the level of the individual academic, making it a part of their identity that they need to do better:

[A]t the same time the sort of pressure and the sense of forever being assessed and therefore watched, and the sort of feelings of anxiety and persecution and not good enoughness that can come up, I was just reminded of all that the other day.... I was looking in my email and [saw that] in preparation for the next REF[14] we have to begin to do annual tracking of our research activities. And I was thinking, oh fuck, I haven't got anything for the last year. Oh no, I've got a talk, yeah, I did that. And then I thought it's OK, I was actually sick for half of it, so phew. But you know, that pressure, the perniciousness, the toxicity of the new regimes is insane.

(Gloria)

In the new world of academia there is little space for the critically subversive academic. We are only expected to emphasise the positive. Ruth again:

People actually said to me well, the vice-principals [like to hear] good news, if you become another group of people who moan at them, then they target you for punishment, whereas if you tell them a good story about how many brilliant new ideas you've got, then they like you and give you money. That's fine, but it means that you have to keep on saying everything's wonderful when it's not.

Interviewees often also talk about the increased salience of public relations, rankings and assessments in academic life, and the resulting changing quality of relationships among staff, as well as between staff and students, with students becoming less engaged and more instrumental in their approach to university education. As Thomas put it,

> I don't know if it was caused by [the increase in fees] or it was just contemporaneous with it and caused by wider cultural things, but there was more the sort of a sense that we owe students certain things, so we need to, as providers of the service, do them in the way they would like them done. And is this because you are paying fees and you think of yourself as a customer? Never, you'd never say that explicitly, but I wonder if it's in part because there are more student feedback things now than there used to be, and these forms ultimately filter back, and there's no policing mechanism but there's a slight pressure to get the feedback higher.... And I think at a subconscious level that inflects one's decisions somewhat. It's not quite the customer is always right but it's probably not worth annoying the customer too much.

In some cases these kinds of experience are contrasted with a more favourable past. Martin talked about his experience of working in a social science department in the mid 1990s, implicitly contrasting this with the more authoritarian approaches to management that now prevail:

> [It was] very decentralized, it felt schools had a lot of power, there were no faculties, no deans, it didn't feel very managerial. I had a lot of colleagues who sort of protected us, a very democratic department.... It felt like my family rather than a place of work.

Steven remembers that in the past academics had more space and time to spend on developing their ideas into meaningful publications as opposed to the 'competent but mechanical work' that is so often encountered currently:

> one thing that I feel, and I know most of my colleagues feel, is that it's hard to see when we could ever have the time to do any... reading that is not immediately on the task in hand. Whatever it is that makes for good intellectual work, it's... meditating on things, coming at them from an unusual angle, seeing connections, finding significance in detail that have been in front of your eyes for a long time but somehow the moment wasn't right for you to see it. That kind of intellectual creativity depends upon reading around, it depends upon space, depends upon conversation... And if your work is so focused all the time... preparing that bit of teaching, preparing that grant application... I think the danger is of producing competent but mechanical work... And I say it

to be provocative, but some degree of idleness is in the end essential to the focus that produces very good work. And because we've got busier, because the external requirements of measurement have got greater, because professionalization is such a strong internalized force, I think, it's become harder to find the space for that to happen.

Heather talks about a change in the nature of relationships between students and lecturers and a change in the sort of person attracted to an academic career:

[When I was a student] you would knock on the professor's door… and they would invite you in for a cup of tea, and although it was very formal… they absolutely wanted you to be there… Now, I think a lot of people have been attracted into academia that never would have before. Career academics… not academic academics.

This dominant account of what is happening to academic lives and identities suggests a reconfiguration of academic virtue, which has to do with being productive, bringing in money, promoting the university's brand and the brand of one's own work, being ready to compete as a department, as a member of the university, and ultimately as an individual.

## Disrupting the simple story

Our findings suggest that there are good reasons to be sceptical about this simple story. In what follows we argue that the contrast between an idealised past and a corrupted present is crude and misleading in important respects and that the story of a neoliberal juggernaut crushing everything of value in its wake and colonising the souls of academics is too one-dimensional and overly deterministic. We will use our data to show that academic identities[15] operate in different intersecting spheres each of which creates different possibilities for compliance and/or contestation. Underlying our account is a caution about neo-Foucauldian analyses that inform so much of the critical literature on HE and that are implicit in some of our respondents' narratives. As Wacquant (2013: 8) suggests, such analyses can confuse the ideology of neoliberalism with its sociology. Arguably these somewhat homogenised portrayals of academia and the virtues of a 'good academic' stem from some of the flaws to be found in governmentality theories which treat neoliberalism as a ' "generalised normativity"… that "tends to structure and organize not only the actions of the governing, but also the conduct of the governed themselves" and even their self-conception according to principles of competition, efficiency and utility' (Wacquant 2012: 70). Our approach to understanding the 'neoliberal university' falls closer to that of Wacquant and others, who view the neoliberal project as more 'open-ended, plural and adaptable' (Peck 2008: 3).

Although there are examples in the life history narratives of the past being idealised, there are often also examples of poor practice, either experienced first-hand or witnessed – examples of lack of support, neglect, bullying, bad teaching and overwork – and a 'pick and choose' system in which if you found a good mentor it might have worked for you, otherwise not.[16]

> The quality of teaching was very bad. There were only about twenty undergraduates for my year, and twenty staff, so it's interesting that the lecturers didn't have very much to do but they still didn't manage to do it very well...
>
> (David)

> In terms of my academic career, everything before the age of 35 I remember as extremely negative. Incredibly horrible things used to happen [in the '60s, '70s and early '80s] to women, to junior people, things you couldn't imagine happening now, and the atmosphere was very hostile for all sorts of people, including black people... just like sort of straightforward racism.
>
> (John)

Other narratives challenge the image of an idealised past not from a student-experience perspective, but from a management perspective, arguing that academics used to be 'unproductive' and got away with 'doing nothing' for decades, so they had to be held to account – 'managed' – to start doing their jobs. An excerpt from Donald's life history, a university manager and academic himself, exemplifies well this type of narrative:

> British academics of the '60s were more cosseted than even in the '40s and '50s. You'd written a book that got you the professorship and you never publish again, it was a well-known syndrome. So of course when any of that cake was taken away the reaction was quite strong.... So they'd all been moaning, but at somewhere like where I worked, given that they weren't being made redundant, they were being propped up by the income generating activities of our management, then I think eventually most of them would say yeah, OK, maybe it's not so bad after all.

Where accounts of a better past do feature, rather than taking them at face value it might sometimes be more accurate to view them as imagined pasts functioning as a means of re-asserting how things ought to be. In her study of the lives and experiences of academic biomedical scientists, Kerry Holden goes further, arguing that narratives of imagined pasts – lamentations over the loss of a 'golden age' – can play a depoliticising role, operating not only as a means of building a secure and cohesive identity in troubled times but also as a means of motivating 'people to apply their labour to academic science without challenging the conditions in which they work' (Holden 2015: 42).[17]

Just as the past was not perhaps as rosy as some of the accounts suggest, so the present is in some respects less bleak than is conveyed by the simple story. The data – and our own experience – suggest a much more complex picture reflecting the fact that processes of neoliberalisation are not complete, the structural pressures and discursive influences are variegated; and there are multiple possibilities for agency and/or for counter discourses. For example, the introduction of successive research assessment exercises in the UK can be read as a negative move that creates a 'factory model' of academic production in which academics are put under immense pressure to churn out publications conforming to narrowly defined quality expectations at regular intervals whether or not they have anything of real significance to say. However, there are also more positive readings of these exercises. Pat Sikes (2009: 135), for example, has shown how, for colleagues working in new universities in the 1990s/2000s, the Research Assessment Exercise (RAE) 'brought recognition and self-affirmation for those who want to be, and be seen as being, researchers' in a context in which teaching had previously been privileged. In an analogous, although contrasting, move within the heavily research oriented Russell Group universities, a greater emphasis on teaching has been brought about by the raising of the tuition fee in 2010 and the increased salience of the National Student Survey, which ranks universities according to how satisfied their students are. Like the RAE this instrument has been widely castigated for its corrosive effects on academic work, resulting, as one critic puts it, in 'the subordination of education and scholarship to the arbitrary imperative of student satisfaction' and a far less challenging educational experience for students who are constituted by the survey as passive consumers rather than active, engaged, independent learners (Furedi, 2012). On the other hand, however, the keen attention paid by university senior managers to the survey results has served to confer legitimacy on the kind of teaching-focused identities that previously tended to be marginalised in Russell Group institutions. For example, Martin was turned down for promotion twice, he believes, at least in part because of his focus on teaching. But then: 'The sector got more interested in teaching, and therefore I, who had always been very interested in working with students, became able to have a career.'

Similarly, the recent focus on measuring and rewarding 'social and economic impact' can and has been criticised for reinforcing an instrumentalist approach to research and teaching. However, there are also positive stories to tell about how this move has lent validation and recognition to forms of community outreach and scholar-activism that might once have gone unnoticed and unrewarded by university managers.

More generally, despite the many pressures towards conformity and the internalisation of market-oriented norms, and despite the multiple processes of bureaucratisation and technologisation that keep academics apart and weighed down by a continuous flow of seemingly pointless tasks, many UK academics tell more uplifting stories – of inspirational teaching and academic role-modelling, of colleagues' extreme dedication to students, of supportive mentoring, collegiality, sociability and friendliness and a spirit of critical dialogue all being alive and well in their departments and institutions. In other words, there are many positive currents that suggest the alleged neoliberal takeover is far from complete.

Moreover, the fact that academic identities operate in different spheres makes for complex patternings and combinations of compliance and contestation. These spheres include: the content of academic writing and 'professing'; day to day practices at a micro level, for example, relationships with students and immediate colleagues, and comportment within teaching, administration and research projects; institutional citizenship/service activities; and extra-institutional or national or international activism. An academic might be critical and subversive in one sphere, for example, their academic writing, while fully compliant or at least unquestioning in another, for example, in the sphere of institutional citizenship, or while acting in ways that are uncollegial in their day to day relationships with colleagues or that reflect an ethos of competitive individualism. David's story reflects well such contradictions. A critical scholar in his writing and in his socially engaged projects, he describes how we can nevertheless fall prey to self-regarding, careerist orientations:

> I was put in for early promotion for reader, and I was turned down... And I wasn't very good at [dealing with it]. I was given it the next year, but it didn't matter to me because I'd been, you know, turned down. And [very soon after this episode] I took a professorship at a different university... and to keep me, my own university offered me a professorship, but it was too late. So I'm quite egotistical and it's easy now, because I've got a posh job, but... I don't think in hindsight it's very good behaviour.

There are many examples in our data of social scientists engaging in multiple modes and spheres of contestation including: local micro-resistances, for example, subverting or inflecting bureaucratic demands, or ironic distancing combined with superficial compliance; propagating, sustaining and/or recovering counter-discourses, for example, within research groups, departments or more diffuse academic networks; refusals, protests and industrial action; and the creation of alternative spaces with non-dominant norms either outside of conventional HE boundaries or within pockets of HE institutions. For example, George decided early on not to have a partner and children and take only part-time jobs to free up time to engage in alternative initiatives. His life has been extremely precarious; at one point he was homeless for 8 months being unable to earn enough to pay rent. However, he says that, although he is part of the 'ever-growing academic precariat' with all the resulting anxieties, he at least is free to do his activist-scholar work. He also talks about doing things 'under the radar' in the university:

> [T]he victories amount to what you can get in under the wire, and I was taught a very good lesson by a massive inspiration who works at X University... he said we are getting these emails about the university's new mission statement and we know it's a lot of nonsense so we ignore them. Never ignore them. You can write one sentence different, because most folk are going to ignore them, so if you can change one sentence you can make a massive difference. And they put a sentence into the university's mission statement, that said something about the university's public democratic mission to the community, and the next ten years they pointed to that sentence and were able to use rooms in the university for free, and bring the community in that they wouldn't have been able to have done otherwise...

> Everyone says that critical thinking is important, is part of your employability agenda... so there's one where you can get stuff in under the wire in recent times, because if you get to teach critical thinking you can actually get to encourage people... and even if you've touched one person in the class that's going away saying I'm just a little bit thinking differently [that means that] there is room to do something.

Others we spoke to have left academia altogether. For example, Daniel tried to be a full-time academic, but became disaffected after a financial mismanagement case and now does part time work in further education, to save time for his projects, for example, working with/for homeless people. As he explains,

> I never had any debts because of having a cautious approach to money... so making decisions hasn't been based on finances. And the things I valued didn't cost me much money. The relationships that I've been in I haven't had children. So the responsibilities that I've had have been fairly minimal, so I haven't had to commit to things that would incur debt or put one in a position where you had no other choice than to take on loans or additional responsibilities financially.

Angela and Alan also left academia entirely and now make their livings by giving paid talks, working as journalists, and consulting – also to leave time for their projects that are related to HE. Silvia permanently left the UK and now works as an academic abroad. After experimenting with alternative educational projects and engaging in union politics to resist changes, she ended up being disillusioned with fellow UK academics who did not resist and were not, as she saw it, sufficiently self-reflexive when it came to their own environment.

Jonathan, Martin and Sophie tried to change the system from within, creating an innovative university-wide curriculum project that sought to inculcate more collectivist and critical pedagogies. In direct opposition to the culture of passivity and commodification of education that they attributed to the National Student Survey and the wider HE market, their project positioned 'students' as engaged and active scholars who can – and are expected to be – equals of academics in research and learning. But, when this became increasingly difficult and tuition fees rose, they moved beyond the walls of academia creating a new extra-institutional HE project and establishing close links and networks with other, similar movements both in the UK and abroad. They all still work for mainstream universities but – as Martin sees it –for his actions to be consistent with his ideals, 'to be part of a collective political project', he needs to commit 'professional suicide and make [himself] invisible', by giving up his high-ranking position(s) within the university: 'I'm... going into the shadows, sharing a little office here. I used to have a big office on the top floor, but this is where I want to be now, in the shadow. Working towards sabotaging neoliberalism.'

Jim and Simon describe their involvement in HE campaigns and movements that use social science methodologies to produce evidence to challenge the premises of HE policy initiatives. These movements have not been successful in disrupting the marketisation and financialisation of UK HE but, despite feeling very disillusioned, they do carry on networking and building new activities and projects designed to bring about positive change. As Jim explained, his most important question now is how to mobilise academics around certain issues:

> One of the things I'd learned is that if you lose a battle and you are kind of pressed down, the way for you to break out is to form alliances outside... and there are some things you can see coming and you are never going to push them back, but you can create a niche beyond it; the way to do it is to mobilise other people with information. It helps to have a particular target, like when you know that a policy is going to come out, you can to some extent predict what's in it, so you write your response before you get it and then when you get it you check your response, and because you've done quite a bit of background preparation you are immediately out with a thing...

Paul and Karen are involved in broader social movements beyond the walls of academia, while Thomas, Roger and Julie tell stories of small scale resistance – such as not letting managers colonise their time. As Thomas explained, in his situation,

> The outer pressure of family life erodes one's capacity to work at home or at the weekends, and then there's the sort of inner pressure of academic life which would push in the other direction. And in my own case I think probably the outer pressure of family life has sort of crushed the academic pressure, so I tend not to work in the evenings or at weekends...

Roberta, Jack and Karen practised another kind of contestation from within. In different ways, each has used their positions in university management to promote and enact at least some of their educational ideals. As Karen put it,

> If you don't have a professorial title then you need to go to look at a leadership management role, and [my experience in academia is that] having a title is great but having access to [a] budget is even better. So having the budget and having the positional authority I think is, for what I want to do, which is ensure that equality issues are embedded, so actually having the budget would make me do more on that than a professorial position.

## Exploring tensions between contestation and compliance in narratives and practice

Making the simple story part of the assumptive world of HE scholarship can become a recipe for defeatism and a self-fulfilling prophecy. If we continually reproduce the pessimistic representations reflected in the simple story, we risk failing to reflect the kinds of practices represented in the previous section, which are making a difference through, for instance, 'under-the-radar' actions and initiatives. On the other hand, there are dangers associated with celebrating complexity and playing up the significance of refusals and contestations, which, in effect, are often localised one-on-one initiatives that are no real match for the concerted and highly efficient efforts of neoliberal politicians and university executives. For in doing so, we may end up obscuring the value of arguably stronger forms of resistance, for example, mass refusal to comply or mass industrial action.

In this final section, therefore, we want to use our data to try to make sense of what Jones refers to as 'low level' and 'sporadic' organised discontent among UK academics. In doing so we draw on Set Jansen's analysis (Jansen 2014) as to why people sometimes 'yearn for the state'. According to Jansen, critical social science scholarship often posits the state as an imposed externality, reinforcing the assumed boundary between 'state' and 'society'. As a result, much scholarship focuses on how people 'evade' state structures, and does not sufficiently explore peoples' practices of 'non-evasion of state grids' (Jansen 2014: 238–241). Jansen suggests that in order to understand people's 'strong yearnings for "normal lives" and, as part of that, for incorporation into a "functioning state" ' researchers need to reformulate currently existing conceptualisations of 'state-making around a singular "standard grid" into a more multi-layered, dynamic and plural understanding' where grids can 'capture the intimate ways in which efforts to restore routines of "normal life" are implicated in the production and functioning of ordering frameworks' (Jansen 2014: 243). Jansen's findings show that when the people he studied sought incorporation into state grids, they wanted it 'on their terms, and yearned-for "normal lives" were projected to be calibrated by a degree of predictability. Grid evasion existed in tension with grid desire' (Jansen 2014: 255).

Jansen developed his analysis to make sense of the 'hope for the state' he observed among the inhabitants of a wartime Sarajevan suburb in the 1990s, which contrasted starkly with the narratives of anti-statist resistance foregrounded in many anthropological studies. This approach can also, we suggest, helpfully illuminate the very different context of UK HE, in which most of our interviewees, although unsatisfied with and critical of various aspects of academic working conditions and present-day HE institutional structures, did remain within the system and – given the option – in one form or other wished to continue to stay in mainstream HE. If we examine our data through this lens, we observe that academics – experiencing the 'disruptions' generated by policy and institutional restructurings – often tried to re-establish rhythms and trajectories of 'normal lives' by creating new/ alternative grids on which they could rely. However, in order to reduce precariousness in their lives, they also sought to connect their grids 'upward and outward into "institutional statecraft" ' (Jansen 2014: 257).

When student fees were increased in 2010 and new providers were allowed to enter HE, practices of institutional incorporation for staff and students suddenly started to change across the sector. Some academics – more often those with secure contracts and/or in the old, wealthy universities – remained comfortable with the changing practices of 'incorporation' because, for them, it meant an increased level of security and wealth transfer. Many others – most often those with precarious contracts and/or in former polytechnics and smaller universities – felt that the changes were threatening their existence. As David put it,

> My colleagues were all really scared. What had happened [when the cap on student numbers was lifted] was that half our students hadn't turned up, fifty percent of the students of the entire social science faculty. So if this happened again and again we'd have to sack half our staff, so these people were scared, and when people are worried about losing their jobs, they can behave very differently.

As our interviews indicate, this divergence in attitudes became an impediment to developing alternative 'grids' that could have underpinned a more concerted and collaborative effort at the national level. Jim reflects on these contradictions:

> Lots of academics were worried about, well if we don't have fees we'll have cuts... and that's when we lost some academics. But... wanting to have fees, and not to take cuts, would be for the professoriate to wish to be in the top ten percent rather than being satisfied with lower incomes. And... quite a lot of people didn't like those aspects [the prospect of cuts to incomes and/or jobs].... So it was almost as if representing the students as consumers contained contempt for students, whereas it wasn't students who were becoming consumers because of their instrumental attitude, we were complicit in their instrumentalisation.

This excerpt highlights how an idealised understanding of what 'students' should be was linked with a newly established oppositional category, the 'consumer', constructing and reifying a binary divide between the (ideal-typical) student and (ideal-typical) consumer. Such oppositional categories helped transpose academic–student relationships to a more instrumental level, and – as Jim pointed out – made it possible for many academics to accept the high fees and withdraw from contestational movements. Thus, academics who continued to feel secure in terms of institutional and financial support often withdrew from such movements after initial involvement, leading to the weakening and fragmentation of these networks. Others, whose precariousness increased, either did everything in their power to improve their position (e.g. changed jobs to be in large and well-funded research universities), or formed new cross-institutional and cross-national/international alliances to reach out to others and reduce precariousness. However, most of these movements did not seek a total 'evasion' of state grids: many academics involved kept their jobs in mainstream universities and worked to develop new movements and structures that at some point could be linked back and 'incorporated' into institutional grids. But, they wanted this to happen on their own terms and by challenging existing norms and structures. One good example is the cooperative university movement, in which a reoccurring discussion explored how the movement could issue degrees/diplomas to participants that would be recognised by academics and employers, and thereby push the state into recognising the legitimacy of such alternative structures, and – possibly – lead to a rethinking of university fee policies.

Interesting patterns also emerged when we did a keyword search in our interviews for the term 'normal/normality' and then – to understand contextual uses –analysed the narrative sections where these keywords were embedded. The results indicate that in many cases 'normality' was located outside of what was happening in universities or the everyday lives of academics. The term 'normal' was used within a comparative framework that allowed academics to talk about their hopes for a 'normal life' and distance themselves from aspects of the HE system that were most objectionable. In addition, by establishing what 'normal' ought to be, they were better able to articulate their anxieties, prompted by the recent experiences of disruption in their academic lives and fears of 'falling off the grid', that is, being fired and not being able to get another job in the sector. This comparative framework was then used by interviewees to construct a narrative space for discussing both their analytical-critical engagement and their practices of compliance and contestation, without feeling as if the two were contradictory. At the same time, this framing created space to articulate what 'inside' and 'outside' meant in relation to HE, and on what grounds interviewees thought 'leaving' or 'staying' should take place. Sophie's account reflects this complex framing:

> I decided to leave, and people thought I was crazy, because I was the only one of my PhD cohort that had any stable work at all… It was hard, but I was very unhappy, and really sort of deeply depressed in that place. [But I was asked to do certain things and I felt] this just isn't appropriate, and I thought I don't want to become this person… And part of it is maybe that I am just maladapted, you do wonder this; other people seem less injured by it. And I think that's one thing I've tried to work on a lot… getting away from this wounded attachment to an image of the university which the university is clearly not… so I can work critically within it until such point as I decide not to… And I think that was a couple of years ago that I really did do a sort of taking stock because someone asked me, well why do you stay then? And I thought that's a fantastic question, as a way of gaining some perspective on the critique, because sometimes it is difficult but there are reasons that I'm here and it's useful for me to look at over time… and I think whether those have to [do] with habitus and privilege and stability and fear or whether it has to do with the fact that I think this is still a space of possibility and joy and social importance, you know, and so yeah… I think it's a combination of both.

It was those whose dissatisfaction with the system caused them to move 'outside' – either temporarily or permanently – that seemed more comfortable with making stronger arguments of contestation and evasion. However, for many of these academics, 'outside' only meant moving to 'parallel grids' – for example, the state HE system of another country, another university/ educational establishment, HE consultancy, HE journalism – and they used their positioning in these parallel structures to establish and keep 'inside' links with both mainstream and alternative HE institutions and movements. In actual practice, despite all the dissatisfactions narrated in their life histories, very few of our interviewees left the system/grid voluntarily; most needed an 'institutional push' to do so, for example, when their job was terminated, their contract expired, or they got into irresolvable tensions with heads of programmes and/or management and they felt, as Martin put it, that

> [n]ow it is not possible to be a critical, by which I mean functioning, academic, inside an English university, there is no space, it's gone. And I like to think of cracks and dialectics, but the space has been so shut down that we have to embed the institution somewhere else, in a different form.

## Conclusion

We began by highlighting the apparent contradiction between the strength of the critique of neoliberal HE reforms within UK social science scholarship and the seeming ineffectiveness of social scientists' ground-level political responses. In seeking to illuminate and explain that contradiction, we contrasted the simple story of HE change with a more complex and variegated story that gives emphasis to the multiple possibilities for, and combinations of, compliance and contestation at different times and in different spheres and places. But, while recognising this complexity, we have also sought to caution against accounts of contemporary academic practices, which celebrate complexity and thereby, either implicitly or explicitly, perhaps exaggerate the potential for small-scale, fragmented and diffuse refusals and contestations to counter the neoliberalisation of UK HE in meaningful ways.

In attempting to understand the lack of a concerted and unified organised opposition, we shifted our focus from contestation to the 'non-evasion of state grids' among critical social scientists. This helped us to see much more clearly that academic practices present a complex and interconnected pattern where there is no clear 'inside' and 'outside' as was constructed and implied in the narratives. Such binary oppositions are shared narrative devices that can help academics to establish strategic positions and construct meaningful identities (Harms 2011). But, we suggest, these binary oppositions can become essentialising and reified and might contribute to limiting the space in which such concepts can be more fully explored and deconstructed to allow for common ground to be found on which broader HE movements can be efficiently organised.

As for the relevance of our findings beyond the British context and in Europe, we think our research demonstrates the need to pay close attention to specific cases and contexts in different spheres and levels of the academy. Such an approach helps us to understand in more detail what the constraints and possibilities are for academics who are differently positioned in academia and who are working in and across different spheres of action. A detailed analysis of cases and contexts coupled with an analytic frame that acknowledges the motivational power of yearnings for 'normality' also has some explanatory potential, helping us make sense of the apparently contradictory co-existence of contestation and compliance within the social sciences.

## Acknowledgements

We are grateful to our research participants for such interesting and inspiring conversations and for giving so generously of their time to take part in the project. We would also like to thank Chris Newfield, Tania de St Croix and Joss Win for very helpful comments on an earlier draft of this chapter.

## Notes

1 The names of the authors are in alphabetical order. This is a fully co-authored chapter.
2 These include the free and cooperative university movements, 'debt' movements, and the 'rethinking economics' movement.
3 Parts of the UK picture are relatively distinctive. In particular, successive governments have made deliberate attempts to sideline critical voices in universities, deriding them as protecting public sector or producer interests, or as mindlessly oppositional in ways that suggest they should be ignored, defeated and dissolved.
4 Scotland, Wales and Northern Ireland set their own HE policies and so the funding reforms discussed below were not implemented in these jurisdictions. However, many other restructurings – brought about by marketisation – were implemented, often altering institutional structures and changing the conditions of academic work.
5 As analysts of HE finances made clear (McGettigan 2013), the government, by giving out £9,000 'income contingent repayment loans' to students and allowing universities to recruit as many students as they wished put in place a new system that in the short and medium-term was more costly than before the funding decrease and was likely to prove more expensive in the long term as well.
6 Universities UK, *Developing Future University Structures: New Funding and Legal Models*, September 2009 (Universities UK 2009).
7 Universities UK, in its report, *Where Student Fees Go*, describes: 'major capital investment[s] … in what students say matter most to them, including state-of-the-art teaching facilities, additional staff, improved libraries and flexible and informal study areas where students can work in an environment that suits them' (Universities UK 2013: 1, 5).
8 For example, Middlesex University's philosophy programme was transferred to Kingston University, so Middlesex could focus its resources on developing branch campuses overseas (McGettigan 2013).
9 One such high-profile example is the case of University College London and the Institute of Education: the two institutions 'merged' in 2014. UCL's 'acquisition' of IoE meant that they now 'managed' a school of education, consistently ranked as first in the world by QS World University Rankings, and a large portfolio of buildings located in the middle of Bloomsbury, currently among the most valuable real estate in the world.
10 Fraudulent practices were exposed by investigative journalists, not by government oversight (*The Guardian*, 14 December 2014: *Thousands of 'fake' students at UK's new higher education colleges*, http://www.theguardian.com/education/2014/dec/02/students-private-higher-education-colleges-taxpayer-subsidy-benefits-nao-loans, Times Higher Education, 30 October 2014: *Uncontrolled expansion: how private colleges grew*, https://www.timeshigher education.co.uk/features/uncontrolled-expansion-how-private-colleges-grew/2016579.article [Both accessed 2 September 2015].

11  The interviews ranged between 1 and 3 hours, with the majority lasting 2–3 hours. We interviewed academics working in English and Scottish universities, but not Wales or Northern Ireland. In order to incorporate a wide range of academic life trajectories, we also interviewed academics who had moved abroad, and/or left academia altogether. The names of all our informants were changed. To conceal identities further we decided not to indicate the types of institutions where interviewees worked.

12  For a discussion of campus novels and their film adaptations see Moseley (2007).

13  For example, see Cribb and Gewirtz (2013).

14  The REF (Research Excellence Framework, previously known as the Research Assessment Exercise) is a system of research quality assessment periodically conducted by the HE funding bodies for England, Scotland, Wales and Northern Ireland to determine the allocation of research funds to universities.

15  We use the term 'identity' not as an analytical tool, but rather as a 'category of practice' as defined by Brubaker and Cooper according to whom, identity, 'is used by "lay" actors in some (not all!) everyday settings to make sense of themselves, of their activities, of what they share with, and how they differ from, others' (Brubaker and Cooper 2000: 4).

16  The variegated picture that emerges from our interviews in part may reflect our methodology that took a holistic life history approach. That is, rather than just focusing on the working life experience of academics (which might have reproduced simple stories of loss), we also asked about the personal dimensions of their lives and their earlier (student) experiences.

17  In some of these cases, accounts of deteriorating work conditions might also simply reflect changes relating to the career stage of those being interviewed.

## References

Brubaker, R. and Cooper, F. (2000). Beyond "identity". *Theory and Society*, 29(1), 1–47.

Cribb, A. and Gewirtz, S. (2013). The hollowed-out university? A critical analysis of changing institutional and academic norms in UK higher education. *Discourse*, 34(3), 338–350.

Furedi, F. (2012). Satisfaction and its discontents. *Times Higher Education*, 8 March, Available at: https://www.timeshighereducation.com/features/satisfaction-and-its-discontents/419238.article [Accessed 29 September 2015].

Harms, E. (2011). *Saigon's Edge: on the margins of Ho Chi Minh City*. Minneapolis: University of Minnesota Press.

Higher Education Funding Council for England (2015). HEFCE allocates £3.97 billion to universities and colleges in England for 2015–16. Available at: http://www.hefce.ac.uk/news/newsarchive/2015/Name,103785,en.html [Accessed 29 September 2015].

Holden, K. (2015). Lamenting the golden age: love, labour and loss in the collective memory of scientists. *Science as Culture*, 24(1), 24–45.

Jansen, S. (2014). Hope for/against the state: gridding in a besieged Sarajevo suburb. *Ethnos: Journal of Anthropology*, 79(2), 238–260.

Jones, K. (2011). Patterns of conflict in education: France, Italy, England, in Green A. (ed.). *Blair's Educational Legacy: thirteen years of New Labour*. New York: Palgrave Macmillan.

McGettigan, A. (2013). *The Great University Gamble: money, markets and the future of higher education*. London: Pluto Press.

Moseley, M. (ed.) (2007). *The Academic Novel: new and classic essays*. Chester: Chester Academic Press.

Peck, J. (2008). Remaking laissez-faire. *Progress in Human Geography*, 32: 3–43.

Sikes, P. (2009). In the shadow of the research assessment exercise? Working in a 'new' university, in Gewirtz, S., Mahony, P., Hextall, I. and Cribb, A. (eds). *Changing Teacher Professionalism*. London: Routledge.

Skultans, V. (1997). Theorizing Latvian lives: the quest for identity. *The Journal of The Royal Anthropological Institute*, 3(4), 761–780.

Skultans, V. (1998). *The Testimony of Lives: narrative and memory in Post-Soviet Latvia*. London: Routledge.

Universities UK (2009). Developing Future University Structures: new funding and legal models. Available at: http://www.universitiesuk.ac.uk/highereducation/ Documents/2009/FutureUniversityStructures.pdf [Accessed 29 September 2015].

Universities UK (2013). Where Student Fees Go. Available at: http://www.universitiesuk.ac.uk/highereducation/Documents/2013/WhereStudentFeesGo.pdf [Accessed 29 September 2015].

Wacquant, L. (2012). Three steps to a historical anthropology of actually existing neoliberalism. *Social Anthropology*, 20(1), 66–79.

Wacquant, L. (2013). Constructing neoliberalism: opening salvo. *NEXUS: Newsletter of the Australian Sociological Association*, 25(1), 1, 8–9.

# Chapter 11

# Losing the plot, plotting the lost

## Politics, Europe, and the rediscovery of lifelong learning

*John Holford*

## Introduction

One of the oddities of international lifelong learning over the past couple of decades has been the European Union's enthusiastic distancing of itself from what Europe has contributed – through education – to western civilisation. That this has coincided with the EU's coming of age as an educational agent makes it all the odder. Until the early 1990s, education was very much at the margins of the union's activities; it was only in the early 1990s the European Commission established a directorate general for education (and culture) for the first time. One might have imagined that the new band of European educational civil servants, tasked with developing a new 'European dimension' in education, would encourage growth from distinctively European roots. Far from it: their first major statement – the White Paper *Teaching and Learning: Towards the Learning Society* (European Commission 1995) was virtually indistinguishable from a host of other policy papers, which emerged in the 1990s from international organisations such as the OECD, UNESCO and the Group of Eight industrial nations: 'in essence', Field (2000: 8) observed, 'they said much the same'.

This chapter does not address the question of why EU policies on education and lifelong learning have been so similar to those across the 'developed' world. Although this is far from fully understood, the broad contours of the explanation – the apparently inexorable advance of marketisation and neoliberal ideology, the globalisation of policy-making – have been widely rehearsed. The focus instead is on what this abandonment of European achievement and traditions in education has meant for the nature of education policy (in particular what this has meant for the field of the education of adults), and on the importance of ensuring that these achievements are not consigned to the 'dustbin of history'.

## The consensus: markets, competitiveness, employment

The essential message international organisations sought to convey from the early 1990s was that 'globalisation' required individuals – and just as urgently, economies – to be 'flexible'. The future was change; success would go to enterprises and economies that adapted most quickly and best. People would have to change through the life course: they could no longer expect to work in a single job, or even a single sector, for life: and to be able to move from one occupation to another, they would have to develop new skills. To stay employed, they had to remain employable, and this required constant training and retraining. And just as the capacity for constant change was an imperative for individuals, so it was for the economy and society as a whole. No longer was it good enough for educational systems to decide what people should be taught; it was individuals themselves who could best decide what they had to learn. Markets sent the best signals: provided people became self-motivated lifelong learners, they themselves would know what was best for them.

The problem – on this view – was that educational institutions, and educational systems, did not, on the whole, recognise this new reality. Hide-bound by traditional thinking, controlled by professionals and bureaucrats, they were far too rigid and resistant. They had to become more adaptable. This was the message adopted by the EU. In a 'permanently changing economy', the European White Paper argued, the 'crucial problem of employment *compels* the education and training system to change' (European Commission 1995: 25; emphasis added). Education and training strategies had to address work and employment as 'a central preoccupation'. International organisations sang the same tune. 'Everyone is convinced of the need for change'. Employment and the needs of business and the economy provided the over-riding purpose of education; as the economy was permanently changing, so education must be permanently flexible. 'The central question now is how to move towards greater flexibility in education and training systems, taking take account of the diversity of people's demands' (European Commission 1995: 23). Leaving aside whether 'everyone' really did indeed agree (in the early 1990s it was common to overlook even the possibility of alternatives to the 'end of history'), the brute fact is clear: from the mid-1990s onward it became increasingly difficult, across most countries, to justify the public provision of education for wider purposes than generating a more efficient economy and a more employable workforce.

To students of educational policy, this is all pretty commonplace: the rise, over the past quarter century, of a new commonsense about education. In this, the needs of the economy (sometimes framed as employment or employability) are primary. 'Everyone' knows they need to be flexible in a permanently changing economy. The 'flexibility' of education and training systems – whatever that may mean – has increased (although some think much remains to be done): partly through the development of new approaches to public sector management; partly through 'marketisation', privatisation and the growing penetration of private sector enterprise into educational provision at all levels. (It is probably in the education and training of adults that marketisation has gone furthest.) And partly, of course, through what has been called the retreat of the state: the preference for low tax levels, lower levels of state provision, poorer welfare, the apparently inexorable advance of neoliberal ideology.

Many have described this 'global imaginary' (Rizvi and Lingard 2010), and explained both its increasing dominance and its effects. Viewed through a 'global' lens, the EU's adoption of this perspective calls for no special explanation; indeed, it would be remarkable if it had done anything very different. Some suggested, in fact, particularly in the early years of the present century, that the EU's version of globalisation was in some ways distinctive: either through its development of a potentially more democratic European educational 'space' (Nóvoa and Lawn 2002), or through its greater emphasis on social inclusion and 'citizenship' – a heritage, perhaps, of the European social model. Vida Mohorčič Špolar and I have pointed to the continuing presence, albeit residual, of 'non-economic themes – equity, social inclusion, social cohesion, citizenship, and so forth' in EU lifelong learning policy (Holford and Mohorčič Špolar 2012: 41). It would be wrong to deny that European education policy has given prominence to particular features that have a citizenship or inclusion dimension. The 1995 White Paper's emphasis on 'proficiency in three European languages' is clearly part of this; social inclusion remains a central element of EU policy rhetoric.

Whether EU education policy was ever really as different from the global mainstream as these authors imagined (or hoped) remains debated, but since the 2004 'crisis' of the Lisbon Strategy, and the post-2007 financial crash and depression, global trends have clearly dominated (Dale and Robertson 2009). European policy, and EU policy, of course does have its own particular features: a global consensus on policy does not mean global uniformity. At the EU level, policy-making has been marked by particular features – the need to work with a wide diversity of member states, the problem of achieving some kind of unity of policy amid this diversity, while doing justice to the principle of 'subsidiarity'. There are, of course, a host of unique mechanisms which make EU policy processes fascinating – the 'open method of coordination', the European semester, and so forth (Milana and Holford 2014). In trying to establish a common direction, the EU has encountered the deep resilience of national institutions: a single model of lifelong learning across Europe seems as unlikely today as it did to observers (Holford *et al.* 2008) a decade ago; perhaps less so. But this diversity should not blind us to the common trend: justification by competitiveness.

Few educational policy-makers, national or international, now dissent from this conventional wisdom that the principal purposes of education, both initial and lifelong, are related to work. In 1995 the EU White Paper saw this as 'proof' of the 'demise of the major ideological disputes on the objectives of education' (European Commission 1995: 23). As Grubb (1996: 535) wrote, 'vocationalism is rampant again': the idea that 'public education should be more "relevant" to our... economic future is widespread'. While this label (vocationalism) does some violence to the richness of the concept – for instance, to the insights into the notion of 'vocation', which have derived from Weber – it is common, and must serve us here.

## Adult education and the 'learning turn'

The education of adults was hit by vocationalism in the 1990s. Initially, this was somewhat masked. Many adult educators were optimistic about a 'learning turn'. Lifelong learning was endorsed and adopted by international organisations – the OECD, the European Union – as key to public policy. Corporations, which had long been encouraged to treat training seriously, were now falling over each other to become 'learning organisations'. In the words of one contemporary:

> Everyone has heard the story. Being a learning organization or engaging in lifelong learning is now essential to economic health. It enables organizations to compete in the global economy. Moreover, by properly deploying technology such as the worldwide web, individuals can all be linked into learning networks. Now everyone has access to education without having to endure the indignities of admissions procedures, let alone authoritarian and disciplinary teachers.
>
> (Boshier 1998: 3)

Adult educators soon discovered, however, that there was a price to pay for these enthusiastic new supporters: it was vocationalism. In recent decades, 'lifelong learning' has become as strongly vocational as education more generally – probably more so. Tongue in cheek, Boshier suggested that adult educators 'must be delighted': their ideas had 'moved out of church basements, extension offices, institutes of adult education and community groups and into corporate boardrooms'. But those who had helped UNESCO and others build 'an architecture for lifelong education' were discovering that lifelong learning was 'recurrent education or human resource development (HRD) in drag'. It might, he said, 'look splashy and alluring; it can preen and prance and strut its stuff. And it goes out at night. But what you see is not necessarily what you get. Remember what your mother said about going out with strangers?' (Boshier 1998: 4).

Boshier's argument was that the lifelong education, as formulated by the Faure Report (Faure *et al.* 1972), had been 'a blueprint for educational reform', a 'master concept' developed in 'response to the ferment of the 1960s [and]... launched on a wave of protest spawned by student activists, grave concerns about ecological catastrophe, crisis in French education and politics and the toxic remnants of the Vietnam war'. In the 1990s, however, 'architects of the new right' had 'hijacked some of the language and concepts' of lifelong education while ignoring its central purpose: 'developing civil society and democracy'. And, Boshier pointed out, in doing so they also challenged longer-standing adult education traditions. 'In some ways the Faure Report echoed the British Ministry of Reconstruction 1919 report, also billed as a "design for democracy" (Waller 1956)' (Boshier 1998: 4); we shall return to the Ministry of Reconstruction below. In fact, as Lee *et al.* (2008) have shown, this 'new neoliberal context' was beginning to mark international policy communities' discussions of lifelong learning as early as the 1980s – a decade they see as 'an important formative period out of which emerged a neo-liberal discourse on lifelong learning' (Lee *et al.* 2008: 448).

While contributions since the 1990s have added detail, texture and theoretical bells and whistles to Boshier's argument, the essentials remain. A 'neo-liberal' tide, premised on a 'global imaginary' (Rizvi and Lingard 2010) and the political economy of free markets, has swept the democratic, humanist and liberal dimensions of lifelong education aside. With them have been lost professional discourse and expertise, institutional practices, beliefs, principles and memories – sacrificed on the altar of market efficiency, victims of narratives of 'creative destruction' originating in Schumpeter (1942), but developed and popularised in more recent US strategic management theory (Christensen *et al.* 2002). If vocationalism is now common sense, it is partly because so many of the social bases for alternatives, and for critique, have been razed.

## The worlds we have lost

This chapter explores how we might develop a basis for refusing this common sense. We do so – in part – by drawing on historical perspectives. One of the vanities imposed on political (and to some extent intellectual) debate by the 'global imaginary' is the notion that the modern world is entirely different from the past – and that historical insight is therefore a priori irrelevant. At political and managerial levels, this is associated with a range of incontestable tropes – 'modernisation', 'change', 'flexibility', and the like. Even at the level of theory, we find the notion of a 'learning society' portrayed as descriptive of a novel world. Jarvis (1998) identified three main interpretations in the literature. There was the learning society 'as reflexive society', based on understandings of modernity (or for some, late or post-modernity) as risky and in constant flux; learning becomes an essential coping strategy for individuals, organisations and even nations. The learning society as a market phenomenon emphasises the invention or reinvention of knowledge as a 'desirable' and tradeable commodity: learning therefore becomes something to be demanded in markets, rather than provided as a matter of public policy. Radical perspectives – such as Faure *et al.* (1972) – were posited on the learning society as novel – an as yet unrealised, perhaps even utopian, future.

It is worth adding, perhaps, that framing change as implying the desirability of the new, and the past primarily as impediment to change rather than source of understanding, has long been a favoured view among moderniseres. 'History', Henry Ford is widely said to have said, 'is bunk'. He continued: 'It's tradition. We don't want tradition. We want to live in the present and the only history that is worth a tinker's dam is the history we made today'.[1] Whatever he really thought (his actual words – 'History is more or less bunk' – were a little more qualified), he has been quoted, or misquoted, often enough since to demonstrate the lasting rhetorical value of his claim.

Our case goes roughly as follows. First, we draw attention to the fact that today's vocational common sense would have seemed odd not only to most educators of adults, but to significant political thinkers on left and right, through most of the twentieth century (not to mention earlier). We do this through a case study of twentieth century British (in fact, mainly English) adult education. No claim is made that British experience is representative: merely that it is illustrative. The hope is that through pointing to some of the richness of this tradition, we will encourage researchers to explore, rediscover and recover the traditions and practices that marked adult education in other European countries. Towards the end, we draw attention to the fact (not, apparently, so self-evident as one might assume) that the problems facing Europe and the world today are by no means only – in the narrow sense – economic: they are in very real ways cultural, social and political.

## Comparative perspective: learning from adult educations past

It may, today, be common sense to seek vocational rationales for lifelong learning, but common sense, as Gramsci (1971: 196–198) taught us, is ideological, and located in specific social and historical milieux. For most of the twentieth century, assumptions about the proper content of (post-school) education for adults were rather different. We sketch an account based on British examples. No doubt similar stories could be told about other European countries – each would, of course, have its own particular inflection, and no student of European history could doubt that some of the inflections would be substantial.

Of course, nominally the EU has valued its links with great European educators of the past. Socrates, Grundtvig, Erasmus and Comenius are preserved in the names of programmes and funding mechanisms. While we may wonder whether this reduction to sources of Euros leads their contributions to be better understood, or even better remembered, such names give some small clue to the richness of the traditions Europeans have inherited. And behind the names – and these are four among many – lie not only philosophies and programmatic statements, but centuries of practices shaped by people – students, teachers and others – institutions, ideologies, movements, revolutions. The difficulty involved in encapsulating the diversity and history of European educational systems is immense. Arguably, the compilation by Jarvis and Griffin (2003) was in some ways an attempt to revalorise the European tradition in the education of adults: they found five volumes insufficient to it justice.

The case we examine here is that of English adult education. I have argued elsewhere that

> Policy development for a learning society in England could have drawn on rich traditions in further and higher education, and perhaps especially in adult education. During the twentieth century, these traditions had been particularly strongly entwined with the politics, ideology and thinking of the labour movement, though they had also been widely endorsed on the political right.
>
> (Holford and Welikala 2013: 146)

The specific formation we shall explore here is the form of working class adult education developed in the early twentieth century as a result of pressure on universities from – broadly – the labour movement. The particular vehicle for this pressure was the Workers' Educational Association (WEA), a body that has remained at the centre of adult educational activity since its establishment in 1903. The WEA was formed by students in university 'extension' courses, who argued that universities and government should devote resources to the education of working class adults and children. What its founder – Albert Mansbridge – and its early members valued above all was liberal education. This was 'true education': it 'directly induces thought, which permeates the whole of society'. In contrast, most education provided to the working classes promoted only 'unthinking absorption of facts', putting people 'at the mercy of the opinion of the hour, however irresponsible', and leaving them susceptible to 'flights of mere rhetoric' (Mansbridge 1944: 1). The specific form in which this education was provided was the 'tutorial class': relatively small classes (a maximum of 30) of mainly working class students, which met weekly, normally for two hours on each occasion, over 24 weeks in each of three successive years.

From a modest start, this quite quickly became a substantial movement. Universities – first Oxford, then others – were persuaded to organise and subsidise classes in industrial towns, often far away from the university itself. In 1907, the Board of Education had set in train arrangements (which were to persist until the 1990s) whereby universities and other bodies, particularly the WEA, were provided with public funds 'in aid of part-time courses in subjects of general as distinct from vocational education' (Statutory Rules and Orders 1919: 31). The Great War cemented this – although the amount of money involved was always modest. As the war progressed, and the soldiers died, government established a Ministry of Reconstruction to contemplate and plan a post-war world 'fit for heroes to live in'. The ministry appointed a committee on adult education, which itself produced a large – and landmark – report in 1919. This made strong assertions about the content of education. 'Technical education', it argued 'must be an integral part of our educational system'. However, it 'is not an alternative to non-vocational education. The latter is a universal need; but whether the former is necessary depends on the character of the employment' (Ministry of Reconstruction 1919: 174). The committee also argued for the liberalisation of technical education by

> the inclusion in the curriculum of pure science and of studies which enable the student to relate his own occupation to the industry of which it is a part, to appreciate the place of that industry in the economic life of the nation and the world, and to interpret the economic life of the community in terms of social values, i.e. of economic history, economics and sociology.
>
> (Ministry of Reconstruction 1919: 174)

Following the war, this became an established and influential (if small) feature of the English educational system. In 1918, as we have seen, 'adult education' was defined in law as involving 'general as distinct from vocational education' (Statutory Rules and Orders 1919: 31), and over the following half-century the term adult education developed in Britain connotations of 'specifically liberal education' (Jarvis 2004: 44). This had a wider influence: in 1921, for instance, the Board of Education issued a booklet on *Humanism in the Continuation School*. Continuation schools were newly established institutions for compulsory part-time study by adolescents. In this, the Board declared:

> ... the world in which we find ourselves to-day is something very different from that upon which the eyes of men have been accustomed to rest for ages past, so different indeed, and so recent in its coming upon us, that the human mind, and still less the machinery of education, have hardly begun to adjust themselves to it in any conscious fashion. Yet if the necessary readjustment is not made our civilisation is doomed, as any civilisation must be in which material progress outruns the intelligent control of the human spirit. It is not technical instruction we stand in need of so much as an informed humanism...
>
> (Board of Education 1924: 6)

This is hardly the place to explore in detail this tradition, but it is worth mentioning that the commitment to liberal adult education for workers spread across the political spectrum, and lasted into the 1970s. In the early 1950s Winston Churchill famously wrote that 'no branch of our vast educational system... should more attract... the aid and encouragement of the State than [liberal] adult education'. It ranked, he said, 'far above science and technical instruction... [and] demands the highest measures which our hard-pressed finances can sustain'. The 'whole range' of evidence considered by the Ashby Committee, was 'unanimous' that liberal adult education was 'still essential' (Ministry of Education 1954: 33):

> adult education students represent in relation to the community at large a social and intellectual asset the loss of which would be deplorable; and we put on record our hope that their genuine educational needs will never go unfulfilled through lack of funds.
>
> (Ministry of Education 1954: 34)

As late as the early 1970s, a major government report (the report of the Russell Committee of Inquiry) was adamant that adult education should not be judged by its vocational outcomes:

> The value of adult education is not solely to be measured by increases in earning power or productive capacity or by any other materialistic yard-stick, but by the quality of life it inspires in the individual and generates for the community at large. It is an agent changing and improving our society: but for each individual the means of change may differ and each must develop in his own way, at his own level and according to his own talents. No academic subject or social or creative activity is superior to another provided that those engaged in it develop a greater awareness of their own capacities and a more certain knowledge of the totality of their responsibilities as human beings.
>
> (Department of Education and Science 1973: xi)

Forty years on, it is perhaps quaint that Russell thought it helpful and relevant to emphasise the value of the views expressed by a previous major government investigation: the Ministry of Reconstruction 50 years earlier (1919). The achievements of the [English] educational system since 1900 had been 'spectacular', and 'nowhere more perhaps than in the growth of technical education in the last twenty years' (Department of Education and Science 1973: 3). But 'lifelong continuance' of education was essential, and the Russell Committee quoted at length 'words from our predecessors' report' which it thought 'even more relevant today than when they were written in 1919' (Department of Education and Science 1973: 4):

> We do not wish to underrate the value of increased technical efficiency or the desirability of increasing productivity; but we believe that a short-sighted insistence upon these things will defeat its object. We wish to emphasise the necessity for a great development of non-technical stud-ies, partly because we think that it would assist the growth of a truer conception of technical education, but more especially because it seems

to us vital to provide the fullest opportunities for personal development and for the realisation of a higher standard of citizenship. Too great an emphasis has been laid on material considerations and too little regard paid to other aspects of life.

(Ministry of Reconstruction 1919: 153; quoted in Department of Education and Science 1973: 4)

Sketching the broad parameters of this tradition does not, of course, do justice to the nature and richness of its educational and societal contribution. Within this space there evolved a network of educational institutions and practices, which intersected with social, economic and political institutions at a range of levels. We have seen its deep connections with the trade union and labour movement: the WEA was central and – although always constitutionally neutral as regards party politics – always gave succour and comfort to socialists and trade unionists. We have touched on its particular pedagogical character: the tutorial class. There were other features: a marked reverence for 'residential education', so adult education was marked by residential summer and weekend schools; emphasis on Socratic dialogue and discussion; strong reliance on books and strong links with the educational mission of public libraries.

## The limits of vocationalism

Let us turn back to the educational challenges facing Europe. According to the European Union these are – in the spirit of vocationalism – essentially to support the EU's economic aims. In 2000 the Lisbon Strategy announced that Europe would become 'the most competitive and dynamic knowledge-based economy in the world... with more and better jobs and greater social cohesion' by 2010. The strategy failed. Instead, Europe in 2010 was facing a 'global recession' (perhaps more accurately described as a European and North Atlantic depression). The EU's response was 'more of the same': the Europe 2020 strategy is built around similar aims:

- smart growth – developing an economy based on knowledge and innovation;
- sustainable growth – promoting a more resource-efficient, greener and more competitive economy;
- inclusive growth – fostering a high-employment economy delivering economic, social and territorial cohesion (European Commission 2010: 8).

Although the aims are similar, in practice social concerns have been – at least initially – played down. There was a renewed emphasis on economic competitiveness – particularly through strengthened mechanisms of 'soft governance', such as the European semester (Holford and Mleckzo 2013).

The Commission's communication *Rethinking Education* (European Commission 2012) spoke loudly of such thinking: education and training have a 'broad mission', which 'encompasses objectives such as active citizenship, personal development and well-being', it admitted. But 'against the backdrop of sluggish economic growth and a shrinking workforce due to demographic ageing, the most pressing challenges for member states are to address the needs of the economy and focus on solutions to tackle fast-rising youth unemployment' (European Commission 2012: 2). These meant concentrating on 'developing transversal skills' (p. 3), 'particularly entrepreneurial skills' (p. 3), on 'STEM related skills' (p. 4). Curricula should be made 'more relevant to the workplace' (p. 11), partly through 'a reinforced partnership approach' between public and private sectors (p. 13). Vocationalism rules.

Five years into 'Europe 2020', do the strategy's achievements seem more impressive than Lisbon's? The EU's economies have been stagnating for the best part of a decade; the 'employment problem' remains unsolved. The crisis of the Eurozone continues, despite the punishment inflicted on the people of Greece (and, if to a lesser degree, other peoples). If education has been serving the economy, its success has been limited. This may, of course, be because – as Wolf (2002) and Brown *et al.* (2011) have in different ways argued – what education can achieve is limited. But at roughly the same time, the EU has been facing the most profound political and social challenges. Until 1995 the EU had 12 member states; by 2007 it had 27. Its population grew from roughly 350 million people to over 500 million. The changes were profound. The countries of the EU have very diverse economies, polities, societies and histories. Four have populations in excess of 60 million each; 13 have populations smaller than that of London, the continent's largest city. In 2010, 86 per cent of EU GDP came from the 12 countries that were member states before 1995.

It is hardly surprising that this rapid growth and social change generated crisis. Manuel Barroso (quoted in Charter 2007) compared the EU 'to the organisation of empires': 'We have the dimension of empire', he said (although in contrast to empires, which were made 'with force' and 'a centre imposing diktat', EU members had 'fully decided to work together and to pool their sovereignty'). The management of Europe's diversity must be profoundly difficult, and the European Commission's growing enthusiasm for mechanisms that will provide simple but reliable ways of describing and measuring social phenomena is probably a natural result. The rejection in 2005 of the constitutional treaty by the peoples of France and the Netherlands in popular referenda threw the political project off course; the crisis of the Euro has stressed the relationship between richer and poorer member states virtually to destruction. At the same time, growing migration has been matched by newly assertive far right political parties, often of a highly 'Eurosceptic' kind. Political instability in the Middle East and Afghanistan, the growth of

'Islamist' political movements, not to mention the west's 'war on terror' have challenged Europe's sense of identity. And in 2015 the refugee crisis grew to a scale unknown since the late 1940s.

This suggests, of course, that many of the challenges facing Europe are not economic after all; and 'economics' may not provide all the answers. A recognition of this – or perhaps a partial recognition – is apparent in the Paris Declaration of EU education ministers (March 2015), 'Promoting citizenship and the common values of freedom, tolerance and non-discrimination through education'. This began:

> In response to the terrorist attacks in France and Denmark earlier this year, and recalling similar atrocities in Europe in the recent past, we reaffirm our determination to stand shoulder to shoulder in support of fundamental values that lie at the heart of the European Union: respect for human dignity, freedom (including freedom of expression), democracy, equality, the rule of law and respect for human rights. These values are common to the Member States in a European society in which pluralism, non-discrimination, tolerance, justice, solidarity and equality between women and men prevail.
>
> (European Union Education Ministers 2015)

The ministers continued in similar vein, with a ringing endorsement of their collective commitment to 'protecting and strengthening Europe's spirit of freedom, a spirit which values critical thinking as much as respect for others in line with the values of the Union':

> we have a special duty to ensure that the humanist and civic values we share are safeguarded and passed on to future generations. We remain united in our efforts to promote freedom of thought and expression, social inclusion and respect for others, as well as to prevent and tackle discrimination in all its forms.
>
> (European Union Education Ministers 2015)

The Paris Declaration was, in fact, issued in the name not only of education ministers, but of the European Commissioner for Education, Culture, Youth and Sport. And the Commission's communication, *New priorities for European cooperation in education and training* (European Commission 2015), acknowledged that the 'pressing challenges' of 2012 (the economy and youth unemployment) have broadened. Europe, it says, now faces 'a number of urgent tasks': not only 'restoring job creation and economic recovery, achieving sustainable growth; bridging the investment gap' but 'enhancing social cohesion; giving radicalisation and violence priority attention' (European Commission 2015: 2). There is a renewed emphasis on education's 'important role in fostering inclusion and equality, cultivating mutual respect and embedding fundamental values in an open and democratic society' (p. 2), and the need 'to prevent and tackle marginalisation and radicalisation' (p. 5).

So far, the spirit of the Paris Declaration pervades the 2015 communication. But when we look for practical policies to these ends, it falls considerably short. While there are extensive recommendations on the theme of 'quality and relevance of learning outcomes is key for skills development' (European Commission 2015: 3), the section entitled 'Education must contribute to social cohesion, equality, non-discrimination and civic competences' does little more than reassert what the ministers had declared in Paris five months earlier. Some of its assertions are important – if only because of their new, or renewed, prominence:

> Inequality is at its highest level in 30 years in most European and OECD countries, and has a negative impact on educational outcomes, as education systems tend to reproduce existing patterns of socio-economic status. Breaking the intergenerational cycle of low qualifications must therefore be a priority. While a majority of Member States has taken measures to improve access to education for disadvantaged learners, a significant educational gap persists and access to good quality mainstream education and training remains a challenge in many parts of the EU.... Gender gaps in education must be tackled and gender differences in educational choices addressed.
>
> (European Commission 2015: 4–5)

But rhetoric is seldom enough, and in these areas the commission's ability to suggest concrete measures – its policy imagination – has served the peoples of Europe poorly. There will, it says, be 'funding from the Erasmus+ programme, in line with the four areas identified in the Declaration'[2] (p. 5). But on the whole – for the Commission – moving ahead on the Paris agenda seems likely to involve travelling along its well-established vocational tracks. For example, in relation to 'violent extremism', it asserts education and training's 'important role in fostering inclusion and equality, cultivating mutual respect and embedding fundamental values in an open and democratic society'. Quite so. But the mechanisms it envisages are only 'reaching out' to the most disadvantaged with education and training 'to prevent and tackle poverty and social exclusion and discrimination': 'step up efforts to improve access to quality learning for all, thereby fostering upwards social convergence' (p. 2). Few would disagree that education for all is important. Any education, even the most narrow and vocational, probably helps to 'build a foundation on which active citizenship rests' (p. 2). But education – especially European education – has much more to offer. It is time the European Commission educated itself about the practical and professional knowledge that European educational systems, movements, institutions and traditions have developed in areas outside vocational education. It might then be able to make meaningful suggestions about curriculum and methods for 'cultivating mutual respect and embedding fundamental values in an open and democratic society'.

In this context, it is salutary to consider whether the destruction of non-vocational expertise and knowledge in education – and here we refer in particular to adult education – might have been an error. And in this respect, it is well to refer back to our English example. Until the mid-1980s, as we have seen, all British governments endorsed and funded liberal adult education. They did so in part for reasons which today might be labelled 'citizenship' or 'inclusion'. This came from different directions. Liberal adult education had a strong ethos of 'service'; its leading intellectuals were strongly influenced by idealist philosophers such as T.H. Green and Benjamin Jowett, which 'elevate[d] public service, whether to government, empire, church or community, as the highest ethical and professional imperative' (Goldman 2000: 299; see also Steele 1994). We can see this in one of the movement's foundational speeches: by John Mactavish, a worker in Portsmouth Dockyard, at a conference at Oxford University of academics and 'working class representatives'. He began with a claim for rights:

> I am not here as a suppliant for my class. I decline to sit at the rich man's table praying for crumbs. I claim for my class all the best of all that Oxford has to give. I claim it as a right – wrongfully withheld – wrong not only to us but to Oxford.

There has always been an ambiguity in the claim: was it for his class (in the sense of his fellow adult education students), or was it for the working class? But it was not just an assertion of right; he was also making an argument about the role of higher education in society, and of society's need for 'service':

> What is the true function of a university? Is it to obtain the nation's best men, or to sell its gifts to the rich? Instead of recruiting her students from the widest possible area, she has restricted her area of selection to the fortunate few.... We want workpeople to come to Oxford [and]... to come back as missionaries.... The sons of the working-man come to Oxford to escape from their class, not to lift it. We want Oxford to open wide her doors to the best of our people, and take them in. We want her to send them back as doctors whose business will be health-giving, not wealth-getting; we want her to send them back to us as lawyers whose business will be justice not fees; we want her to send them back to us as living teachers, not mechanical manipulators of child-life. We want her to inspire them not with the idea of getting on, but with the idea of social service....
>
> (Mactavish quoted in Mansbridge 1913: 194–197)

This was one perspective on citizenship and inclusion: there were others. By the mid-1920s Lord Eustace Percy, President of the Board of Education, argued in a memorandum to a colleague 'that £100,000 spent annually' on liberal adult education through the WEA 'would be about the best police expenditure we could indulge in...' (quoted in Fieldhouse 1985: 123). But this was by no means the only perspective on the political right. Thirty years later, Churchill wrote:

> I have no doubt myself that a man or woman earnestly seeking in grown-up life to be guided to wide and suggestive knowledge in its largest and most uplifted sphere will make the best of all the pupils in this age of clatter and buzz, of gape and gloat. The appetite of adults to be shown the foundations and processes of thought will never be denied by a British Administration cherishing the continuity of our Island life.
>
> (Churchill 1953: 173)

The point of this chapter is not to say that English adult education has 'the answers' to Europe's problems. Like all other forms of education, it had strengths and limitations; and of course, it was 'of its time'. It generated a wealth of literature about itself – some of it, in the positive sense, research-based, some much more normative, some celebratory, some highly self-critical. Its practitioners argued about matters of policy and practice for the best part of a century. The point, rather, is to suggest that the historical traditions and institutional forms of education – from all of Europe's nations – should be reviewed and sympathetically reassessed. They are, and should be treated as, a treasure chest of experience and insight, from which new forms of education able to address the continent's social and political challenges can evolve. If this is to be achieved, the European Commission, and indeed policy-makers across the continent, should acknowledge their need to learn; and to learn from the past – critically, of course – as well as from today's 'best practice'. A non-vocational Cedefop, dedicated to adult education for 'fostering inclusion and equality, cultivating mutual respect and embedding fundamental values in an open and democratic society'? Encouraging – and supporting – research on European educational traditions would be a good start.

## Notes

1 Interview with Charles N. Wheeler, *Chicago Tribune*, 25 May 1916. Burlingame (1957: 9) quotes Ford as asking John Reed, 'How can anyone claim to know the truth about history?' when it is 'rewritten every year from a new point of view'.
2 These are, according to the commission: '(i) promoting the acquisition of social, civic and intercultural competences, enhancing ownership of Europe's fundamental values, and fostering active citizenship; (ii) enhancing critical thinking and media literacy; (iii) fostering the education of disadvantaged children and young people; and (iv) promoting intercultural dialogue'. (European Commission 2015: 5) The

educational ministers' phrasing was slightly different: '(1) Ensuring that children and young people acquire social, civic and intercultural competences, by promoting democratic values and fundamental rights, social inclusion and non-discrimination, as well as active citizenship; (2) Enhancing critical thinking and media literacy, particularly in the use of the Internet and social media, so as to develop resistance to all forms of discrimination and indoctrination; (3) Fostering the education of disadvantaged children and young people, by ensuring that our education and training systems address their needs; (4) Promoting intercultural dialogue through all forms of learning in cooperation with other relevant policies and stakeholders' (European Union Education Ministers 2015).

# References

Board of Education (1924). *Humanism in the Continuation School.* London: HMSO.

Boshier, R. (1998). Edgar Faure after 25 Years: down but not out, in Holford, J., Jarvis, P. and Griffin C. (eds). *International Perspectives on Lifelong Learning.* London: Kogan Page, pp. 1–20.

Brown, P., Lauder, H. and Ashton, D. (2011). *The Global Auction: the broken promises of education, jobs and incomes.* Oxford: Oxford University Press.

Burlingame, R. (1957). *Henry Ford.* London: Hutchinson.

Charter, D. (2007). Call for Vote on "Europe Empire". *The Times,* 11 July. Available at: http://www.timesonline.co.uk/tol/news/world/europe/article2056576.ece [Accessed 24 August 2011].

Christensen, C.M., Johnson, M.W. and Rigby, D.K. (2002). Foundations for growth: how to identify and build disruptive new business. *MIT Sloan Management Review,* 43(3), 22–31.

Churchill, W.S. (1953). Letter to Sir Vincent Tewson, in *Report of Proceedings at the 85th Annual Trades Union Congress.* London: TUC, pp. 173–174. (Reprinted in Ministry of Education 1954, pp. 66–67.)

Dale, R. and Robertson, S. (eds) (2009). *Globalisation and Europeanisation in Education.* Didcot: Symposium Books.

Department of Education and Science (1973). *Adult Education: A plan for development. Report of a committee of inquiry... under the chairmanship of Sir Lionel Russell.* London: HMSO.

European Commission (1995). *Teaching and Learning: towards a learning society.* Luxembourg: Office for Official Publications of the European Communities.

European Commission (2010). *Europe 2020: a strategy for smart, sustainable and inclusive growth.* Communication from the Commission. Brussels: COM(2010) 2020.

European Commission (2012). *Rethinking Education: investing in skills for better socio-economic outcomes.* Communication from the Commission. Strasbourg: COM(2012) 669 final.

European Commission (2015). *New priorities for European cooperation in education and training. Draft 2015 Joint Report of the Council and the Commission on the implementation of the Strategic framework for European cooperation in education and training* (ET 2020), COM(2015) 408 final.

European Union Education Ministers (2015). Declaration on promoting citizenship and the common values of freedom, tolerance and non-discrimination through education. Paris, 17 March. Available at: http://ec.europa.eu/education/news/2015/documents/citizenship-education-declaration_en.pdf [Accessed 27 November 2015].

Faure, E., Herrera, F., Kaddoura, A.R., Lopes, H., Petrovsky, A.V., Rahnema, M. and Champion Ward, F. (1972). *Learning to Be: the world of education today and tomorrow*. Paris: UNESCO.

Field, J. (2000). *Lifelong Learning and the New Educational Order*. Stoke-on-Trent: Trentham Books.

Fieldhouse, R. (1985). Conformity and contradiction in English responsible body adult education 1925–1950. *Studies in the Education of Adults*, 17(2), 121–134.

Goldman, L. (2000). Intellectuals and the English working class 1870–1945: the case of adult education. *History of Education*, 29(4), 281–300.

Gramsci, A. (1971). *Selections from the Prison Notebooks*, in Hoare, Q. and Nowell Smith, G. (eds). London: Lawrence & Wishart.

Grubb, W.N. (1996). The new vocationalism: what it is, what it could be. *Phi Delta Kappa*, 77(8), 553–546.

Holford, J. and Mleckzo, A. (2013). Lifelong learning: national policies from the European perspective, in Saar, E., Ure, O.-B. and Holford, J. (eds). *Lifelong Learning in Europe: national patterns and challenges*, pp. 25–46.

Holford, J. and Mohorčič Špolar, V. (2012). Neoliberal and inclusive themes in European lifelong learning policy, in Riddell, S., Markowitsch, J. and J. Weedon, J. (eds). *Lifelong learning in Europe: equity and efficiency in the balance*. Bristol: Policy Press, pp. 39–61.

Holford, J. and Welikala, T. (2013). "Renaissance" without enlightenment: New Labour's "Learning Age" 1997–2010, in Saar, E., Ure, O.B. and Holford, J. (eds). *Lifelong learning in Europe: national patterns and challenges*. Cheltenham: Edward Elgar.

Holford, J., Riddell, S., Weedon, E., Litjens, J. and Hannan, G. (2008). *Lifelong Learning: policy and practice in an expanding Europe*. Vienna: Lit Verlag.

Jarvis, P. (1998). Paradoxes of the learning society, in Holford, J., Jarvis, P. and Griffin, C. (eds). *International Perspectives on Lifelong Learning*. London: Kogan Page, pp. 59–68.

Jarvis, P. (2004). *Adult Education and Lifelong Learning: Theory and Practice*, 3rd edn. London: Routledge Falmer.

Jarvis, P. and Griffin, C. (eds). (2003). *Adult and Continuing Education: major themes in education*, 5 volumes. London: Taylor and Francis.

Lee, M., Thayer, T. and Madyun, N. (2008). The evolution of the European Union's lifelong learning policies: an institutional learning perspective. *Comparative Education*, 44(4), 445–463.

Mansbridge, A. (1913). *University Tutorial Classes: a study in the development of higher education among working men and women*. London: Longmans, Green and Co.

Mansbridge, A. (1944). *The Kingdom of the Mind: Essays and Addresses 1903–37*. London: J.M. Dent and Sons.

Milana, M. and Holford, J. (eds) (2014). *Adult Education Policy and the European Union: theoretical and methodological perspectives*. Rotterdam: Sense Publishers.

Ministry of Education (1954). *The organisation and finance of adult education in England and Wales. Report of the Committee appointed by the Minister of Education in June 1953* (Chairman: Eric Ashby). London: HMSO.

Ministry of Reconstruction (1919). *Adult Education Committee: Final Report*, Cmd. 321. London: HMSO.

Nóvoa, A. and Lawn, M. (eds). (2002). *Fabricating Europe: the formation of an education space.* New York: Kluwer.

Rizvi, F. and Lingard, B. (2010). *Globalizing Education Policy.* Abingdon: Routledge.

Schumpeter, J.A. (1942). *Capitalism, Socialism and Democracy.* New York: Harper and Row.

Statutory Rules and Orders (1919). *Regulations for Technical Schools &c., dated August 24, 1918, made by the Board of Education, for Technical Schools, Schools of Art, and other forms of Provision of Further Education in England and Wales.* No. 2231. London: HMSO.

Steele, T. (1994). The colonial metaphor and the mission of Englishness: adult education and the origins of English studies, in Marriott, S. and Hake, B. (eds). *Cultural and Intercultural Experiences in European Adult Education: essays on popular and higher education since 1890.* Leeds: University of Leeds Department of Adult and Continuing Education, pp. 70–91.

Waller, R.D. (1956). *Design for Democracy: an abridgment of a report of the Adult Education Committee of the Ministry of Reconstruction commonly called the 1919 Report, with an introduction 'the years between'.* New York: Association Press.

Wolf, A. (2002). *Does Education Matter? Myths about Education and Economic Growth.* London: Penguin.

# Chapter 12

# How are European lifelong learning systems changing?

## An approach in terms of public policy regimes

*Eric Verdier*

## Introduction

In 2000, the strategy adopted by the European Council in Lisbon for the building of the 'knowledge society' made lifelong learning (LLL) a key instrument of economic competitiveness combining innovation and social cohesion. The term 'lifelong learning' places the emphasis explicitly on the multiplicity of sources and forms of knowledge. The intention is clearly to emphasise that what is at stake is the individual's entire learning trajectory, regardless of age, from the first steps in nursery school to the senior citizen programmes at university: no institutional sanctuary, such as basic instruction, is to escape the re-examinations called for by this exhaustive view of the lasting or occasional ways and opportunities for learning.

While the European Council in Lisbon defined the open method of coordination (OMC) as the means of 'spreading best practices and achieving greater convergence towards the main EU goals, 'it stressed that its purposes in the area of education and training may be defined as a way of enabling mutual comparison and learning, and thereby of limiting the risks inherent in change and reform' (European Commission 2002). The title of the resolution adopted by the European Council held in Brussels in 2003 – 'Different systems, shared objectives' – clearly attests to the need for open cooperation to come to terms with the diversity of national schemes. This realistic political orientation underlines the fact that any attempt to compare national LLL systems comes up against the constraint of complexity. First of all, vocational education and training (VET) schemes are embedded in other social sub-systems (e.g. labour relations, basic education, higher education, the labour market and company management) (Bosch and Charest 2009). In rhetorical terms, the expression 'lifelong learning' both reflects this complexity and accentuates it still further insofar as it endows this resource with a new purpose, namely that of helping to ensure career paths and job transitions, to the point of making it a new 'pillar' of the social welfare systems.

The first section of this chapter puts forward an approach in terms of public policy regimes in education and LLL that is capable of taking account of societal dynamics. Each LLL regime is identified on the basis mainly of the principles of justice informing the institutions responsible for its regulation. These ideal types attach prime importance to the action targeted by the social and political actors; this perspective aims to introduce a semblance of order into a societal diversity that is considerably more complex. The second section applies this approach to the transformations that have occurred in several national systems that are emblematic of European diversity in education and LLL.

## Towards a comparative approach in terms of lifelong regimes

The contribution of available typologies of education and training systems to the understanding of LLL is undeniable but they are not very efficient to explain the hybridisation of the LLL national systems; they reduce the complexity of national constructions to the peculiar homogeneity of such a cluster of countries; consequently they make it difficult to analyse the transformations they undergo in the course of time. That is the reason why it is necessary to construct ideal types of LLL regime (and not ideal types of cluster of countries).

## Scope and limits of comparative typologies

Thus the comparative approach through varieties of capitalism (Hall and Soskice 2001) emphasises the structural relationship between the education and training arrangements and the economic structuring of the different capitalisms (Estevez-Abe *et al.* 2001), highlighting in particular the links between the formation of skills and the dynamics of innovation (incremental versus radical). In addition, with the ideal type of coordinated market economies, it shows that employers' organisations, major actors in societal configurations, have every interest in cooperating with the trade unions and the state so as to have access to a workforce whose skills will be the source of a long-term comparative advantage in globalised markets. The extension that Green *et al.* (2006) have given it makes it possible to link each cluster of countries to a societal configuration of social cohesion and inequalities, whether in the distribution of knowledge or the quality of access to jobs and, more generally, income. Dualist approaches emphasise that one and the same process – whether reunification in Germany or decentralisation in France – will give rise to such different regional dynamics as to call into question the pertinence of works that regard the national level as the reflection of a societal homogeneity. Works cast in the socio-historical mould make it possible to understand how the training for trades that prevailed within the framework of guilds could be recycled to become a decisive resource for the rapid industrialisation that Germany underwent in the second half of the nineteenth century; for the more recent period, it sheds light on the conditions in which the German industry-oriented dual system has been able to adapt to the accelerated mutations of globalised capitalism, the challenges of reunification and the emergence of a society in which service activities have taken a major role (Culpepper and Thelen 2008).

The fact remains that these various works suffer from two major difficulties. First, with the notable exception of the dualist approaches, they tend to impose on each national model an assumed coherence that makes it difficult to understand the changes that cause them to evolve and sometimes reconfigure them, except by referring to exogenous causes – globalisation – and neglecting endogenous factors. This difficulty is even greater when, to increase the power of the ideal types, the analysis emphasises a primordial structuring dimension, for example, in the case of the 'varieties of capitalism', the employers' strategies leading to incentivising rules that will shape individual behaviours in education and training. In this particular case, the training system loses all autonomy vis-à-vis the structural choices of the employers' organisations and must necessarily adapt to them. In contrast it could be argued that the education system is imbued with a dynamic that is specific to it – for example, an internal organisation designed to produce equality of outcomes, even if this keeps at arm's length the employers' preoccupations in terms of skills and qualifications.

The socio-historical approach does indeed pertinently retrace the long-term evolutions that have led to the current societal configurations. Moreover, considering that institutions are not only formal rules but also result from the interpretations and adaptive implementations that the actors make of them, Streek and Thelen (2005) show that significant transformations can result from a gradual process of adaptation of institutions to realities. But it is striking that in order to account in the recent period for the transformations of national LLL systems, this approach has particularly focused on the German case (Culpepper and Thelen 2008) in order to explain – admittedly, in fine detail – why, ultimately, the latter had changed so little....[1]

Comparative analysis has to deal with the fact that several factors favour an increasing hybridisation of national VET systems. In a context of economic uncertainty and demands for effective public spending, these include the successive attempts of public policy and politics to respond to recurring educational and labour market challenges, especially the early school leaver phenomenon, the school-to-work transition and long-term unemployment. Quite often, the reforms undertaken in the area of education and training draw their inspiration – more or less unofficially – from (supposed) 'successes' developed within reference countries. Along the same lines, the transformations specific to general education lead to a repositioning of initial VET schemes within young people's study programmes because of their increasing access to higher education. Last of all, European education and training policies coming under the OMC create a favourable context for hybridisation (see Verdier 2008). Without imposing requirements, the OMC organises the circulation of ideas and 'good practices' and encourages member states to undertake initiatives aimed at attaining the objectives jointly defined on the basis of the so-called Lisbon Strategy and then the Europe 2020 strategy. The European approach leads member states to engage in reflexivity when, for one thing, considering European and international assessments (notably of the OECD with the PISA test) and, for another, drawing up the activity reports they prepare every 2 years to describe the actions aimed at fulfilling the joint objectives.[2]

## Five regimes of lifelong learning

Each LLL regime is identified on the basis mainly of the principles of justice informing the institutions responsible for its regulation. They have been constituted on the basis of socio-historical analyses of the national systems in order to bring out the political principles which, at a given phase in their history, have spurred a reorganisation of education and training for young people. These ideal types are reconstructions of social and political trajectories in the area of LLL; they provide a schematic description of reality that makes it possible to move beyond the tension between the diversity of particular historical occurrences and the general nature of these national evolutions. These regimes are built around responses to a series of political issues, with a minimum level of coherence established among the various choices by virtue of the institutional complementarities and solidarities among actors which these regimes generate.[3]

---

**Box 1**

LLL regime as a combination of political principles, actors' logics, rules and instruments

Every regime entails more or less explicit responses to highly political questions:

1. Which principles of justice and efficiency are to be applied in the area of education and training?
2. Is the individual as conceived within the regime integrated into a professional community, line organisation, network or social citizenship?
3. Who takes responsibility for qualification and employment-related risks (unemployment, precariousness, obsolescence of skills, etc.): the individual and/or social insurance/the state?

4. What kind of governance is needed: what configuration of private and public players (degree of decentralisation, role of private training establishments and companies)?

5. How should education and training be organised: continuity or separation between initial and continuing training? What place for vocational training in the initial curriculum?

6. What conception of knowledge is to be applied: primacy of academic knowledge, work-related knowledge, or absence of distinctions between the different kinds?

7. What regulatory institutions are put in place: provision of information, schemes compensating for initial inequalities, rules for selection of individuals, negotiated collective agreements?

8. What are the means of access to both initial education and training (e.g. accessibility of tertiary education) and continuing training (cf. the question of guidance)?

9. What is the nature of the training to be provided for young people: vocational, general, organised by levels?

10. Who funds the different kinds of education and training (public authorities, companies, families or individuals)?

The principles of justice and efficiency underlie the legitimacy of the rules in this area, all of which depend on various forms of justification (Boltanski and Thévenot 2006): vocation (*Beruf*), academic meritocracy, solidarity, utility of the service, transparency of the quality–price ratio. As representations of the common good, these conventions encompass different conceptions of what is 'efficient and fair' in collective action concerning LLL. In the course of action, they can be invoked by any player in order to justify its choice. These conventions, which are used by private and public players, are associated with different cognitive, financial and organisational resources that take concrete form as instruments, rules, social technologies and so on, all of which help to stabilise the regulations at work. Notwithstanding their individual specificities, these five regimes can be grouped into two categories in terms of their linkages with market rules. Three of them are more or less based on 'decommodification' (Esping-Andersen 1990).[4] They are described as 'academic', 'corporatist' and 'universal', respectively. The other two are market oriented but have different conventions or principles and are described as 'pure market competition' and 'organised market' regimes, respectively.

## Three 'decommodified' LLL regimes

Above and beyond compulsory schooling, the three decommodified regimes make initial education and training a central focus of the collective action, which is decisive for both individual and collective destinies, but they draw on quite dissimilar rules: selection, vocation and cohesion (see Table 12.1). They also decommodify education and training to varying degrees. The academic regime is built around two processes: first of all, school-based competition between individuals, the fairness of which must be guaranteed by a public actor invested with incontestable political legitimacy. It also relies on an objectified criterion, academic performance, which, in principle, is not sensitive to local market influences (Duru-Bellat 1992). The corporatist regime relies on occupational identities sustained by individual commitment to a vocation, as well as on highly involved social actors (Vinokur 1995). The latter are in fact called upon to make a political commitment to the creation of vocational training qualifications so that they may enjoy high social esteem and become the rules governing occupational labour markets (Eyraud *et al.* 1990). The universal regime is based on a principle of solidarity that attempts to compensate at an early stage for inequalities stemming from a disadvantaged social environment (Wiborg 2009).

## Two conceptions of market regimes

Both of these regimes, the pure market competition regime and the one 'organised' around networks linking public and private actors, approach training in utilitarian terms (see Table 12.2). In the former, a price marks the successful matching of service supply and demand in the market of education and (further) training; in the latter, a quasi-market (Bartlett and Legrand, 1993) plays a predominant role: its workings are subject to a body of rules intended to guarantee the transparency of quality–price relationships for all the protagonists in order to control possible information distortions and arrive at the fair price. In this case, we can speak of a market 'organised' by public intervention, which then has to guarantee the reliability of the information and the quality standards supporting the transactions taking place in the organised market.

It is important to underline that each national system results from a compromise between several possible regimes, even if one of these ideal types may predominate. It is supported by specific coalitions of public and private actors. This societal arrangement may be more or less sustainable depending on the endogenous social dynamics and capacity to cope with external changes.

## The evolution of European LLL systems: what challenges and hybridisations?

The characterisation of each national LLL system and its evolution relative to the five ideal types is based, first, on a body of information and analyses concerning the political principles, actors' logics, rules and instruments and,

Table 12.1 'Decommodified' LLL regimes

| | Corporatist | Academic | Universal |
|---|---|---|---|
| Justice principle | Access to an occupational or craft community (vocation) | School-based merit system ('rank' and selection) | Compensation for initial inequalities ('solidarity' and social inclusion) |
| Conception of skills in initial education or training | Overall mastery of a trade or occupation | Education levels | Reconciliation of basic knowledge and practical skills |
| Certification | Recognised qualification | Certification by an academic authority | National diploma |
| Nature of programme | Contents determined by negotiation | Subject-based standards | Interaction between different kinds of knowledge |
| Area of recognition | Occupational labour market | Internal and hierarchical market | 'Multi-transitional' labour market |
| Key actor in initial education or training | Company | Academic education institutions | Community of partners |
| Objective of initial education or training | Occupational rules | Indicators of abilities | Social citizenship |
| Main risk | Stigmatisation of those without qualifications | Sharp inequalities in schooling | Increased collective costs |
| Key actor in institutional regulation | Social partners at industry level | Educational institution | Public authorities |
| Continuing training objectives | Higher levels of occupational mastery | Short-term adaptation of skills | Social autonomy |
| Political responsibility for employability | Collective agreements at occupational branch level | Companies and public bodies | National tripartism |
| Funding of continuing training | Vocational training schools and individuals | Companies and employers' associations | Public agencies and mutual funds |

Source: Author.

*Table 12.2* Market LLL regimes

|  | Market competition | Organised market |
| --- | --- | --- |
| Principle of justice | Utility of services provided | Fair price for quality |
| Objective of initial (vocational) education | Human capital | Social capital |
| Conception of skills in initial education and training | Meeting a demand (possibly on the job) | Portfolio of operational skills |
| Certification | Level of remuneration (matching) | Attestation of skills |
| Nature of programme | N/A (not available or inadequate) | Quality procedure |
| Area of recognition | Immediate transaction (spot market) | External 'organised' markets |
| Key actor in initial training | Individuals as consumers | 'Guided' individuals |
| Main risk of failure | Under-investment in training | Inefficient incentives |
| Key actor in institutional regulation | Invisible hand | Public regulatory and accreditation agencies |
| Conception of continuing training | Utility of service provision | Diversified skills portfolio |
| Political responsibility and employability | Individuals | 'Active' individuals and agencies |
| Funding | Direct payment or loans for individuals | Training vouchers, individual training accounts |

Source: Author.

secondly, on a series of statistical indicators to describe several dimensions given that, a priori, the presence of a particular regime should manifest itself in a specific (upward or downward) trend for each indicator:

- access to the different levels and courses of education and training (see Table 12.3);
- the internal selectivity of the education system and the pupils' level of achievement (see Table 12.4);
- the expenditure on education and training: the weight share of private expenditures, the per capita expenditure on primary pupils and on higher education students (see Table 12.5);
- the school-to-work transition should (proportion of young people not in education, employment or training (NEETs) for instance) (see Table 12.6);
- access to LLL (see Table 12.7).

The trends in the indicators must be correlated with the reforms implemented to account for the effectiveness of new hybrid forms (in this sense, the analysis connects with the approach of Streeck and Thelen (2005), who advocate distinguishing the processes of change from the results of change).

*Table 12.3* Access to different kinds and levels of education 2000 and 2012 (per cent)

| Countries | Educational attainment below upper secondary (25–34 year olds) | | Upper secondary students in general education | | Upper secondary students in vocational combined school and work-based | | Tertiary education graduates (25–34 year olds) (short tertiary) | | Tertiary education graduates (55–64 year olds) | |
|---|---|---|---|---|---|---|---|---|---|---|
| | 2000 | 2012 | 2004 | 2012 | 2000 | 2012 | 2000 | 2012 | 2000 | 2012 |
| Germany | 15 | 13 | 39 | 52 | 47 | 42 | 22 | 29 (9) | 20 | 26 |
| Denmark | 13 | 18 | 53 | 54 | 46 | 44 | 29 | 40 (5) | 18 | 29 |
| France | 24 | 17 | 44 | 56 | 11 | 12 | 31 | 43 (16) | 13 | 20 |
| Sweden | 13 | 9 | 47 | 51 | – | | 34 | 43 (9) | 23 | 29 |
| UK | 33 | 2 | m | 61 | m | | 29 | 48 (8) | 19 | 33 |
| EU 21 | 23 | 16 | 46 | 47 | 15 | 14 | 24 | 37 (9) | 14 | 22 |

Source: OECD 2014a.

*Table 12.4* Internal selectivity and quality of achievements (PISA results)

| Countries | % of students repeated a grade in primary, lower or upper secondary school | | % of students below level 2 in maths in PISA | | % of students below level 2 in reading in PISA | | Student-level score-point difference associated with one-unit increase in ESCS (maths) | |
|---|---|---|---|---|---|---|---|---|
| | 2003 | 2012 | 2003 | 2012 | 2000 | 2012 | 2003 | 2012 |
| Germany | 21,6 | 20,3 | 21,6 | 17,7 | 22,6 | 14,5 | 44 | 43 |
| Denmark | 3,6 | 4,7 | 15,4 | 16,8 | 17,9 | 14,6 | 39 | 39 |
| France | 39,5 | 28,4 | 16,6 | 22,4 | 15,2 | 18,9 | 43 | 57 |
| Sweden | 3,5 | 4 | 17,3 | 27,1 | 12,6 | 22,7 | 36 | 36 |
| UK | m | m | 19,8 (2006) | 21,8 | 19,6 (2006) | 16,6 | m | 41 |
| OECD | 13,8 | 13,3 | 21,5 | 22,2 | 19,3 | 17,7 | 39 | 39 |

Source: OECD 2014a. ESCS refers to the PISA index of economic, social and cultural status.

This approach is put to the test by the transformations that have taken place in some national education and LLL systems since the early 2000s, chosen for the emblematic places they occupy in the typologies available. Sweden has been selected because its education system is presented as typically social-democratic and is, moreover, embedded in a strongly redistributive welfare state. The German system is regarded as the flagship of a corporatist

*Table 12.5* Expenditures in education

| Countries | Annual expenditure per primary student/upper secondary | | Expenditure on educational institutions as a percentage of GDP | | % of private expenditure on educational institutions for all education levels | |
|---|---|---|---|---|---|---|
| | 2004 | 2011 | 2000 | 2011 | 2000 | 2011 |
| Germany | 0,63 | 0,63 | 4,9 | 5,1 | 13,9 | 13,6 |
| Denmark | 0,77 | 0,86 | 6,6 | 7,3 | 4,0 | 5,5 |
| France | 0,71 | 0,53 | 6,4 | 6,1 | 8,8 | 10,6 |
| Sweden | 0,88 | 0,93 | 6,3 | 6,3 | 3,0 | 2,8 |
| UK | 0,64 | 1,52 | 4,9 | 6,4 | 14,8 | 25,1 |
| EU21 | 0,78 | 0,89 | 5,2 | 5,8 | 7,9 | 10,6 |

Source: OECD 2014a.

orientation underpinning a 'coordinated' variety of capitalism. Denmark is interesting in two respects: its model of flexicurity has been strongly promoted by the European Commission on account of its capacity to prevent long-term unemployment and quickly reintegrate the unemployed into employment, in particular through training throughout active life; moreover, although embedded in a universal-style welfare state, its educational system makes strong use of training in apprenticeship of corporatist inspiration. France is a priori the symbol of an academic and selective training of young people and has developed a model of LLL based on a tax paid by employers, very rare in international terms. Finally in the late 1990s the United Kingdom was the country in which a market system of education and lifelong training was most likely to be favoured by the reforms of the Conservative and then New Labour governments.

## Sweden: predominance of the universal regime but for how long?

In the early 2000s, Sweden accumulated a set of features corresponding to a LLL regime with a dominant universal orientation: high rates of access to the various levels of education; modes of funding and organisation reflecting a political determination to channel the effects of the market, academic selection and corporatist closure; student performances generally less uneven than in comparable countries. All of these findings and practices are inseparable from the 'individualised model of integration', which regulates the long common core of the Swedish education system by combining 'integration through common objectives and differentiation of pathways' (Mons 2007: 119). At upper secondary level, one of the basic objectives was to reduce as much as possible the gulf between vocational training and general education in order

Table 12.6 From school to work

| Countries | Unemployment rate of 15–24 year olds | | (1) Unemployment rate of 25–34 year olds with educational attainment below upper secondary | | (2) Unemployment rate of 25–34 year olds with tertiary education | | (1)/(2) | | % NEETs 15–29 year olds | | Relative earnings of 25–34 year olds by educational level in 2012: •Below upper secondary education | •All tertiary education (upper secondary = 100) |
|---|---|---|---|---|---|---|---|---|---|---|---|---|
| | 2000 | 2012 | 2000 | 2012 | 2000 | 2012 | 2000 | 2012 | 2000 | 2012 | | |
| Germany | 8.5 | 8.0 | 14.6 | 18.8 | 2.7 | 2.8 | 5.4 | 6.7 | 13.3 | 9.9 | 78 | 148 |
| Denmark | 6.7 | 14.1 | 10.6 | 14.8 | 4.2 | 7.7 | 2.5 | 1.9 | 5.8 | 12.0 | 78 | 112 |
| France | 20.6 | 23.6 | 21.7 | 23.2 | 6.6 | 6.8 | 3.2 | 3.4 | 15 | 16.6 | 80 | 138 |
| Sweden | 9.5 | 23.6 | 13.1 | 21.4 | 3.2 | 5.4 | 4.1 | 4.0 | 7.9 | 9.7 | 78 | 110 |
| UK | 12.0 | 21.2 | 9.1 | 17.2 | 2.0 | 4.2 | 4.5 | 4.1 | 14.2 | 16.3 | 70 | 149 |
| EU 21 | 18.3 | 23.1 | 16.8 | 24.2 | 5.7 | 8.5 | 2.9 | 2.8 | 7.9 | 14.8 | 81 | 138 |

Source: *Education at a Glance*, 2014, OECD 2014a.

*Table 12.7* Access to continuing training and education

| Countries | % of 30–39 year-olds in education | | Participation rate in continuing training | | Access to continuing training tertiary graduates / non-qualified | |
|---|---|---|---|---|---|---|
| | 2005 | 2012 | 2007 | 2012 | 2005 | 2012 |
| Germany | 2,5 | 4,0 | 43 | 53 | 5,0 | 3,9 |
| Denmark | 7,8 | 9,0 | 38 | 66 | 1,7 | 1,9 |
| France | 2,6 | 3,0 | 32 | 36 | 2,3 | 3,3 |
| Sweden | 13,3 | 14,0 | 69 | 66 | 2,6 | 1,9 |
| UK | 15,8 | 7,0 | 40 | 48 | 3,1 | 2,2 |
| OECD | 5,7 | 6,0 | 34(EU21) | 51 | 3.3 | 3,0 |

Source: OECD Education at a Glance 2007, 2009 and 2014.

to offer all pupils access to higher education. In terms of access rates, the Swedish results were among the best in Europe: (1) they were high for pre-primary school, which was effective in reducing educational inequalities due to social background and gender disparities; (2) like Denmark, Sweden was characterised by a low rate of early school leaving (Table 12.3); (3) it also had a fairly good level of access to higher education, above the European average. Sweden was also characterised by the lowest share of private expenditure on education and only a slight difference between individual expenditure on higher education and that on primary schools (Table 12.5), with the overall average significantly higher than in Germany and France. Adult education is part of the public education system: a very dense network of public centres devoted to adult education (Abrahamsson 1999) limits disparities by qualification, gender and age (Table 12.7). Public policies in training have been focused on less well educated populations: from 1997 to 2002, a vast public programme – called 'knowledge lift' – aimed to bring participants up to upper secondary school level, thereby enabling them to go on to higher education as well. In all, some 230,000 people, equivalent to 75 per cent of the young people in upper secondary education, took part in the programme (Stenberg 2003). While the unemployment rate for those without qualifications was fairly high, the differences in earned income by level of qualification were considerably lower than in Europe as a whole (Table 12.6). With the changes that have taken place in the last ten years, the universal orientation of the LLL system has been significantly weakened, so much so that one may wonder whether there is not a structural change under way with the introduction of rules belonging to the 'organised market' regime. Some characteristic features of universalism are still present: strong access to higher education and 'second chance' education, a limited role for the private sector, etc. But the slippage of results in the OECD PISA test is striking, particularly as regards the increased proportion of young Swedes scoring poorly in reading literacy and mathematics, which is now (2012) distinctly above the OECD average (Table 12.4). This trend must no doubt be seen in relation to the reforms introduced by the conservative coalition in power from 2007 to 2014 (Wiborg 2010), although they sometimes did no more than systematise measures introduced by the Social Democrats: education vouchers, liberalisation of choice of school, reduced help for pupils in difficulty in the city suburbs, etc. Faced with the growing difficulties of young people on the labour market,[5] the government undertook in 2011 to give a corporatist inflection to secondary education: access to the second cycle made conditional on school results; a sharper distinction between general and vocational streams; a new curriculum designed to favour the development of apprenticeship in companies.[6] In a sense it was calling into question the pursuit of equality of outcomes at the end of secondary education, the emblematic objective of the anchoring of the universal regime.

## Germany: maintained societal coherence of a corporatist system but increasing limitations

Until the end of the 1990s, the predominant corporatist regime of branch-level 'private governments' (Hilbert *et al.* 1990) linked apprenticeship to occupational certifications during working life through the intermediary of the *Berufsakademies* ('vocational academies'). From the outset, the system has been based on a market in apprenticeship places, which is itself highly regulated by quality standards constituted at federal level in the tripartite context of trade unions, business organisations and government. The predominance of corporatist regulation helps to explain: (1) the low rate of youth employment (Table 12.6) maintained by this 'regulated integration' on the labour market (Garonna and Ryan 1991); (2) the stagnating rate of university graduates among the younger generation at a time when the increases were very rapid in many other European countries (Table 12.3). Since the mid-1980s, the German-style 'primacy of professional know-how' has sought to integrate the growing versatility of competences by considerably diminishing the number of diplomas and accelerating the rate of curriculum revisions and creation of new qualifications (Bosch 2009). But while it remains attractive to young people, the dual system as a whole has faced increasing pressures from: (1) the structural shortage of apprenticeship places at the expense of the 36 per cent of young people exiting at best with a certificate from the shortest lower secondary programme (*Hauptschule*, ISCED level 2), or without any qualification at all; the issue is all the more important in social terms given that in Germany, more than elsewhere, lack of qualification increases the risk of unemployment; (2) the erosion of promotion prospects for holders of qualifications acquired in the course of their careers in the continuity of their apprenticeship training.

The declining access to recognised further qualifications (e.g. *Meister* and *Techniker* federal certifications) explains the current low rate of access to education during working life. This societal situation reflects a model of separation, which is opposed to secondary education models of integration (Mons 2007). In addition, the relative lack of access to pre-elementary school (in 2000, it was still four points below the EU average and 25 points lower than in France) reversed the European objectives of 'facilitating access for all to education and vocational training' and reconciling working life and family life (see Salzbrunn 2007).

As for the continuing training of the unemployed, recent reforms (Hartz IV) are clearly based on a regulation in 'organised market' terms in order to favour a quick return to employment regardless of its quality. The upgrading training provided to the unemployed by federal agencies was sharply reduced (Bosch *et al.* 2008).

The 'PISA shock' (the poor results of young Germans in the first OECD PISA survey), which gave rise to debate among politicians, led to the introduction of both federal and regional retraining programmes for young people excluded from the dual system.[7] Some other measures aimed to: (1) improve teacher professionalism, particularly regarding skills in diagnosing students' difficulties and in teaching methods; (2) subsidise all-day schools (*Ganztagsschule*) (one in ten schools were all-day schools in 2002; more than half in 2012); (3) merge the two vocational tracks of lower secondary; (4) make the pre-school education system universal: it has been widely carried out even if a relatively small proportion of pre-primary pupils in Germany attend these programmes in public institutions.

Evidence of these efforts is the fact that per capita spending on pupils has more particularly risen in Germany, especially since 2008. Moreover, in the last decade, the improvement in the PISA scores of young Germans has been fairly spectacular: in mathematics they have moved from below to significantly above the OECD average. The performances of young people with an immigrant background have significantly improved (Table 12.4).

Admittedly, these various trends do not testify to a structural change but rather to a touch of universalism, which, for the moment, does not call into question the coherence of a system that overall is clearly corporatist (see Bosch 2009). All the more so, in the short term, because the results in terms of employment are excellent: in contrast to other OECD countries, unemployment has declined sharply for all levels of qualification since the onset of the economic crisis, the unemployment rate for young people with an end of secondary schooling certificate is half the OECD average (5.3 per cent as against 10.6 per cent), and the proportion of NEETs is one third lower. Lack of a qualification has never been more penalising, which is consistent with the predominance of the corporatist regime. Nonetheless, one feature suggests that important recomposition could take place in the background: the proportion of young people completing higher education, while still distinctly below the European average, has grown significantly since 2000 (+13 points as against an OECD average of 10) in the context of demographic decline.

## Denmark and its virtuous compromise: the good European student?

The Danish model constitutes an original compromise between a historically corporatist convention (especially in initial education and training) and an increasingly more universal one (Méhaut 2013). Formally, apprenticeship predominates within upper secondary education (Table 12.3), but unlike the German case, it is associated neither with high rates of early school leaving nor with very unequal outcomes in the PISA evaluations, or obstacles to entering higher education. But taking into account the radical changes in apprenticeship based on reforms towards more comprehensive schooling in the 1980s, 'it is no longer possible to speak of "apprenticeship" but rather of basic vocational training' (Méhaut 2013:102). Indeed, the share of private funding, in secondary and higher education alike, is quite limited, which reflects the universal principles strongly defended by the state. The same is true for continuing training, where funding is essentially provided by the public authorities. This approach yields high rates of access to continuing training, whether it leads to certification or is directly related to the job (Table 12.7); it also turns out to be considerably more egalitarian than in OECD countries overall.[8] This country nonetheless remains an inevitable reference for societal benchmarking on questions of training and unemployment. The specific concept of *folkeoplysning* (literally 'popular enlightenment') is not foreign to this situation to the extent that, bringing together 'personal development, the sense of community, education, vocational training and individual responsibility within the democratic process' (Meilland 2006), it offers a complex alchemy.

It gives rise to a group of institutions intended to encourage the free choice of individuals, and particularly that of young people, so as to allow them to experiment in the course of their studies and working lives alike (Van de Velde 2008). Thus, as soon as they are of age, Danish young people benefit from a system set up by the state to guarantee them broad financial independence, whether they are students or in employment, through two funding sources associating an allowance and earned income. In the 2000s, more than 55 per cent of the 15–24 year age group combined work and studies, and many university students punctuated their studies with work experience segments.

Nonetheless, despite the generous budget allocation to education and training, some evolutions are disturbing. The school-to-work transition is facing a dramatic increase in drop-out rates from upper secondary vocational training and education (Table 12.6). Initial training pathways are marked by the discrimination encountered by young people of non-community origin in terms of access to and participation in apprenticeship (Wiborg and

Cort 2010): it could be linked to the 'very large performance gap between students born in Denmark and first-generation migrants, and even larger between those born in Denmark and second-generation migrants' (European Commission 2014c).

## France: an uncertain compromise between academic and corporatist regimes

The academic regime ('everything is played out before age 25', after which companies adapt individual skills to their needs, with the active support of the public authorities) is historically prominent. First, 'French meritocracy' is based on rigorous selection throughout the school career (see Table 12.4). The upper secondary cycle is structured around a three-way segmentation (vocational/technological/general) and although there has been undeniable progress, the democratisation of the education system is so ambiguous that some authors speak of 'segregative democratisation' (Duru-Bellat and Kieffer 2001). Access to higher education has significantly expanded and the proportion of graduates in the 25–34 year age group is as high as in Sweden, but this is due to the development of short vocational degree programmes (France remains behind many European partners in terms of the share of graduates at masters or PhD level) and there has been no change in the predominance of the highly selective *Grandes écoles*, which still shape the 'scholar gentry' (analysed by Bourdieu). Indeed, the influence of social origin on the PISA results is the highest among the OECD countries.

Nevertheless, in the course of 30 years of successive reforms, which addressed youth unemployment and a demand for more democracy in education, France's educational policy has developed vocational certifications integrated into the hierarchy of general education levels while promoting alternating training in the form of apprenticeships or school-based programmes. In this respect, the creation of the vocational baccalaureate marked a major turning point: for the first time, a vocational high-school curriculum could not dispense with work placements. 'Integrated vocationalism' was thus developed as a compromise between, on the one hand, a corporatist regime and, on the other, the historically dominant academic one (Table 12.3).

Indeed, the vocational stream is still subject to the standards of general education, and notably the hierarchy of training levels. A form of channelling towards VET schemes by default is still widely practised. The logic operating within this academically inspired system is that of placement rather than vocation or 'calling'. The school-to-work transition phase (Table 12.6) is all the more risky for young people with low training levels (17 per cent of exits without qualifications) who are forced to go back and forth between studies, odd jobs and unemployment (European Commission 2014d). This transition remains marked by the chronic inability of the schemes to curb youth unemployment.

Since 1971, continuing training (Table 12.7) has been run on a tripartite basis (government, trade unions and employers), which has made short courses more accessible to the most skilled employees (Verdier 1994). Thus the role of business in the organisation of training is predominant but the rate of access to training during working life is less than half the European average and is very unequal. Three industry-wide agreements on 'lifelong learning' (2003, 2009 and 2014), which were written into laws, have not really changed the situation even if they create first an individual right to training and then an individual training account (it enables employees to accrue a total of 120 hours of training – very far from a real education right along the life course).

## United Kingdom: a complex mix of academic elitism, organised market and universal principles

The British system is probably the one that has undergone the greatest transformations in the last ten years. Within a regime that is academic (centred on 'Oxbridge') and secondly corporatist (with the former apprenticeships), Margaret Thatcher's reforms promoted a quasi-market logic but one that was organised from the outset around standards for certification. The NVQs (national vocational qualifications) were the figurehead, in terms of both initial and continuing training, and the programmes themselves were thus left to the free initiative of the training providers. From 2000, moreover, the Labour government invested in the development of initial education and training within a 'redistributive' logic devoted to people without qualifications but within an 'organised market' logic. The aim is notably to reduce the proportion of young people who, at the end of compulsory schooling, find themselves unemployed, inactive and outside of any training programme to the point of falling into social exclusion (European Commission 2014e). If the main activation programme – the New Deal for Young People – privileged the target of a 'first job', various schemes like the 14–19 Strategy (ensuring that each young person finds a suitable study programme after compulsory schooling) to some extent reflect the emergence of a universal convention.

From this standpoint, the results have been unequal. On the one hand, the proportion of young people with a level of education below the second cycle of secondary schooling has strongly declined, bringing the United Kingdom up to the European average, while public investment has increased, even since 2008, with a view to providing a basic level of education for all pupils – with some success, as shown by the improved PISA scores of British youngsters. But, on the other hand, the fall in rates of schooling between the ages of 16 and 19 years remains significantly higher than in neighbouring countries, while the proportion of NEETs among 15–29 year olds has remained stable and thus significantly above the European average (Table 12.6). In addition, The UK has a relatively low proportion of upper secondary students enrolled in initial VET schemes, which is lower than the European average and 'in contrast with the wider EU trend, initial vocational education and training graduates in the UK have an employment rate that is 2.4 percentage points lower than their counterparts from general education' (European Commission 2014e: 4).

Moreover, 'while the main activation programme for young people in the United Kingdom – the New Deal for Young People – has helped many youth return to work, sustainable employment outcomes have proved difficult to achieve' (OECD 2009: 2). One in five young people finding work through the programme held a job lasting less than 13 weeks. Under the coalition government (2010–2015), the role of charitable foundations and private entities in providing services to NEETs was developed.

In a general way, the United Kingdom differs from other European countries in the very high proportion of private expenditure in overall education spending – two and a half times as great – a gap which widened significantly during the 2000s (Table 12.5). It is particularly spectacular as regards higher education (70 per cent private expenditure as against 21 per cent for the European Union overall). This British specificity undeniably testifies to the weight of the rules of the market in the functioning of the educational system. But it has to be borne in mind that the repayment of the loans that British students take out is underwritten by the state (which protects against the personal bankruptcies that are common in the United States). The configuration is therefore that of an organised market requiring a strong commitment by the public authorities through the loans system. The effectiveness of this arrangement is undeniable, as the proportion of graduates among 25–34 year olds has risen by 20 points and is now significantly above the European average. There is a similar configuration in LLL, because the rate of returns to education among 30–39 year olds has remained significantly higher than in Germany and France, again thanks to a mix of private resources and public aid; moreover, while lower than in clearly universalist countries, the rate of access to LLL is higher than in Germany and France and, in addition, it is less inegalitarian – at the expense of the less educated – than in those two countries.

## Conclusion

Analysis of national systems of education and LLL in terms of regimes confirms that these systems do not spring from a single logic, as the available typologies suggest. Not only does each of these systems prove to be the result of historically constructed compromises between ideal type regimes, but the analysis of their evolutions often reveals a growing complexity of their societal configurations, even if not of equal magnitude. In Europe, the last quarter century has seen a growing hybridisation of national training systems. Among the countries examined, Denmark has seen the construction over a long period of an original compromise between universal and corporatist learning regimes, which is the basis of the flexicurity promoted as an example to follow by the European Commission. This compromise has, if anything, been strengthened in the last ten years though major collective investments, even if significant problems remain: a relatively high drop-out rate and difficulty in fully integrating young people with an immigrant background into the corporatist regime that prevails in initial vocational training. Through a growing individualisation of pathways through education in basic schooling, Sweden has set itself apart by a growing convergence of vocational training and general education curricula, manifesting a growing universalism of education oriented towards the widest possible access to higher education. But it would seem that the amplification by the conservative governments (2007–2014) of an 'organised market' within general education has played a part in the decline of the PISA scores of young Swedes and a growth in inequalities. In reaction to this, recent reforms, whose impact cannot yet be easily measured, have aimed to stimulate the development of apprenticeships with employment contracts. In Germany, the changes have so far been more limited: helped by demographic decline and the economic success of the 'made in Germany' label, the corporatist regime, linked to a market in apprenticeship places, has been able to adapt to the general trends, showing greater responsiveness in modifying the content of training and creating new vocational qualifications linked to the emergence of an increasingly service-based economy. In the future, the increased proportion of young people going into higher education will very probably present a new challenge for this system, especially if training in the course of a career does not provide certifications equivalent to higher education qualifications. In France, the academic regime has not seen a structural challenge to its pre-eminence, but a succession of reforms, particularly inspired by Germany, have set up an original system, called 'integrated vocationalist', superimposing, in the same occupational area, certifications of different levels, including higher education. In parallel, access to higher education has been substantially widened while offering very variable prospects of employment, depending on the degree of selectivity of the courses. Despite recent reforms, the introduction of a universal regime within compulsory schooling is proving difficult. In the United Kingdom, the Thatcher era inaugurated a partial entry into an organised market regime whose effectiveness principally concerned persons in transition (young people and the unemployed), while the last decade has given rise to large public–private investment in compulsory schooling, which is universalist in inspiration, but struggles to combat a strong dualism in education and in the labour market.

Finally, if there is convergence, it is mainly in the trend towards a growing hybridisation of national systems that is favoured by European strategies. At the national level, the actual form taken by the combination of various ideal type regimes of LLL remains quite country specific. This evolving peculiarity explains why the same reform, of neoliberal inspiration for example, will take on a different meaning depending on the societal context involved. This maintained diversity of sociopolitical constructions illustrates the relative strength of the European OMC developed within the context of the Lisbon Strategy. As in the case of active employment policies, such European perspectives cannot be reduced to the neoliberal viewpoint alone (Barbier 2002). In any event, this European approach leaves the way open to varied interpretations depending on the national contexts. However, the European orientation imposes itself, or, in any case, becomes an unavoidable reference, for both their content (i.e. their consistency with the union's priorities in terms of objectives) and their ability to generate, or at least permit, the development of theatres of dialogue at the different levels of policy-making.

## Notes

1 The main reason lies in the repeated capacity of apprenticeship to assert itself as a virtuous social compromise, both for firms and for young people, in a societal context perturbed by the effects of reunification.
2 As an example, Germany experienced what was called the 'PISA shock', when the first wave of this OECD survey showed that the performances of young Germans in terms of competences were significantly below the average for the participant countries.
3 The presentation that follows is a summary (see Verdier 2013 for more details).
4 The concept of decommodification comes from the idea that, in a market economy, individuals (and their labour) are commodified. Decommodification refers to activities and efforts (generally by government) that reduce individuals' reliance on the market and their labour for their wellbeing.
5 Even if 'up to 50% of unemployed young people are full-time students searching for jobs and Swedish youth tend to spend comparatively short periods unemployed' (European Commission 2014a: 4).
6 But since 2011, 'apprenticeships have suffered from low take-up, high drop-out rates and a lack of interest by both students and employers' (European Commission 2014a: 5).
7 Under the neocorporatist coordination of the training pact formed between the government and social partners (*Ausbildungspakt*) (see European Commission 2014b).
8 The participation rate of adults in formal and/or non-formal education is considerably above the OECD average (OECD 2014b), see Table 12.7.

## References

Abrahamsson, K. (1999). *Vocational Education and Training in Sweden*. Thessaloniki: Cedefop.
Barbier, J.-C. (2002). Peut-on parler d'"activation" de la protection sociale en Europe? *Revue Française de Sociologie*, 43(2), 307–332.
Bartlett, W. and Legrand, J. (1993). The theory of quasi-markets, in Bartlett, W. and Legrand, J. *Quasi-Markets and Social Policy*. Houndmills: MacMillan Press, 13–34.

Boltanski, L. and Thévenot, L. (2006). *On justification: economies of worth*. Princeton: Princeton University Press.

Bosch, G. and Charest, J. (eds). (2009). *Vocational Training: international perspectives*. New York: Routledge.

Bosch, G. and Weinkopf, C. (2008). *Low-Wage in Germany*. New York: Russell Sage.

Bosch, G. (2009). The revitalization of the dual system of vocational training in Germany, in Bosch, G. and Charest J. (eds). *Vocational Training: international perspectives*. New York: Routledge, 131–161.

Culpepper, P. and Thelen, K. (2008). Institutions and collective actors in the provision of training: historical and cross-national comparisons, in Mayer, K-U. and Solga, H. *Skill Formation, Interdisciplinary and Cross-National Perspectives*. Cambridge: Cambridge University Press, 21–49.

Duru-Bellat, M. (1992). Evaluer les trajectoires sociales à l'aune de la méritocratie. *Savoir*, 3, 453–468.

Duru-Bellat, M. and Kieffer, A. (2001). La démocratisation de l'enseignement en France: polémiques autour d'une question d'actualité. *Population*, 55(1), 51–80.

Esping-Andersen, G. (1990). *The Three Worlds of Welfare Capitalism*. Princeton: Princeton University Press.

Estevez-Abe, M., Iversen, T. and Soskice, D. (2001). Social protection and the formation of skills: a reinterpretation of the welfare state, in Hall, P. and Soskice D. (eds). *Varieties of Capitalism: the institutional foundations of comparative advantage*. Oxford: Oxford University Press, 145–183.

European Communities (2002). Council Resolution of 27 June 2002 on lifelong learning. *Official Journal of the European Communities* C 163/1.

European Commission (2014a). *European Training Monitor Sweden*. Available at: http://ec.europa.eu/education [Accessed 4 October 2015].

European Commission (2014b). *European Training Monitor Germany*. Available at: http://ec.europa.eu/educationdate [Accessed 4 October 2015].

European Commission (2014c). *European Training Monitor Denmark*. Available at: http://ec.europa.eu/educationdate [Accessed 4 October 2015].

European Commission (2014d). *European Training Monitor France*. Available at: http://ec.europa.eu/educationdate [Accessed 4 October 2015].

European Commission (2014e). *European Training Monitor United Kingdom*. Available at: http://ec.europa.eu/educationdate [Accessed 4 October 2015].

Eyraud, F., Marsden, D. and Silvestre J-J. (1990). Occupational and internal labour markets in Great-Britain and France. *International Labour Review*, 129(4), 501–517.

Garonna, P. and Ryan, P. (1991). The regulation and deregulation of youth Economic activity, in Garonna, P., Ryan, P. and Edwards, R. (eds). *The Problem of youth: the regulation of youth employment and training in advanced economies*. London: MacMillan, 35–81.

Green, A., Preston, J. and Janmaat, J.G. (2006). *Education, equality and social cohesion: a comparative analysis*. Houndmills: Palgrave MacMillan.

Hall, P. and Soskice, D. (eds). (2001). *Varieties of Capitalism – The Institutional Foundations of Comparative Advantage*. Oxford: Oxford University Press.

Hilbert, J., Südmersen, H. and Weber, H. (1990). *Berufsbildungspolitik – Geschichte, Organisation, Neuordnung*. Köln: Editions Opladen.

Méhaut, P. (2013). Formal or actual convergence? Three cases of hybridisation, in Janmaat, G., Dura-Bellat, M., Green, A. and Méhaut, P. (eds). *The Dynamics and Social Outcomes of Education Systems*. Houndmills: Palgrave MacMillan (Series: Education, Economy and Society), 94–115.

Meilland, C. (2006). Danemark: la formation continue des adultes, instrument de politique de l'emploi et enjeu des négociations collectives. *Chroniques internationales de l'IRES*, 101, 23–29.

Mons, N. (2007). *Les nouvelles politiques éducatives. La France fait-elle les bons choix?* Paris: PUF, coll. Education et Société.

OECD (2009). *Jobs for Youth, United Kingdom*. Paris: OECD.

OECD (2014a). *Education at a Glance 2014*. Paris: OECD.

OECD (2014b). *Country Note Denmark Education at a Glance 2014*. Paris: OECD.

Salzbrunn, M. (2007). Entre autonomie et insertion. Les grands dispositifs de la politique de la jeunesse et de la famille en Allemagne. *Horizons Stratégiques*, Avril, 43–69.

Stenberg, A. (2003). An evaluation of the adult education initiative relative labor market training, doktorsavhandling, *Ekonomiska studier* nr. 609, Nationalekonomiska Institutionen, Umeå Universitet.

Streeck, W. and Thelen, K. (2005). Introduction: institutional change in advanced political economies, in Streeck, W. and Thelen, K. (eds). *Beyond Continuity: explorations in the dynamics of advanced political economies*. New York: Oxford University Press, 229–254.

Van de Velde, C. (2008). *Devenir adulte. Sociologie comparée de la jeunesse en Europe*. Paris: PUF.

Verdier, E. (1994). Training and enterprise in France. *International Journal of Manpower*, 15(5), 38–54.

Verdier, E. (2008). L'usage des idées floues. L'Education et la formation tout au long de la vie' in Giraud, O., Muller, P. and Warin, P. (eds). *Politiques et démocratie. Mélanges en l'honneur de Bruno Jobert*. Paris: La Découverte (Coll. Recherches), 109–135.

Verdier, E. (2013). Lifelong learning regimes versus vocational education and training systems in Europe: the growing hybridisation of national models, in Janmaat, G., Duru-Bellat, M., Méhaut, P. and Green, A. (eds). *The Dynamics and Social Outcomes of Education Systems*. Houndmills, Palgrave MacMillan (Series: Education, Economy and Society), 70–93.

Vinokur, A. (1995). Réflexion sur l'économie politique du diplôme. *Formation Emploi*, 52, 151–183.

Wiborg, S. (2009). *Education and Social Integration. Comprehensive Schooling in Europe*. New York: Palgrave MacMillan.

Wiborg, S. (2010). Swedish Free Schools: Do they work?, *LLAKES Research Paper* 18. Available at: http://www.llakes.org/wp-content/uploads/2010/09/Wiborg-online.pdf.

Wiborg, S. and Cort, P. (2010). The vocational education and training system in Denmark, in Bosch, G. and Charest, J. (eds). *Vocational Training. International Perspectives*. New York: Routledge, 84–109.

# Index

Bold page numbers indicate figures, *italic* numbers indicate tables.

3-5-8 model in higher education 112

*A Nation at Risk* (Gardner) 16–17
Abelès, Marc 2
academics: corporatisation, impact on 159–62; role in HE reforms 95; *see also* working conditions for academics
accountability and standards 17
actor-network theory 3; *see also* networks of collaboration
adaptability 177
administrative costs, reducing 40
adult education: crisis in Europe 186–7; history, learning from 180–5; learning turn 179–80; liberal education 182–5, 189–90; vocationalism 178–9, 185–90; for workers, early 20th C 182–5; *see also* lifelong learning
AHELO project 113–14
Amsterdam Treaty 21

Balint, Tim 37
Barroso, Manuel 44, 186
Baschet, Jérôme 150–1
'Baumol-disease' 17–18
Beck, Ulrich 122, 123–5
Beckert, Jens 135, 135–6
benchmarking: and expertise 83–5; governing by 146–7; *see also* facts, governing by
better regulation: agenda 33–8; economic/quantitative interpretation 43–4; Mandelkern group 36, 41–2; member states 39–44; OECD 45; standard cost model (SCM) 40, 44
Biesta, Gert 6

big data 94
Bobbitt, J.F. 16
Bologna Process 21, 105, 106–7, 114
Bologna Working Group on Qualifications Framework (BWGQF) 113
Boltanksi, Luc 8
Boshier, R. 179–80
Bowker, G.C. 3

Camp, Robert C. 147
Canada, regulatory impact assessment (RIA) 35
capitalism: and lifelong learning regimes 195–7; risk and the university 123, 132–6
Carbone, Luigi 45
change, capacity for 177
choice 124
Churchill, Winston 190
class, risk and the university 132–7
commensuration space 19–26
comparability 54, 62
convergence of policies *see* policy transfers
cooperation in education and training, development of 19–26
corporatisation, impact on academics 159–62
critical stance on lifelong learning 8–10
Crouch, C. 134
Cusso, R. 111

Daston, Lorraine 141
datafication of education 23–4

decision-making as
    numbers-based 99–100
Denmark as lifelong learning regime
    203, 208–9, 211–12
Desrosières, Alain 145, 149
diploma supplement 107, 117n6
Directorate of Education and Culture
    (DGEAC) 86–8
dissemination of policy models
    *see* policy transfers

economic development and education
    policies 93–4
education and training 2010 work
    programme (ET 2010) 24–5
education and training strategy 2020
    (ET 2020) 25–6, 61, 64–5, 185–6
*Education at a Glance* (OECD) 23
educational contestation 157
Elliott, A. 124
enterprise risk management
    (ERM) 126–7
'Entrepreneurship360' 63
epistemic community 75, 80–3
epistemic/non-epistemic governance of
    HE 93–4, 97
epistemic objects, standards as 14–15
EQAR *see* European quality assurance
    register (EQAR)
Erasmus programme 105
ESG *see* Standards and guidelines for
    quality assurance in the European
    Higher Education Area (ESG)
ET 2020 25–6, 61, 64–5, 185–6
European Commission: higher education
    106; ranking lists in higher education 99
European credit transfer system (ECTS)
    107–10, *108*, 112, 117n7
European quality assurance register
    (EQAR) 111
European Research Council
    (ERC) 97–8
European space of education,
    development of 19–26
evidence-based approach 65–6; *see also*
    benchmarking; facts, governing by
evidence-based policy 145
evidence-based research and policy 80–3
experimental facts 145
expertise: benchmarking 83–5;
    Directorate of Education and Culture
    (DGEAC) 86–8; entities producing

74; epistemic community 75, 80–3;
    evidence-based research and policy
    80–3; institutional 86–8; learning
    in the shadow of hierarchy 75–6,
    86–8; NEXUS network 86–8; policy
    learning 74–6; reflexive learning
    75; regulatory powers of policy
    makers 73; social interaction 75; and
    technocracy and politicisation 74;
    think tanks 76–80

fabrication of European space of
    education 19–26
facts, governing by: experimental facts
    145; Foucault 143–4; historically
    142–3; imagination 149; philoso-
    phy 143; proliferation of 140–1; real
    utopias 151; realistic possibles 147–8;
    as resistance source 147–51, **150**;
    statactivism 148–9; statistics 144–5;
    systems producing facts 141; *see also*
    benchmarking
Faure Report 179–80
fields 96
financialisation 135
Fisher, Ronald 145
flexibility 177
Foucault, Michel 143–4
Fourcade, M. 128
France: as lifelong learning regime 203,
    209–10, 212; Mandelkern group 42
freedom of thought, challenges to 92–3
Friedberg, E. 115
funding of HE 97–8

Galison, Peter 141
Genel, Katia 143
Germany as lifelong learning regime
    202–3, 206–8, 212
Gorga, A. 112
governance, risk 122, 125–8
government and universities 159
Green, A. 195
Grek, Sotira 38, 39, 61
Grubb, W.N. 178

Haas, P. 81
harmonisation and standards 3
higher education: 3-5-8 model 112;
    academics, impact of quality control
    instruments on 112–14; Bologna
    Process 105, 106–7; conformism
    in 108; corporate practices,

implementation of 156–7; diploma supplement 107, 117n6; educational contestation 157; Erasmus programme 105; European Commission 106; European credit transfer system (ECTS) 107–10, *108*, 112; European quality assurance register (EQAR) 111; funding restructuring in UK 156–7; international organisations, intervention in 105–7; learning outcomes 113, 115–16; mobility of staff and students 105–7; organised anarchies 115–16; privatisation 156; quality control instruments 107–11, *108*; Sorbonne Declaration 105–6; specialisation of tasks 116–17; standardisation instruments 107–11, *108*; Standards and guidelines for quality assurance in the European Higher Education Area (ESG) 110–11; tuition fees 156; *see also* ranking lists in higher education; risk and the university

Holden, Kerry 163
Holford, J. 182
Horkheimer, Max 143
Huber, C. 130, 131
human capital theory 23, 24

imagination 149
individualisation 124
integration, European 97–8
intergovernmental organisations (IGOs) and standards 18–19
international indicators and evaluation of education systems project (INES) 23
international organisations, intervention in HE 105–7
international standard classification of education (ISCED) 18
ISCED (international standard classification of education) 18
Italy: better regulation 42–3; Mandelkern group 42–3

Jansen, Set 168–9
Jarvis, P. 180
Jeanpierre, L. 148
Jones, Ken 157

Karkatsoulis, Panagiotis 45
Kearns, David T. 147

King, R. 131
Kinnock, Neil 41
Knill, Christoph 37
Knowledge Centre for Evidence-Based Technologies (KCEBT) 80–3
knowledge development 17–18; datafication of education 23–4; numbers, governance by 94
Kok Report 25

labour flexibility and insecurity 134–5
learning in the shadow of hierarchy 75–6, 86–8
learning outcomes 113, 115–16
learning society 180
Lee, M. 180
liberal education 182–5, 189–90
life histories approach 158
lifelong learning: abandonment of European achievement 176; academic/corporatist compromise regime 209–10; capitalism and regimes of 195–7; change, capacity for 177; characteristics of regimes 199, 201–3, *202*, *203*, *204*, *205*; corporatist regimes *200*, 206–8; corporatist/universal compromise regime 208–9; crisis in Europe 186–7; critical stance on 8–10; decommodified regimes 198–9, *200*; Denmark as lifelong learning regime 208–9, 211–12; economic needs as primary 177–9; globalisation 177–9; history, learning from 180–5; hybridisation of systems 211–13; learning society 180; learning turn 179–80; liberal education 182–5, 189–90; limitations of vocationalism 185–90; Lisbon Strategy 185, 194; market regimes 199, *201*; mixed type regime 210–11; neoliberalism 180; open method of coordination (OMC) 194; regimes of 197–203, *200*, *201*; universal regimes *200*, *203*, 205–6; vocationalism 178–9, 185–90
Lisbon Strategy 22, 25, 185, 194

Maastricht Treaty 21
Mactavish, John 189
Mandelkern group 36, 45
Mansbridge, A . 189
Mayrgündter, T. 114

member states and better
regulation 39–44
Meyer, J.W. 115
mobility of staff and students 105–7
monitoring instruments, PISA as source
of 62–3
monopolies 95
Musselin, C. 115
mutual surveillance see Programme
for International Student
Assessment (PISA)

national actors and better
regulation 39–44
National Student Survey 164
neoliberalism: lifelong learning 180;
risk and the university 132–6;
standards 17
Netherlands: better regulation agenda
40; standard cost model (SCM) 40
networks of collaboration: datafication
of education 23–4; emergence
of 21–2
new public management 96, 122
NEXUS network 86–8
numbers, governance by 94, 99–100

objectification of education
practice 13, 18
OECD see Organisation for
Economic Co-operation and
Development (OECD)
open method of coordination (OMC)
22, 25, 194
Organisation for Economic
Co-operation and Development
(OECD): better regulation 35–8,
38–9, 45; comparability with EU
63–5; densification of EU relations
60, 62; Education at a Glance 23;
evidence-consequence sequence 66–7;
interdependence with EU 37, 38;
Mandelkern group 45; models and
recommendations 66–7; peer reviews
45; PISA and policy alignment
with EU 61–2; PISA collaboration
54; PISA in European documents
63–7; and policy transfers 32–3;
public management committee
(PUMA) 35–6; Reference Checklist
for Regulatory Decision-Making 36;
relationship with EU on education
38–9; standards and 18–19

Padoan, Peir Carlo 42
Papatsiba, V. 105
Paris Declaration 187–8
Parker, L. 111
Pepin, L. 19
performativity and standards 17
Piketty, Thomas 133
PISA see Programme for International
Student Assessment (PISA)
policy learning: epistemic community
75, 80–3; reflexive learning 75, 80; in
the shadow of hierarchy 75–6, 86–8;
social interaction 75, 84–5
policy transfers: better regulation
agenda 33–8, 38–9; in Europe
31; Mandelkern group 36, 41–2;
member states and better regulation
39–44; national/international public
authorities 44–6; OECD and EU
relationship 32–3, 38–9
political entrepreneurs 84
politicisation and expertise 74
Power, Michael 126, 127
precautionary principle 35
'Preparing for life - How the
European Commission supported
education, youth, culture and
sport (2010-2014)' (European
Commission) 61–2
PriceWaterhouseCoopers 127
privatisation of higher education 156;
see also capitalism; neoliberalism
Programme for International Student
Assessment (PISA): comparability 54,
62; context-specific uses 56–8; crossing
effects 58–60; densification of EU/
OECD relations 60, 62; educational
policies, reception and effects on
55–60; ET 2020, support for 61;
European level, reception and effects
of 60–3; evidence-based approach
65–6; evidence-consequence sequence
66–7; literacy framework 60–2;
meta-policy 58–9; mutual surveillance
through 68; new geographies 58–60;
new governing modes 58–9; OECD
as body of expertise 65–6; OECD
collaboration 54; OECD comparability
with EU 63–5; OECD/EU policy
alignment 61–2; OECD models and
recommendations 66–7; OECD/
PISA in European documents 63–7;
as source for monitoring instruments

62–3; and standards 18–19; transnational dynamics 56–8
property ownership 134
Prpich, G. 128

quality control instruments in higher education 107–11, *108*; academics, impact on 112–14; learning outcomes 113, 115–16
quality politics, standards 3–5

Radaelli, Claudio 43, 75
ranking lists in higher education: convergence/divergence tendencies 95; decision-making as numbers-based 99–100; economic basis of HE 92–3; economic development and education policies 93–4; epistemic/non-epistemic governance of HE 93–4, 97; European Commission 99; fraud 101–2; freedom of thought, challenges to 92–3; funding structures 97–8; governance mode of HE 93; increased numbers of 100–1; integration, European 97–8; larger units, creation of 98; mapping as alternative 102; numbers, governance by 94; quality and reliability of data on 102; risk and the university 131; scholarly/non-scholarly discourses 95; transformations in HE 93; transnational field of HE 96–9; U-Multirank 100–1
real utopias 151
realistic possibles 147–8
Reay, D. 129–30
red tape scoreboard project 40
reflexive learning 75, 80
reflexive modernisation 124
regulatory impact assessment (RIA) 35, 43
regulatory intervention *see* better regulation
research, critical stance in 8–10
Research Assessment Exercise (RAE) 164
'Rethinking education' initiative 63
risk and the university: calculation, risk 131; and capitalism 123, 132–6; class 132–6; crisis 136; critical approach to risk 128; differentiation between universities 129–30; embedded in regulation, risk as 125–6; enterprise risk management (ERM) 126–7; future,

recommendations for 137; governance, risk 122, 125–8; international students 130; introduction of risk management 128–30; motivation for risk management in 130–1; ranking of universities 131; reputational risk 131; risk-based external quality assurance 130–1; risk society 122, 123–5; solutions sold to universities 122, 126, 132; standards, risk 126
risk society 122, 123–5
Rothstein, H. 125
Rowan, B. 115

Sayer, A. 135
Schiller, F. 128
scientific management 15–16
Scott, James C. 150
Scott, W.R. 111
Shore, Chris 2
Sikes, Pat 164
Skornicki, Arnault 142
Skultans, Vieda 158
social efficiency movement 15
social inequalities 132–7
social interaction 75, 84–5
Sorbonne Declaration 21, 105–6
specialisation of tasks 116–17
standard cost model (SCM) 40, 44
Standards and guidelines for quality assurance in the European Higher Education Area (ESG) 110–11
standards and standardisation: academics, impact of quality control instruments on 112–14; accountability 17; 'Baumol-disease' 17–18; datafication of education 23–4; defining standardisation 3; epistemic objects, standards as 14–15; European space of education 19–26; and harmonisation 3; higher education, instruments 107–11, *108*; intergovernmental organisations (IGOs) 18–19; international standard classification of education (ISCED) 18; knowledge development 17–18; Lisbon Strategy 22; neoliberalism 17; objectification of education practice 13, 18; origin and development of 15–19; performativity 17; and quality politics 3–5; risk 126; scientific management 15–16; social efficiency movement 15; Taylorism 15–16

Star, S.L. 3
statactivism 148–9
statistics 144–5
story telling and think tanks 76–80
Streeck, W. 134, 135, 196

Taylorism 15–16
teaching: greater emphasis on in HE
    164; testing and accountability as
    damaging 9
technocracy and expertise 74
technologies of evidence 80–3
Thelen, K. 196
Thévenot, Laurent 8
think tanks 76–80
Thompson, J.D. 115
3-5-8 model in higher education 112
Torriti, Jacopo 38
transfer of policies *see* policy transfers
transnational field of HE 96–9
Treaty of Rome 20–1
Tremblay, K. 116

U-Multirank 100–1
UNESCO *see* United Nations
    Educational, Scientific and Cultural
    Organisation (UNESCO)
United Nations Educational,
    Scientific and Cultural Organisation
    (UNESCO) and standards 18–19
United States: origin and development
    of standards 15–17; regulatory impact
    assessment (RIA) 35

universities: government 159;
    *see also* higher education; risk and
    the university

vocationalism 178–9; limitations
    of 185–90

Wacquant, L. 162
Welikala, T. 182
Wolf, Adam 45
Workers' Educational Association
    (WEA) 182, 185
working conditions for academics:
    analytic approach 158; complexity of
    present situation 164–8; contestation,
    spheres of 165–8; corporatisation,
    impact of 159–62; different spheres
    of identities 162, 165; funding
    restructuring in UK 156–7; idealised
    past, challenges to image of 163–4;
    imagined pasts 163; life histories
    approach 158; National Student
    Survey 164; new identities and virtues
    159–62; organised discontent 168–72;
    Research Assessment Exercise (RAE)
    164; social and economic impact,
    focus on 164; state grids, 168–72;
    ttension between compliance and
    contestation 168–72
Wright, Erik Olin 151

Xerox 145, 146, 147